Market Values

by

Gerri Moore

Grosvenor House
Publishing Limited

This book is published by
Grosvenor House Publishing Ltd
28-30 High Street, Guildford, Surrey, GU1 3EL.
www.grosvenorhousepublishing.co.uk

A CIP record for this book
is available from the British Library

ISBN 978-1-908596-80-2

This book is dedicated to
my brother, Gregory Shaw,
Adventurer, wit and altogether good egg.

Chapter 1

Terry O'Malley flung open his son's bedroom door and caught it, by his fingernails, before it banged against the wall. One fingernail pulled away and it hurt like hell. He closed the door quietly and walked over to the bed.

"Colin," he said, hitting the off button of an alarm that had been beeping incessantly for four minutes, "you've got precisely three minutes to get your backside out of that pit." The bedclothes moved a fraction so Terry tore open the curtains and flung wide the window. A blast of cold air rushed in to displace the warmth. A pale white hand reached up from the depths of the blankets and pulled them tighter round the neck of the occupant.

"OK," said Terry through clenched teeth, "sure you want to play it that way?" He grabbed a handful of blanket and jerked it away from the body.

"Bloody hell, dad," Colin's voice was a whine, "are you trying to kill me?"

"A bit of cold air never killed anyone, Colin," Terry replied, "but an angry father, now that's a different matter." He dropped the blankets on the floor and stood inspecting his only child. Colin was thin, smaller than others of his age and white as a supermarket loaf. Terry shook his head as he wondered how he'd managed to produce such a puny specimen. Colin's long unkempt hair was fair and spread out over the pillow. Terry could see an ear ring piercing one lobe. Colin's eyes were tightly shut and he wrapped his arms around his shivering body.

"Dad," he whimpered, "I didn't get in until two this morning."

"And it's now five o'clock," replied Terry without feeling, "I told you last night I needed- needed, mark my words- not wanted, your help this morning. Would I have asked a superstar for help under normal circumstances? Couldn't you have missed rehearsals for once? Or got in earlier? I told you Brendan had to go to the doctors." Terry left the room. He waited for thirty seconds at the top of the stairs and then re-entered the room. Colin had rolled out of bed onto the still warm blanket on the floor. Terry reached down, grabbed his son's arm and yanked him to his feet, hauled him into the bathroom, pushed him bodily into the shower and turned on the cold water. It had the desired effect. Colin couldn't scream out nor shout, as he was too busy trying to draw breath but he was quick enough to turn the tap to hot and then he mouthed "bastard" to Terry's retreating figure. Five minutes later Colin came down dressed in a white T-shirt, blue jeans and a pair of soft leather shoes.

"Are you seriously thinking of going to the wholesalers with me dressed like that?" his father asked, "Are you completely mad?"

"Yes, why not?" replied Colin, "and no, I'm as sane as anyone can be at this ungodly hour."

"You'll freeze your nuts off," said Terry, "you know they're cooled warehouses, don't you? Won't you at least put on a coat and some boots? Do we need two invalids in the family?"

Colin, irritated by his father's usually amusing habit of asking question after question, went to the cupboard in the hallway and found a padded jacket and boots. He put them on and walked back into the kitchen, glancing at the clock on the wall.

"It's not five o'clock yet!" he exclaimed. Terry grinned.

"So," he said, "I lied, son. Now come on."

Colin grabbed a piece of toast and threw half a cup of tea down his throat and followed his father outside. The truck's engine was already running. Colin got in and slammed the door closed. Terry gritted his teeth. He wound down the window and turned on the radio.

"Dad, its bloody freezing in here," said Colin, "put the window up."

"Aren't you forgetting something?" said Terry.

"Please," Colin said through clenched teeth. Terry wound the window up. Twenty minutes later they arrived at the wholesale market. Terry jumped down from the truck, eager to get his hands on the best produce available. Colin closed his eyes and pulled the collar of the jacket up around the lower part of his face. He'd decided to grab a few minutes more sleep. The door next to him opened and a hand pulled him out of the truck.

"Stick with me, kid," his father said, "you might learn something useful." Reluctantly Colin followed his father into the massive warehouse. His appearance was greeted with some good-natured calls and one wolf whistle accompanied by a shout of "he's brought his girl along." Terry strolled over to the man who had whistled and squared up to him.

"You got something to say?" he said sarcastically.

"Brought the girl along, that's what I said," the man puffed out his chest and set his feet squarely. He matched Terry in height and was obviously not afraid of him.

"This," Terry said, pointing at Colin, "is my son and you'll show him some respect." The man

laughed in his face.

"Respect!" he exclaimed, "for a nancy boy that thinks he's Mick Jagger. Don't make me laugh."

Terry punched him in the stomach, quickly and expertly. The man dropped to his knees, gasping.

"You'll respect that maybe," Terry said and walked away, beckoning Colin.

"Why did you have to do that?" Colin shouted to his father's back, his face red and angry.

"Because you couldn't and wouldn't," his father shouted back at him. A hand gripped Terry's sleeve and he stopped. He turned and faced Colin.

"I don't need respect here," said Colin, waving his hand around the warehouse.

"No, son, you don't," said Terry, gritting his teeth, "but I do." Colin shook his head and remained silent while Terry negotiated with his wholesalers, picking from boxes on display and complaining about yesterday's potatoes. Colin wandered over to a section marked 'specials' and bent over a box of pineapples. One had been sliced and left on the top. The sweet aroma rose to fill his nostrils and he touched one prickly head. He closed his eyes and imagined the sun beating down and women dressed in coloured skirts harvesting the crop. He hummed a melody and curled his toes in his boots. He could almost feel the sand and hear the sea..

"You ready, Colin?" a voice broke into his reverie.

"Pineapples," he replied impulsively, turning to face his father, "have you ever sold pineapples?"

"No," Terry replied, "leave those to the shops. They can store them, we can't. Anyway, they'd be two and six each. You can buy a tin for one and eight. Not what our customers want."

"How do you know if you've never tried?" Colin said. Terry looked at his son's eyes. The pale orbs were shining. He couldn't remember the last time he'd seen his son enthusiastic about anything but music.

"Think you could sell some?" he asked.

"Yes," Colin replied, "I'm sure I could."

"Comes out of your wages if you don't," Terry challenged.

"OK," said Colin defiantly.

"Half a dozen too many?" asked Terry.

"No, six is just right," replied Colin. Terry called the wholesaler over and added six pineapples to his list. The lesson would be good for the boy and Terry imagined the scene when Colin had to eat pineapples every day for a week. He grinned.

"Right, Colin, round the back with the truck, for collection." They walked to the entrance and Colin got in and started the engine. The truck lurched as it rolled forward.

"Shit," he said and looked out of the cab. The front off side tyre was flat.

"I'll kill that bastard next time," Terry swore.

"Listen, dad, it might be a co-incidence," Colin said as he leapt out of the cab.

"Co-incidence, my arse," said Terry, "but we're going to have to move it if we're to sell anything today, let alone bloody pineapples." Colin uncoupled the spare tyre from under the truck while Terry jacked up the front end. They worked together and ten minutes later the truck was up and running.

"Thanks, son," said Terry. He wiped away a smudge of oil from Colin's face with a rag and was transported back to the days when he took his son out playing football, down to the stream looking for tadpoles, out to the woods collecting horse chestnuts to soak in vinegar for conkers.

"Where does time go, lad?" he said quietly.

"Don't know, dad," Colin replied, moving away from him. He was embarrassed.

"Come on," Terry said brusquely, "let's hit the road."

By 6.30am they were outside Dee's house. Deirdre, or Dee as she was universally known, had worked full time for the O'Malley brothers ever since their father, Sean, had dropped dead with a massive heart attack at the age of forty five. She and Terry had both nagged Brendan to go to the doctor when he started with pains in his chest. She nodded at Colin and climbed in beside him.

"How's the band going?" asked Deirdre, peeling a banana and offering some to Colin.

"It's actually going well," he said as he broke a piece off the fruit and stuffed it into his mouth, "one of the guys has met a friend of a friend who knows where The Hollies record and he reckons he can get us in there for a session."

"The who?" asked his father with a laugh.

"Not The Who, dad, The Hollies," said Colin, "you know the song- Jennifer Eccles." Colin's arm swung out in Terry's direct line of vision as he played an imaginary guitar and sang the first line of a song.

"Put your bloody arm down," Terry said, "I'm trying to drive."

"Sorry, dad," Colin said then he turned to Dee, "you've heard it, haven't you?"

"Sounds vaguely familiar, Colin," she tried to hide a smile, "but I don't know much pop music."

Colin continued singing through the song until they pulled up outside the rear of the Market Hall.

"They knew how to build things, those Victorians, didn't they?" said Colin as he looked up at the ornamental frieze running around the building. Buxom ladies in long flowing, Grecian dresses held cornucopias of fruit and flowers. A sturdy shepherd, lamb dangling from his arm gazed towards them from the left. On the right side a fisherman held an enormous cod and scanned the sky for storm clouds, carved into the centre of the frieze stood the coat of arms of the town.

"Yes, and this is only the back entrance, but it will be history soon, and I for one will be glad to have some decent facilities," said Terry. They drove in to the allotted place for O'Malley.

"I'll go on through," said Dee, "see you soon." Terry climbed into the back of the truck and began sliding produce towards Colin until his trolley was full.

"Remember where we are?" Terry asked, "Or should I come with you?"

"Dad, after three generations, I bet this trolley could take me there," said Colin and Terry could hear the annoyance in his voice. Despite Colin's assurance he trundled into the huge Market Hall and hesitated. It looked completely different without the stalls set up.

"Clothes, fancy goods to the rear," he muttered, "cheese, bacon and butchers on the outskirts, fruit and veg....?" He paused and the iron of a trolley caught him on the back of his leg.

"Christ Almighty!" he exclaimed, letting go of the trolley and spinning round, "can't you watch where you're going?" He looked into a pair of dark brown female eyes sparking with fury. Her hair was black and gently curling onto a pair of shoulders covered by an enormous padded trimmed jacket. It had the disadvantage of covering the rest of the body down to the knees. She was, Colin guessed, about his own age.

"Do you have to swear?" she hissed, "as well as stopping without any warning?"

"I, um, I..." stammered Colin and stopped.

"Yes," she said, her eyes now gazing at him calmly, "you what?"

"I'm lost," he said simply. She burst out laughing and he saw two rows of perfect, white teeth. When she had recovered she said, "Where are you trying to find?"

"O'Malley's Fruit and Veg," he said.

"Turn left down here," she pointed, "then two rows down and turn right. Is it your first day here?"

"Thanks," he said, then added, "no, well, yes, well, I'm Terry O'Malley's son." He tore his eyes away from her face and tried to get his brain to work. "Turn left" was all he remembered.

"I hope the foot will be all right," she said as he turned to go.

"Foot?" he said, "oh, yes, the foot." He exaggerated the limp as he wheeled the trolley to the stall.

"Leave those here and go and get the next lot," Dee said, "I can manage." He raced back and looked around wildly for the girl. She was nowhere to be seen. Reluctantly he loaded the trolley and winced as his sock pulled against the drying blood. Half an hour later he had made the trip four times and still he hadn't caught so much as a glimpse of the girl.

"What are these I've found," Dee asked him, and she held a pineapple aloft, "are they a mistake?"

"No," Colin said, "I persuaded Dad to get some. Shall we cut one up so that people can try a piece?"

"Well done, lad," Dee said, "I've been telling him for ages to get something special for the punters. I'll cut one up and buy half so we don't lose all the money on it. It's the smell that will get them going if anything does. Gorgeous, isn't it?" Colin nodded.

"I thought of sun and sand and sea when I saw one at the wholesalers," he said, and he imagined the girl in the trimmed jacket walking along the beach. Dee nudged him in the ribs.

"Then let's hope they weren't grown under glass somewhere in the Midlands," she laughed, "hold the fort while I go and borrow a plate and get some cocktail sticks."

"Give us a hand with the spuds and carrots, will you, Colin," Terry said as he approached the stall.

"Sure, dad," Colin said, still beaming from Dee's praise. They each took a corner of the heavy sacking bag and hauled it to the edge of the stall.

"OK," said Terry, "now lift and forward, shuffling backwards as we go." It was at the critical stage of lifting that the girl walked past the stall. Colin saw her, forgot his orders and the bag tipped sideways under the volition of Terry's heave. Potatoes tumbled, bounced and rolled around Colin.

"Colin!" Terry exclaimed, "what the hell were you thinking of?" Colin saw the girl put her hands to her mouth, chuckle, and then she walked on.

"I'm sorry, dad," he blustered, "I mis-timed the heave." He dropped to his knees and began picking up the potatoes and putting them on the stall.

"Quick," Terry muttered, "we don't want people knowing they've been on the floor."

"They've come out of the earth, dad," retorted Colin, "and that's muckier than this." Dee came back and cut a pineapple in half and wrapped one section in foil, slicing and sectioning the other. She placed the plate at the front and the aroma floated around.

"Morning, love," she said to an elderly couple, "you're out bright and early."

"Aye, well you have to be early to get the best stuff," the old woman replied, "pound of apples please, and from the front, if you don't mind." Dee chuckled.

"I promise you all the apples are the same, love. I polished them myself earlier. The bad one, there was only one, you know, went in the rubbish." Dee carefully selected four apples and showed them to the woman.

"Are the bananas fresh today too?" the woman queried.

"Fresh as a daisy," Dee replied, "and we've the first tangerines in too."

"I'll take four bananas and four tangerines, please." Dee parcelled up the purchases and walked round the stall to load them into the basket. The woman paid her from a battered brown purse.

"Don't go giving me any of that funny dec-i-mated money in my change," the woman said to Dee.

"We've had the new 5p and 10p coins for six months now," smiled Dee, "it's getting difficult to find the old shillings and florins now."

"Aye, well, do your best," retorted the woman, "I'm still not sure those new ones will catch on."

"When can I go for lunch, dad?" Colin asked.

"You've not started work yet lad and you're asking about lunch?" his father said, "if you're hungry, do the tea run. They do bacon sandwiches at the kiosk, that'll keep you going." Dee handed him the cups and he trotted off, following his nose this time. He could smell the bacon and hear it spitting and crisping in hazy fat. He waited for his order, looking at the melee of bodies that were the owners and assistants of the Market Hall. Fishmongers looked as cold as their produce, glassy eyed and with white aprons. Colin shivered and thanked Heaven his dad wasn't in the cold, white tiled section where summer's sun never penetrated. The butchers wore their blue and white striped aprons and looked like a tribe of United supporters. They could all have been bald under the white hats demanded by Health and Safety.

"Bacon and three teas," the woman behind the counter shouted. Colin paid her and took the cups in one hand, the greasy white bag in the other. Three yards later his knuckles had turned from warm to hot to burning. He looked for somewhere to put the cups down but there was only the floor and he wasn't sure he'd be able to bend down and get all three cups to stay upright. Tears pricked his eyes as the cups scalded his skin. He decided he'd have to drop them.

"Let me," said a voice, and two gloved hands held out a battered tin tray. Gratefully he put the cups on the tray, stuffed the sandwich in his pocket and then hopped around, blowing on his fingers.

"Get to the toilets quick and run them under cold water. I'll take these to O'Malley's for you."

The girl from earlier had appeared from nowhere and she had gone before he had time to say anything. He dashed to the toilets and ran his fingers under the cold water. He cursed. Not content with colliding into her trolley, letting her see him grovelling on the floor for potatoes, he had now shown himself to be a complete idiot that couldn't safely deliver three cups of tea. He raised his now frozen hand to the sky in a dramatic gesture.

"Why me?" he asked the sky that was beyond the peeling whitewash and rust stained ceiling.

"Why not you?" said a voice from behind him and he turned in embarrassment to find one of the traders had entered the toilet and was unzipping his fly at the urinal.

"Sorry, mate," said Colin and fled. Arriving back at the stall he saw that Terry and Dee were serving customers and there were others waiting. He began serving and tried out the spiel he'd worked on earlier.

"Wonderful pineapples. Fresh in. Try a piece. We can let you have a whole one, but today only." Plenty of people tried the samples but no one bought. At eleven o'clock Terry told Colin to go for lunch.

"Although you could eat that bacon sandwich I can smell in your pocket," he laughed.

"Crumbs, I'd forgotten all about it," said Colin, "by the way, dad, did that girl say anything when she brought the teas?" He tried to sound casual.

"You mean Elizabeth?" Terry said and he peered sideways at his boy.

"Elizabeth?" said Colin.

"Yes, she and her mother sell baby clothes round the side of the Hall. Not a brilliant position, it's right in the corner, but they do all right." Colin headed in the general direction of the cafes but before he got to the stairs leading up to the balcony level he turned off and walked quickly down the row of stalls that circled the Hall. Because the over-hanging balconies shielded the light, these stalls weren't sought after and the rent was slightly lower. Colin was trying to avoid looking at ladies brassieres and lace panties, dangling helplessly like washing on a wind-free day. He was amazed at how the scraps of material hanging there could ever cover a breast or a bottom. The girls he knew didn't wear bras; they jiggled their breasts with abandon under T-shirts while they danced. They were more than conscious of the effect they were having on the male sex. He concentrated on the traders, seeking Elizabeth, but after a circle of the outer stalls, he couldn't see her. He wandered outside, bought a fresh sandwich and a Coke and sat on a bench in the watery sunshine. He kept looking from left to right in case she passed by. The town hall clock chimed 12 and he started up and ran to the stall. Terry looked at his watch.

"Forty minutes is what we take for a break, Colin, not an hour," he said angrily, "this is not a bloody office, it's a market stall, remember?" Colin said nothing but got on with serving customers. One pineapple had been sold while he was away and Dee had cut up the other half to replace all the samples that had been eaten, but she was only putting out a few sections on the plate.

"Come on, ladies," Colin burst out to the crowd, "make your own fruit salad this weekend instead of a tinned one. The man from O'Malley's says YES."

The customers smiled at him and one woman shouted, "Can I have half a one?"

"If you can find someone to take the other half," quipped Colin, "but then you've probably been married to the other half a long time."

"Cheeky blighter," the woman answered, but her neighbour said, "I'll take the other half." Before the lunch time crowd had gone there were only two magnificent specimens left.

"They'll be gone by tonight," Colin reassured his father.

"I hope so," replied Terry, "because just one left over means no profit. I'm off for lunch." An hour later an extremely well dressed businessman came dashing up to the stall.

"You've got pineapples, I hear," he said.

"We have, sir," said Colin proudly.

"And at a good price," Dee said and she elbowed Colin out of the way.

"Oh, the price is irrelevant," the man said, "my wife has just phoned. She's pregnant and wants fresh pineapple with her celery and Marmite." He pulled a face of complete disgust.

"There's another customer," Dee nudged Colin.

He walked over to where a woman was fingering carrots. By the time he'd got back from serving her, Dee was smiling all over her face.

"That was my sale," Colin protested but Dee opened her hand and showed him the money.

"You sold him two," said Colin and he smiled.

"No, just the one."

"At twice the price!" exclaimed Colin.

"He could afford it," she said, "and anyway pregnant wives are not to be denied at any price."

"I'm not sure that's proper, Dee," said Colin, "but I'll forgive you. We've paid for all of them now and still got one to spare."

"He paid for the samples," she said, "We still need to sell that one." She pointed at the solitary pineapple standing proudly in the centre of the stall and there it stayed. At six o'clock Colin was exhausted. His feet ached and the gash on his leg was hot and throbbing. His white T-shirt, worn so defiantly, was filthy, and he had a tear in his jeans.

"Go and get the truck, Colin," said Terry, "while we clean up and I pay Dee." He threw the keys at Colin who walked wearily to truck. When he got back Terry clapped an arm around his shoulder and said, "We did it, son, sold all the blooming pineapples. Well done, good idea. Thanks, Colin."

"What? Who to?" said Colin.

"Elizabeth," said Dee, "her mother's making a curry and Elizabeth said it would be perfect to enhance the flavour."

"Elizabeth bought it?" Colin groaned and covered his face with his hands.

"Come on, Colin," said Terry, "it's not the end of the world. She's here every market day."

"Yes," replied Colin miserably, "but I'm not." Terry smiled and put an arm around his son's shoulders.

"You could be, son," he said, "if you really wanted."

CHAPTER 2

Elizabeth was cutting up the pineapple in the kitchen and she sucked on her fingers between slicing.

"Don't lick your fingers when you're handling food," her mother Anne laughingly scolded, turning from the dish of curry she was preparing.

"Sorry, mum, promise not to give you any strange diseases though," teased Elizabeth back. Anne listened as her daughter hummed while she arranged the pineapple on a plate.

"You're thinking about that boy again," said Anne and she smiled at Elizabeth.

"Yes, he was really rather cute in a hopeless sort of way," Elizabeth replied, "and I think he was interested in me too."

"Think, or hope," her mother replied.

"Hope," said Elizabeth and she sighed.

"Well, love. There has been no shortage of boys interested in you since you were fifteen."

"Yes, I know," said Elizabeth, "but they were only interested up to a point. When they found out that my dad is an Indian most fell by the wayside, and even more when their parents found out. That Enoch Powell did us no good at all with his damned speech...or, they were only interested in one thing..." Elizabeth ended with a giggle.

"That's not unusual," laughed Anne, "all girls have that problem."

"I know, but just because it's the so-called swinging sixties, it doesn't mean I'm jumping into bed with any old Tom, Dick or Harry. My father wouldn't have wanted that," said Elizabeth primly. Anne smiled to herself but she was not unhappy with Elizabeth's point of view.

"I want to know everything you know about the O'Malleys," said Elizabeth, picking up two plates. They moved into the lounge and sat either side of a table whose drop leaf, when raised, took up too much room. They ate and between mouthfuls Anne told Elizabeth what she knew of the O'Malley family.

"Brendan and Terry's grandfather, whose name was Patrick, came over from Ireland to England. Rumour says he had more money than most Irishmen of that time. He said he won it on the horses, but he never gambled again. He wanted a market stall but there wasn't one free. Remember, this is only what I've heard. I'm not old enough to know it to be true," said Anne

"Carry on," said Elizabeth laughing.

"They say," continued Anne, "that he bribed a council official to get rid of someone and the O'Malley family have had that stall ever since. What happened to Patrick I don't know, but his son, Sean, died of a heart attack behind the very counter you bought this pineapple from..... Sean's son, Brendan, had to run the stall with Dee's help until Terry left school."

"How exciting," said Elizabeth, "but also sad. Tell me more."

"Brendan saw Molly on her father's stall and it is said that he seduced her. They married and went on to have three girls, Michelle, Barbara and Lesley. Terry married Sharon, but she's an outsider and their only son is Colin, whose foot you damaged this morning. From what I hear he passed all his exams and could go to University, but he persuaded his mother, who persuaded Terry, to let him take one year out to pursue his musical interests. Colin does some afternoon shifts in a local garage, pumping petrol, to pay for his board and stop Terry from calling him lazy." Elizabeth giggled.

"He certainly wasn't lazy today," she said, "I saw him running here, there and everywhere."

"Running around looking for you, you mean?" Anne laughed with her daughter; "I've never seen a boy so embarrassed at the sight of ladies underwear. I wondered what you were doing ducking behind the counter when you spotted him."

"Well, it doesn't do to show you're as keen as they are, does it?" Elizabeth said.

"But you went to buy the pineapple," retorted Anne.

"Yes, and he wasn't there," said Elizabeth ruefully.

"Maybe next time," said Anne and she leaned across to touch her daughter's face gently.

"There may not be a next time, mum," said Elizabeth, "maybe today was a once off. I noticed Brendan wasn't there. Colin may just have been filling in. Do you know where he plays his music, or what his band is called?"

"I've no idea," said Anne, "but we can find out. There isn't much the traders don't know and I'm sure they'll be more than happy to talk about Colin. Gossip is stock in trade to most of them."

Her face darkened and Elizabeth reached across to hold her hand.

"They don't gossip about you any more, mum," she said, "you were a nine day wonder and I know they respect you now. You've shown them you can carry on, despite everything."

"It wasn't just me," Anne said sorrowfully, "they talked about you too."

"Listen, mum," Elizabeth said sternly, "you married a man you loved and who loved you..,"

"I thought he did," Anne interrupted.

"He did," Elizabeth responded firmly, "he worked hard, you had me, and we did have a lovely house, I remember it well. With a garden too."

"So where in God's name is he?" said Anne.

"No more, mum" said Elizabeth firmly, "finish your meal, I'll wash the pots, you dry, and we'll go out for a walk. I know it's cold but we need some fresh air. Then I'm going to wash this hair of mine." They did the dishes together and silently in the tiny kitchen. Both were lost in their different thoughts of Mr. Mohammed Patel. Anne remembered when Elizabeth was born. 'Mo', as she called him, had insisted that she be christened in a Church of England. The vicar had not only agreed but had enthusiastically performed the ceremony directly after his last Mass on a Sunday morning.

"Mum," Elizabeth's voice broke into Anne's reverie, "you're supposed to be drying the dishes, not wiping the pattern off the plate."

"Sorry," Anne replied, "you go and get your coat, I'll be ready in two minutes." By the time Elizabeth reappeared Anne was dressed in a long dark coat and her boots. They left the house and walked along the dark streets, illuminated by the odd lamp that was still working. The council made little effort in this part of town, despite complaints. They crossed the road at the bottom and headed into the 'park', as it was known locally. The land was not a designated park; it had neither railings nor facilities but rose grudgingly uphill to a point where you could look down upon the town below. They made their way to the top and Elizabeth ran the last few yards. She was stamping her feet and blowing her fingers by the time Anne reached her. She stood behind Elizabeth for a moment then noticed that her daughter was shivering.

"Come on, race you back to the bottom," she said and set off running. Elizabeth raced after her and had almost caught up with her when she heard Anne cry out and fall heavily to the ground.

"Mum," she cried, falling to her knees at Anne's side.

"Ouch," Anne said, and Elizabeth could see her face distorted with pain, "it's my ankle."

Elizabeth eased Anne's boot off and could see instantly that the ankle was badly wrenched. It was swelling as she watched.

"I'll go and get help," she said, "you stay here and don't move."

"Elizabeth," Anne retorted, "don't be so silly. I'm safer trying to hobble along with your help than lying here helpless on the ground in the dark."

"But you might damage it further," protested Elizabeth.

"I don't care," said her mother, struggling to rise, "I'm not staying here." They heard the dog first, crashing through the nearby bushes. It came bounding up to them. It was a huge mastiff with a studded collar. It stopped and made a low growling sound.

"Heel," called a voice and the dog turned. The man who had called out came into view. He was wearing a black studded jacket, black jeans, black T-shirt and a studded collar. His shaven head seemed to float in the darkness.

"Christ," said Anne, falling to the ground once more and wincing, "that's all we need, a bloody skinhead out with his dog." There was fear in her voice.

"Mother!" Elizabeth exclaimed, "You don't know he is a skinhead. He's probably just bald." The man came closer, leashing the dog as he walked.

"Are you in trouble, ladies?" he asked graciously. Elizabeth heard her mother's sigh of relief.

"Mum's wrenched her ankle," Elizabeth said, "I was going to go for help but she was afraid to be left here on her own."

"She's right," he said, "There are all sorts of people wandering around here at night. You hold the dog," he gave Elizabeth the lead and she took it gingerly.

"It's okay, he won't bite unless I tell him," the man laughed, "right, and can you stand? Anne shook her head. The man simply hoisted her up by her armpits until she was standing on one foot. Then he picked her up in his arms as if she were a feather.

"Right," he said, completely matter of factly, "which way is home?"

Elizabeth giggled and said, "Follow me." Anne remained silent as the man carried her to their front door. Elizabeth opened the door and the dog bounded inside, dragging Elizabeth with him.

"Sorry about that," the man said, "he's probably thirsty. Heel, Rover." The dog turned, looked at his master and began to pant. The man gently placed Anne down on the sofa.

"We could help two at the same time," he said to Elizabeth, "if you'll run a bowl of cold water to put your mother's foot into and give the dog a dish on the kitchen floor." He was kneeling down and gently easing off Anne's long sock.

"That looks nasty," he said, "but I don't think it's broken. Do you mind if I feel at it?"

"No," groaned Anne, "but do you know what you're looking for?"

"Should do," the man replied, "I'm an ambulance driver. I've seen many injuries, a lot worse than this, in my time." He saw Anne's look of surprise and laughed. She found herself blushing. Elizabeth came in with a bowl of water and she gave it to him. He tested the temperature and nodded.

"Icy cold," he said, "this won't be pleasant but it will help." He lifted Anne's foot and put it into the water. She gasped at the contact but kept her foot in place.

"Elizabeth," she said after a moment, "we're forgetting our manners. Please offer Mr..." She looked questioningly at the man.

"David Watson," he said, "but Dave will do."

"Please offer Dave a drink. Will you take tea or coffee?" Anne said, "I'm sorry we don't have anything stronger."

"Tea will be fine," he said, "Mrs..."

"Anne Patel and my daughter is Elizabeth."

"If you can find an old tea towel I can bind up the foot in a cold compress," said Dave to Elizabeth's retreating figure.

"We've plenty of crepe bandages in the cupboard upstairs," said Anne, "I always had a good first aid kit. Well, when you have a child around, it's as well to be prepared." Dave smiled at her.

"You don't have to justify a stock of crepe bandages to me, you know," he said.

"I wasn't," Anne said, defensively, then she saw him smile and added, "well, yes, I suppose I was." She was disconcerted. She felt that she had insulted this man by first of all assuming that he was something he most obviously was not and then by pretending that she had everything she should have just because he was medically trained.

"I should know better," she said, half to herself, but he caught her words.

"Sorry?" he asked.

"I was chastising myself for being a bigot and prejudiced. Of all the people around here, I should know better," she said and pointed to her wedding photograph. Dave picked up the photograph and peered closely at it. It showed a handsome, tall, slim Indian man, proudly arm in arm with Anne on their wedding day. She was in a white shot silk dress and he was immaculate in a navy blue suit, white shirt and pale green tie. The tie exactly matched the shade of Anne's eyes, which smiled adoringly into his face. The contrast between them was all the more striking because of the mane of coppery hair close to the jet black hair of her new husband.

"Good looking man," he said, "I see where your daughter gets it from."

"She has my mouth and nose," Anne blurted out, annoyed.

"Yes, she does. Does she have your temperament too?"

"Meaning?" Anne's voice rose a fraction.

"Calm down, will you?" Dave said softly, "are you always so defensive? I don't give a monkey if you're married to the Man in the Moon. Why do you?" Anne's eyes filled up and Dave took the opportunity to act as if he assumed she was in pain.

"Come on, let's get that foot compressed," he said, "Elizabeth, do you have some painkillers?" For the next few minutes Dave soaked crepe bandages in cold water and bound Anne's foot and gave her painkillers with water.

"I think bed early tonight," he said, "Can you climb the stairs?"

"I think so," Anne replied.

"You'd be better staying there for at least two days. The more rest the better," said Dave.

"I can't do that!" Anne exclaimed, "I have to go to the wholesaler tomorrow. There's a special order arriving. Elizabeth doesn't drive yet."

"Don't worry, mum," Elizabeth interjected, "I'll phone them. I'm sure they'll hold the order."

"But I've promised the goods to customers, I hate letting them down," said Anne.

"Give me the name and address of the wholesaler," said Dave, "I'm on a split shift tomorrow. I can collect the goods for you and take them to the market."

"Oh, we couldn't ask you to do that," said Anne.

"Sorry," Dave said, "you don't know me from Adam, do you? Get the phone book," he looked at Elizabeth, "look me up and check my address. It's 8, Marlborough Road." Elizabeth looked at her mother who nodded. Elizabeth checked the phone book and nodded at Anne.

"Mr. D. Watson, 8, Marlborough Road," she confirmed.

"I'm more than willing to come tomorrow and take Elizabeth to the wholesaler, help her with the boxes and then drop her at the market and bring the van back," he said. Anne looked doubtful but she could see the sense of his plan.

"I'm sure I'll be all right in the morning," said Anne.

"And I'm sure you won't be," said Dave, "but I leave it up to you. Just call me if Elizabeth needs collecting, I can be round in ten minutes. Now, I'd better be off. I'll see myself out. Rover, where are you?" The mastiff trotted into the room from the kitchen and Dave put on his leash. Seconds later he had gone and Anne looked at Elizabeth.

"Well," she exhaled heavily, "that was a peculiar walk in the park, wasn't it?"

"He's nice, mum," said Elizabeth, "but I was scared when Rover came bounding up."

"Me too," said Anne, "more scared than I'd let you know."

"Come on," Elizabeth said, "let's get you up the stairs. Are the painkillers working?" Anne gingerly put her foot to the floor and winced.

"A bit better," she said. She hobbled round the sofa, leaning on Elizabeth's arm and they made it up the stairs.

"See you in the morning," Elizabeth said as she kissed her mother goodnight and drew the curtains.

The next morning Elizabeth made tea and went to check on her mother's condition. Anne tested the foot on the floor but it was still too painful to put her weight on it.

"I'll ring Dave," Elizabeth said, "and you get back into bed." Anne didn't argue. Her face showed signs of a restless night. Twenty minutes later Elizabeth was sitting next to Dave being driven to the wholesalers.

"It really is good of you," she said, "I mean; we didn't even know you until last night."

"It's surprising just how good people can be," he replied, "I see it all the time. You call to a house or an incident and people come out of the woodwork offering tea or blankets or the use of their phones. Then they melt away again. I've had complete strangers standing over me in the pouring rain with an umbrella while I've given oxygen to a patient. Then they vanish." Elizabeth nodded.

"Where was your dad last night," asked Dave casually, "working late?"

"No," Elizabeth hesitated, and then decided on the truth, "he went to India five years ago - and he hasn't come back."

"I'm sorry to hear that, Elizabeth," said Dave sympathetically, "that must be hard for you both."

"It's harder for Mum because she wanted me to go to college but I wouldn't. I left school last year and told her I was going into the business until..." she didn't finish the sentence.

"Until he comes back," said Dave, "and I'm sure he will. No one could leave such a good looking woman and such a pretty girl without good reason."

"Thank you," said Elizabeth.

"We're here," Dave said, "you go in and do the business and I'll wait out front." Elizabeth dropped out of the van and five minutes later she was beckoning him. He carried the boxes, loaded them and they drove to the Market Hall.

"Can you manage all day by yourself?" he asked as he finished carrying the boxes to the stall.

"Sure," she replied, "one of the other traders will keep an eye open when I need to leave the stall. I know the quiet times."

"Right," he said, "I'll take the van back to your mum. Shall I leave it outside and push the keys through the letterbox?"

"Yes, please," said Elizabeth, "I think she'll sleep a lot today. I left her a flask of coffee and sandwiches and painkillers. She should be all right."

"She's a very lucky lady to have you, Elizabeth. You take care," he said.

She watched him walk away, whistling and twirling the keys round his finger.

Chapter 3

Charles Dickens would have been proud of Nathaniel Sharpe. A man ingratiating to his superiors, and a man who perceived himself to be superior to those he was supposed to serve.

The traders called him Nat to his face. What he didn't know was that even the town councillors, also called him "The Gnat" and were thankful for the silent G. Nathaniel was the illegitimate son of Herbert Walker, the previous Market Superintendent. His parents, Mr and Mrs Sharpe, had run a household goods stall and Mrs Sharpe had taken up with Herbert Walker in her twenties. She had flirted behind the stall and winked and blinked her way into his affections. The traders watched as Walker spent more time collecting Mrs. Sharpe's rent than he did any others. Her husband had turned a blind eye and Nathaniel was conceived in the very room that was now his office. He was literally born into the job. Mr. Sharpe acquiesced, with a sidelong glance at his wife's sudden fertility, to his name being on Nathaniel's birth certificate and then died when Nathaniel was ten years old. Mrs. Sharpe collared Herbert Walker on the way back from the funeral and wept onto his best suit. After a decent interval Herbert Walker moved in with them and then Mrs. Sharpe put her claws in. She leaned on Herbert to provide money to send Nathaniel to a private school. Herbert found the money and then, realising that he could end up paying for the rest of his life, persuaded Mrs. Sharpe to let him take the boy at sixteen and train him to be the next Superintendent. She agreed and from then on Nathaniel was to learn, at his biological father's knee, all the tricks and scams that had paid for his education. He learned well. When Herbert Walker died, Nathaniel was only twenty-two and was considered too young to be in charge but he used the influence his father had with people and got the required number of approvals at the next council meeting. He had been in the job for over three decades. His duties were many. One task was to choose an assistant and he selected carefully. The youngsters, always male, were either too dim to realise what he was doing or too bright to stay doing the most boring jobs for longer than a few months. For Nathaniel was, quietly, over a number of years, amassing a considerable amount of money. Hiding his tracks carefully he made sure this money never saw his regular post office savings account or building society account except in figures that he could justify. You would have to know that he held ten separate accounts in three neighbouring towns to realise how lucrative being a Market Superintendent had been for him. His theft had no altruistic motive. He had no children to put through school. He neither smoked nor drank, except a half pint at Christmas. He had no lady friends, nor wanted them. He didn't run a car nor gamble. He negotiated discounts from the traders. His greatest satisfaction came from knowing that he was taking money from under everyone's nose and getting away with it. He always made sure that his back was covered. He kept his account books safely locked away. He never took a day off sick and he encouraged his mother in her hypochondria. When he had to attend council meetings he made sure his assistant was doing something that would keep him occupied for hours. The door of his office was always locked. His hair was receding, his face was long, gaunt and pale, the cheekbones sunken and his eyes were watery. He wore a complete set of dentures and they were immaculately clean and regimentally even. He was tolerated by all, but only a long line of marmalade cats, brought in to mouse, loved him. Marmalade lived upstairs on a blanket and followed him everywhere. His agenda was simple. When his mother died he was going to withdraw all his money and go to Spain or South America. Money would buy him friends.

He was the only man who had read, and could quote verbatim from, the ancient 'Rules for the Administration and Order of the Market Hall and its Occupiers', a weighty tome updated only once since the Victorians had built the Hall.

He quoted its rules frequently, and made up a few. Many a trader had parted with a small 'consideration' for him to turn a blind eye. He always insisted that the wrong be put right as soon as possible and then smiled as he pocketed the money. He loved to check that the scales used on the food stalls were correct. A lump of dirt, eased away from a potato or a crumb of cheese, would be pounced upon.

"We will be keeping these scales clean and therefore accurate, won't we," he would ask, all innocence, "we don't want to be cheating our customers, do we?" A bag of fruit would arrive upstairs later, or better still, a coin. He would rub the coin, a threepenny bit or a penny, and put it carefully into a bag.

"Oh, Mrs. Baker," he would say sorrowfully, "so many empty boxes under the counter. Such a fire risk, don't you think?" Mrs. Baker would flush and set to squashing the boxes flat.

"Let me help," he would say and call for his assistant to take away the offending articles. Mrs. Baker would invariable offer 'something for the lad's help' and Nathaniel would pocket the proffered coin and mutter something about 'making sure he got it later'. The boy never did. Nathaniel's cleverness was in never accepting large amounts of money. He was careful that no one could ever accuse him of taking a bribe. Over eighty per cent of the traders handed over small sums at seemingly random intervals and thought nothing of it. The rest Nathaniel had the good sense to leave alone. Traders came and went and the few who had been in the Market Hall for generations he left alone. Their parents had paid for his education. The pennies and threepenny bits mounted up into shillings and then went into a designated account at the end of each month. The Building Societies were paying 4% interest- tax free. Christmas was the time when younger family members were on holiday and wanting to earn pocket money. Nathaniel would stroll around the market.

"Hello, young man," he would say to a boy nipping to the toilets, "helping out mum and dad today are we?" The innocent child, caught unawares, would nod and grin.

"How long have you got off school this time?" Nathaniel would ask.

"Until January 3rd." Nathaniel would walk back with the child and 'tut-tut' at the parents.

"Under age workers," he would shake his head.

"Oh, come on, Nathaniel," the parent would declare, "He's not doing any harm. It's good for the lad to be learning."

"Well, it's more than my job's worth," Nathaniel would draw his breath in, "but then he does look, I suppose, like a very small sixteen year old."

"Oh, very small indeed," the parent would beam back, "when is it you take your mother's Christmas gift home?"

"There's really no need," Nathaniel would protest, "but normally the end of the week." Nothing more was said but he would expect a card with a coin inside. He always got them. Yes, Christmas was a good time, but only once every 365 days. Today he was collecting the weekly rents when he noticed that Elizabeth was on her own. He wandered over. He knew the health centre had its mother and baby session this morning. Many of the mothers would pop into the Market, to buy new bibs and mittens. Anne would expect a good trade but she was nowhere to be seen. Half a dozen customers stood around waiting to be served. Elizabeth was flustered, as she still hadn't unpacked all the orders.

"It was six of the yellow bibs with ducks on, wasn't it?" she was asking one of the women.

"Yes, but I don't mind these," the woman said, picking up a cheaper design.

"Oh, no," said Elizabeth, "I know they are in here somewhere, mum ordered them especially for you, and they'll look ever so sweet on baby." She dived under the counter and rummaged through the boxes emerging triumphantly with a packet in her hand.

"There, I knew they were here somewhere," she said and began to extract the yellow ones.

"Oh, they're nice," said another woman, "have you three in pink?" Elizabeth wrapped the yellow ones, took the money and turned immediately to get another bag for the pink bibs. Nathaniel saw the toddler's hand reach up over the top of the counter and grab a fist full of mittens and put them in his mother's shopping bag. Elizabeth had no way of seeing as the toddler was lower than the counter and the mother seemed unaware of her child's action. Too unaware.

"Little bugger," Nathaniel thought as he moved in. Here was a golden opportunity.

"Madam," he said, as the woman walked away, toddler in one hand and pram in the other.

"Yes," she spoke sharply as she stopped. Nathaniel was immediately convinced of her guilt.

"Would you like to check your bag," he said, "I think your son has acquired some extra shopping." The woman began to bluster but Nathaniel merely raised his hand and said,

"We can do it here or in my office with a policeman present." Her attitude changed immediately. She checked the basket and found the mittens.

"Oh, my God," she said loudly, so that everyone heard her, "look what this little sod has done. Picked up some mittens. Not even the right size." She laughed a false embarrassed laugh, waved the mittens around and walked back to the stall.

"I'm so sorry," the woman said, "I'd no idea. You can't watch them every single second, can you?" Elizabeth smiled and thanked her. The woman walked away, chastising the toddler and throwing a dirty look at Nathaniel. He walked over and made a show of straightening the mittens.

"Expensive are they?" he asked.

"The best we have," replied Elizabeth, "almost two shillings a pair. Double knit and lined as well."

"So, I've just saved you a considerable amount," he said and stroked his chin.

"Oh, Nathaniel," Elizabeth said, colouring as she grasped his meaning, "thank you so much. Will you, that is, may I offer you a little something as a reward?"

"Oh, I'm sure that's not necessary, my dear," he said but he didn't move away.

"No, no, I insist," Elizabeth said and she leaned over and pressed a coin into his hand.

"Well, that's very kind of you, I'm sure," he said, slipping the coin into his pocket.

"You'll be collecting the rent today?" Elizabeth asked him.

"Yes, that's why I was in this area," he replied. Elizabeth counted out the rent and took the receipt. Nathaniel folded the notes precisely in half and made an entry in his ledger.

"See you," Elizabeth said and dived back down under the counter.

"He's a slimy old sod," said her neighbouring trader.

"You can say that again," replied Elizabeth, "but he did save me from losing some of my stock."

"Aye, at a price," retorted her neighbour, "but he never asked where your mother was, did he?"

Nathaniel continued on his rounds. Nathaniel never interrupted sales and the waiting gave him the chance to spot any infringements of the rules. He waited by O'Malley's stall. They were all busy weighing, wrapping and taking money. He was very precise in his dealings with the O'Malley brothers. Brendan's father had had a run in with Herbert Walker, Nathaniel's father, and had proved that he was no pushover. Nathaniel had seen his father's humiliation and held it against the O'Malleys ever since. One day Brendan O'Malley would pay for his father's so-called success. Nathaniel remembered the day as if it were yesterday....

....It had been a simple case of who had the authority to allocate vacant stalls. The stall adjoining the O'Malleys was being vacated after decades in the same hands. Sean O'Malley wanted to expand and had had his application for a vacant adjoining space on the waiting list for more than three years. Herbert Walker kept the lists in his office. There were three lists: of people wanting to get in to the market, a list of traders needing extra space and another list of traders wanting to move to a more lucrative spot. Whenever there was a vacancy Walker would telephone prospective traders and meet them, away from the office.

"Of course, getting a stall is purely down to the council. They are the elected body, you understand, who decide," he would begin. His companion would nod in agreement.

"But that's not to say that I'm not listened to when it comes to a recommendation," he would continue. At that point the more savvy traders would grasp what was being said and before long a price would have been fixed for Walker's recommendation. The naïve traders never got the point and their names stayed at the bottom of the list. The honest traders gave him short shrift but he was so careful in his use of words that they had nothing concrete to report and their names too stayed at the bottom of the list. Herbert Walker and Nathaniel had gone confidently to the council meeting. Walker's chosen name was at the top of the list and three of the councillors owed him a favour so he did not expect any objections. It was a straight contest between his man and the O'Malleys and he had his arguments ready. It all went to plan and Walker's man got his stall. The next day a furious Sean O'Malley was waiting outside his office.

"A word, Walker," Sean spoke through clenched teeth as he pushed his way into the office.

"Mr. O'Malley," Herbert was calm and collected. He walked around the desk and sat down.

"Take a seat, Sean," he said.

"I'll say what I have to say standing here," said Sean and he leaned across the desk, strong forearms bulging atop massive hands. Walker leaned back in his chair and smiled.

"You can wipe that smile off your face you conniving, snivelling little snot," Sean shouted, "I know, and everybody else knows, that you fixed it yesterday in the meeting. We can't prove anything illegal but we're not going to take this lying down any more. The traders are forming a committee and we're going to approach the council about this waiting list game. In future *we* want to see all the names on the list, and how long they have been there."

"There are rules about the waiting list," Walker said calmly, "that have been in place since the Hall was built. The holding of the list remains in the hands of the Superintendent."

"Then the rules will have to be changed," Sean shouted back, "that's the way we see it. We've got a copy of the rule book, too, you know, and one way or another we'll get the rules changed."

"So that the traders can fix that there isn't any competition?" Walker sneered.

"Is that how you see it?" Sean snorted.

"That's how our forefathers saw it," said Walker, "they knew that given the chance traders would form cartels and keep out anyone trying to undercut them."

"Well, that's not what we want," said Sean, "we want people, all people, to be given a fair chance at a vacant stall."

"You're just angry because you didn't get the stall next door," retorted Walker.

"Yes, I'm angry," replied Sean, "because I want to expand and offer even better value and choice to my customers, and so do a lot of others. It seems that we can never grow our businesses because new traders are given preferential treatment. Or maybe they *give* preferential treatment."

"Be very careful about what you're saying," Walker said quietly.

"I'm damned sure there was something going on yesterday. We're going to stop it," Sean replied and he barged out of the door. Sean worked hard getting the traders to join forces. He cajoled and coaxed people, one by one, to sign his letter asking the council to amend the rules so that the list was published where everyone could see it. Traders wanting to expand were easy to convince but they were afraid that the council would see them as greedy.

"It's not as if we can expand this building," said one of them to Sean, "for every one of us that takes two spaces, we stop someone else making a living. Is that fair?"

"We have to expand or go under," said Sean, chewing the side of his fingernail, "the space we have isn't adequate to hold the volume we could sell. There isn't any storage space. Maybe we should be petitioning for a new Market Hall."

"Slow down, Sean," his companion said, "one thing at a time." For two years Sean badgered away and eventually managed to get an association organised among his fellow traders. He was a thorn in Walker's side on many occasions. His application for an adjoining stall meanwhile stayed on Walker's list. Sean O'Malley and Herbert Walker were both dead and buried before the stall became vacant again and this time Brendan O'Malley was facing Nathaniel Sharpe- son against son.

"Mr. O'Malley," the Chairman spoke precisely and enunciated his words with the care that comes from an upper class education, "you have a problem, it seems." The Chairman looked over his glasses at Brendan, uncomfortable in his best suit and a tie that was too tight. He rose to speak but the Chairman waved him back into a sitting position.

"You're not on trial," he said. Brendan heard a muffled laugh coming from the man sitting next to him and he turned and stared at Nathaniel. It gave him the confidence he needed.

"It's not just me, sir,," he started, "it's many of my fellow traders as well. We need to be expanding to offer our customers better choice and quantity. There is a list of new people wanting to come into the Market and another list that has people wanting to expand. It seems that the new people always get preference. I'm not saying we don't get a hearing, but we never get extra space."

"You think it wrong that we give other people the same chance you've had for, let me see," the chairman glanced briefly at a notebook in front of him, "more than three generations. Your grandfather, Patrick O'Malley *somehow* got a stall, even though he was not from this town, and your own father Sean O'Malley had it until the day he died and you have occupied it since and, presumably, make a good living."

"My father was offering basic fruit and veg., sir. I want to give the people of this town a bit more choice. Don't you think they deserve it?" The point went home.

"The Market Hall isn't big enough to give the existing traders on your list an extra space. It would create less choice and lessen competition," replied the Chairman.

"Then maybe we should be thinking about a new, bigger, Market Hall," replied Brendan, and he paused for a moment to let the idea take root.

"This town is growing fast," Brendan went on, "Factories and businesses that weren't even thought about in Victoria's days are here now. People all need food and clothes at good prices."

The meeting room became animated. The journalist sent to cover what he thought of as yet another boring meeting sat up straight and began taking notes. The councillors sitting around the huge table began whispering. A spectator in the gallery thumped the rail and shouted "Hear, hear!"

"A new Market Hall," said the Chairman "would cost a fortune."

"I'm sure it would," replied Brendan, "but think of the site the current one is sitting on. Right in the middle of town and, some might argue, stopping development of department stores and banks. That land must be worth a small fortune. Once you've got a small fortune a big one's easy to find." The Chairman and the councillors laughed. Brendan coloured and began to bluster but the Chairman held up a hand.

"No, no, Mr O'Malley," he said, "we're not laughing at you. What you've said is truer than you know. We must seriously think about your proposal. But it will take some extensive planning." The Chairman leaned his elbows on the table, cupped his chin in his hands and looked into the distance beyond Brendan for a few moments. The people in the room could almost hear his brain ticking. Then he spoke.

"Yes, I think we should develop this idea. In the meantime I suggest that your proposal about the list be looked at very carefully. Maybe we can find a compromise whereby one stall goes to a new trader and the next to an existing one...and we'll find a way of letting people swap stalls so that they may, over time, get the positions they want. Mr. Sharpe, see to it please." Nathaniel's hand shot up in the air; his fingers spread like inverted icicles. The Chairman nodded in his direction.

"May I add my concerns to those expressed by your good self earlier," he said ingratiatingly, "that we may end up with thirty or more traders with double stalls and less competition."

"Yes, yes, we've already covered that," the Chairman replied testily, "and now we have to move on. Mr. O'Malley has made an interesting new point. The meeting is adjourned and we'll begin looking carefully at the proposal for a new Market Hall." Nathaniel seethed inwardly. Thirty people less to extract money from was not his idea of progress. However, a new Market Hall with more tenants was a good idea, even if it was in the future. He knew the Chairman was Managing Director of a large construction company and the Treasurer of the council owned a firm of architects. He could almost see the pound signs in their eyes as they rose and the chamber emptied. Better accept defeat gracefully and make new plans. He smiled at Brendan but the smile was not returned. A month later the stall came free again and Brendan's name was top of the list and the council were talking seriously about building a new market hall....

....."You want your rent, Nat?" Brendan's voice broke into Nathaniel's reverie.

"Not my rent, Brendan," he said quietly, "the council's rent. I wonder how much they are going to charge in the new hall."

CHAPTER 4

"Mr. O'Malley," said the doctor, "come in and take a seat." The man sitting by the side of the desk was no more than 28 or 29 years old and Brendan was taken aback by the youthful face.

"Are you the doctor?" Brendan asked and his voice betrayed his surprise.

"Yes," the man replied, "Doctor Sharples, at your service, and I do have the papers to prove it."

"You're a bit young, aren't you?" said Brendan as he walked across the room.

"Three years out of medical school and lots of experience," said the doctor, smiling, "Now, what's the problem?"

"A pain, like a stitch but worse. It gets me any time. It's been coming more regularly."

"Will you strip to the waist and get up on the couch, please," said the doctor, who was looking at a thin medical envelope in front of him.

"You're not exactly a regular visitor here, are you?" the doctor said, smiling broadly.

"No. I don't have time to be sick," Brendan replied, "I have a business to run."

"Oh, what kind of business?" the doctor asked him.

"Fruit and veg stall on the market," replied Brendan.

"Ah, long hours, early mornings, humping boxes and sacks, very strenuous," said the doctor.

"Keeps me fit, I think," replied Brendan.

"Smoker?"

"No"

"Drinker?"

"No more than most."

"What's that, then."

"Three pints maybe, three times a week and a whisky or two on a Saturday." The doctor was examining him all the time he was asking questions and then he got out his stethoscope and asked Brendan to cough and breathe while he moved it around his chest and back.

"Any heart trouble in the family?" asked the doctor.

"Dad dropped dead with his heart," replied Brendan. The doctor smiled and asked him what age his father was when he died.

"Forty-five or thereabouts," replied Brendan. The doctor's eyebrows went up ever so slightly and Brendan noticed.

"Well," replied the doctor, "I'd like you to go for tests. It could be that you have the same problem your father had. It's not unusual and it's easy to keep under control these days. Can you go to see a specialist next week?"

"As soon as that," replied Brendan, "can't you just give me some tablets for now?"

"No," the doctor replied, "there is something amiss but the specialist will do some X-rays and tests and we can go from there."

"This is the man you'll be seeing," the doctor said, writing on a card, "you'll get a letter within the week telling you where to go. I'll get the results a few days later. We'll ring you."

"Is there anything I should do, or not do, in the meantime," said Brendan.

"Well, if you can find someone to help with the heavy stuff," replied the doctor, "then you're not putting additional strain on your system, which would help." Brendan shook his head.

"Is that forever?" he said.

"No, Mr. O'Malley," the doctor replied, "just until we've got you sorted. You'll be as right as rain after we've done with you."

"As right as rain, you say," laughed Brendan, "have you ever thought about that expression? What exactly is right about rain?"

"I don't know," said Doctor Sharples, laughing, "Unless you haven't seen any for years."

"Not likely round here, is it?" said Brendan and he held out his hand. The doctor shook it warmly.

"See you soon," he said. Brendan left the surgery and got into the car. It was a fine, bright day and people were smiling in the sunshine as he drove home. He'd told Molly he was going to the accountants. She hadn't said anything just kissed him as he left and said how nice it was to have him around the house when she got up.

"I was up at my normal time," he had protested, "four thirty and not a minute later."

"Yes, I know," she had soothed him, "and normally out at the ungodly hour of five o'clock. I just said it was nice to see you in the morning."

"Oh, right," he'd said. Now, as he parked her car in the drive, he had to decide how to break the news to her. He turned the key in the lock and called through the hallway.

"Is the kettle on?"He heard Molly's voice come through from the kitchen - "It's always on."

He walked into the kitchen and sat at the wooden table that was big enough to seat eight comfortably. It had seen many a family gathering over the years. Molly took her cooking seriously and the table had literally groaned when laden with her dishes. He ran his index finger along the grain. The tree that had been felled for his table pre-dated him by hundreds of years and the table would be here long after he had gone. He liked that idea. Molly placed a cup of tea in front of him.

"It wasn't all that bad, then?" she asked him.

"What?"

"The accountants."

"I wasn't at the accountants, Molly."

"I know," she said simply.

"How do you know?" he asked, and he frowned. Had she been checking up on him?

"Because, Brendan, you left your wallet on the table and I rang them to let you know. They said you weren't expected there today," she said.

"No."

"So," she said, sitting beside him and taking his hand, "where have you been?"

"The doctors," he said and he looked straight at her. Her face remained impassive although he saw fear flicker briefly in her eyes........ Such beautiful eyes, blue as robin's eggs, which had remained as clear and bright as the first day he saw her when she was just sixteen. The same day that he had decided he would marry her. Walking over to her father's stall he had bowed and doffed his cap to her.

"Brendan O'Malley, at your service," he had said and his eyes twinkled. She had blushed pink 'like a daisy's petals kissed by the sun' he told her later and he was smitten.

"What did the doctor say," Molly said and she shook his hand, bringing him back into the present.

"Eh?" Brendan said.

"Where were you?" she said.

"Remembering the first time I saw you, love," he smiled.

"Oh, that's a long time ago," she smiled, "but come on, tell me. I'm getting worried."

"It's my heart," he started and held up his hand to stop her from interrupting, "it's probably faulty like my dad's but the doctor says that these days I can live normally. I've to go and see a specialist next week or so. They'll send a letter." He got up from the table suddenly.

"Fancy a trip to the seaside?" he said.

"What? Now!" she exclaimed.

"Yes, why not?" he replied, "The girls are old enough to take care of themselves. I'll ring the Market Hall and tell Nathaniel to pass a message to Terry. Let's do it." He grabbed her hands and pulled her upwards and then gathered her into his arms. He kissed her head.

"I've a notion to see the sea and why not today?" he said. An hour later they were strolling along the front of the coast of England. Brendan breathed in the salty air and, pulling Molly to him, he gazed out to sea in the direction of Ireland.

"You know, my ancestors came across that sea to work in England. Grandfather Patrick O'Malley arrived with a packet that it was thought he won on the horses. Yet he never gambled again. Strange that, don't you think? Do you think I have relatives over there? Grandfather Patrick was one of four children, my father used to say. I wonder what happened to the others. And odd that Patrick only had the one son, Sean. Really changed when they came over here, didn't they? But my dad never talked about Patrick O'Malley, did he? Sort of clammed up whenever anyone mentioned Ireland. Wonder why?"

"My goodness, Brendan, you sound like your Terry with all these questions. The three left over there will all be long gone now," Molly laughed, "but I guess their descendants are alive. If they had any."

"Should we visit one day, love?" he asked her.

"What, to find them?" she said.

"No, just to see the Emerald Isle that is my heritage," he said.

"Sure, Brendan," she replied in a mock Irish voice, "but not until you've seen the doctor."

"When shall we tell the girls?" he asked.

"Sunday lunchtime, I think that's best," Molly replied, "that's the one time we can be sure they'll all be in one place."

"We've been ever so lucky with them, haven't we?" said Brendan.

"Yes," replied Molly, "Pity one of them wasn't a boy though."

"I'd rather have my three strapping healthy beautiful talented girls than a son like Colin," he said with pride, "why would I need a boy?"

"To take over the business!" she exclaimed.

"There's time yet," he chided, "Barbara or Lesley may decide to become O'Malley Brothers and Daughter."

"More likely Lesley," Molly mused, "Barbara's as fey as Colin. Wants to be a singer too."

"Can she?" asked Brendan and he hummed a tune.

"Can she what?" Molly looked perplexed, "sing or be a singer?"

"Sing," said Brendan.

"Actually, yes she can," said Molly, "she's been in the school choir for over a year now. They've won inter-school competitions and they're doing a musical this Christmas. She's got the lead part."

"Oh, what are they doing?" asked Brendan.

"West Side Story. Barbara's playing Maria. Don't tell me you've not wondered at the music she's been playing recently."

"I only hear a cacophony of noise coming from their three bedrooms. None of it ever sounded like music before," laughed Brendan.

"Maybe it's time you started taking a bit more interest in your girls instead of working morning, noon and night," Molly said gently.

"Yes, love, you're right, I'm not there very often when they do their plays and things, am I?"

"You made it to Michelle's first two Nativity plays, if I remember rightly," said Molly, frowning with concentration, "but then your Dad was alive then."

"Well, there you are," replied Brendan triumphantly, "I've not missed everything."

"That was fifteen years ago," said Molly, shaking her head and smiling, "so tell me..." A sudden rain stopped her in her tracks and they dashed to a cafe for shelter and ordered tea.

"Now, what were you going to say," he asked.

"Well," she started, "seeing as how you were taking an interest in Barbara's singing, I was wondering if I couldn't persuade you to take a little time away from the stall and maybe come to one of her performances." Brendan opened his mouth to protest but she stopped him in his tracks.

"Have you thought about asking Terry if Colin could do one or two days a week? Or even about easing up and getting another assistant like Dee? After all, it's not as if we're short of money."

"With three girls at home and weddings to save up for, you want me to ease up?" he spluttered.

"Yes, I do," Molly said firmly, "I've no inclination to being a widow."

"We'd best talk about all this," said Brendan, scratching his head, "shall we invite Terry's mob for Sunday lunch?"

"Three hardly constitutes a mob," Molly chided him, "but yes, we'll tell our girls the news and then have a family lunch."

Sunday morning brought a clear bright day that promised to burn off the first frost of the year. Brendan and Molly were up with the larks, Molly wanted to make a start on the lunch preparations before the girls got up for breakfast. Brendan offered, as he always did, to do the vegetables and Molly told him, as she always did, to go and read the Sunday paper.

"The last thing you want on your day off is to be handling yet more fruit and vegetables," she laughed. She set to with potato peeler in one hand and a mountain of vegetables on the table. The radio played softly in the background. Michelle was the first of the girls to get up. She wandered into the kitchen wearing an outsize T-shirt bearing the legend "Che Guevara" on the front. She dropped a sleepy kiss on her mother's head.

"Morning, mum," she said, "Want a hand with those?"

"No, love, but I wouldn't say no to a cup of tea," Molly replied.

"When did you ever say no to a cup of tea?" Michelle grinned. Michelle was filling the kettle with water and Molly paused to watch her eldest daughter. Michelle had the strongest resemblance to Brendan's mother of all their three girls. She could only be described as sturdy and wholesome with her rounded face and mass of hair that today was as coppery as Molly's pan bases but tomorrow could be blonde or even black. Her eyes were clear and a green-brown. Michelle had never gone through a spotty phase and her skin glowed with health. She had wanted to leave school straight after her examinations and had begun work at the local police station in a routine administration post. Over six years she had worked hard, proved her honesty and reliability, and was now personal assistant to an Inspector. She couldn't talk about her work at home but she enjoyed the life and had gone out with three or four young policemen. Michelle put the tea in front of her mother.

"Shall I take a cup up to the others?" she asked. Molly glanced at the clock. It was half past eight.

"Was Barbara out late last night?" she asked.

"Oh, come on, mum," Michelle said, "you know you don't sleep properly until you've heard us both come in, but no, I think she was in before eleven."

"Rehearsals again?" asked Molly.

"God, yes," said Michelle, "I'm going to end up singing with her by the time the show starts."

"Go on then, take them a cup and ask your Dad if he wants one too, will you," said Molly. As Michelle was leaving the kitchen, two cups in her hands, the door opened and Barbara walked in. Theatrically Barbara took one cup from her sister and waltzed it around the room singing,

"Pretty, I feel pretty, I feel pretty.."

"Oh, shut up," Michelle said, not unkindly, "is Lesley stirring?"

"She's in the bathroom right now," said Barbara, landing up in front of her mother and kissing her on the cheek.

"Morning mum," she said.

"Good morning, Babs," said Molly, "how did rehearsals go?"

"Fabulous costumes and the singing was great," Barbara said, and then she pulled a face, "although I could wish for a more fanciable guy than Tom Entwhistle playing Tony. I'd rather have had the real Romeo."

"He can sing and dance though, can't he?" asked Molly.

"Oh, yes, like a dream. But he has spots," replied Barbara.

"He won't always have spots," said Molly. She had finished the vegetables and was washing and cutting them and placing them into pans of various sizes.

"Are we having Terry's family round today?" asked Barbara, stealing a piece of carrot and munching on it.

"Yes, so I could do with everyone bathed or showered and down for breakfast in an hour latest, and that means me next." Molly dashed out of the kitchen and up the stairs, catching a glimpse of Lesley leaving the bathroom and returning to the bedroom she shared with Barbara.

"Morning, Lesley," Molly shouted.

"Morning, mum," her look-a-like shouted back. The blonde hair had been washed; 'yet again' thought Molly and Lesley was ruffling it dry through her fingers. Molly showered and dressed with the minimum of fuss and then left the bathroom free. By the time she got downstairs, Brendan had started on breakfast. The table was laid and bacon was ready for grilling, toast was popping and the eggs were about to be dropped into a bubbling poacher.

"No fry up?" she said, hugging him around the waist from behind.

"Healthy living," he said mock sternly, "but how long do poached eggs take?"

"Not that long," Molly laughed, "they'll be like bullets. Go and hurry the girls for me." Thirty minutes later the five of them sat round the table and ate breakfast. As Lesley got up to gather the dishes, her mother put a hand on her arm.

"A minute, Lesley," she said quietly, "your father has something to tell you." Three pairs of eyes were immediately fixed on Brendan and two undeveloped hands went to cover the face of his youngest daughter. Gently he prised one away from Lesley's face and grasped it in his own massive hand.

"It's not what you think," he said gently.

"How do you know what I think?" gasped Lesley.

"Well, tell me the worst," he asked her.

"You and mum are getting divorced," she whispered back. Brendan laughed out loud.

"Pigs will fly before that happens," he said between laughs. Lesley looked relieved but then concerned again.

"Oh, Brendan, tell them quickly before the minds start running riot," said Molly, who saw the pale tenseness on Barbara's face.

"OK," said Brendan, "but only on the understanding that you are not to worry one jot. I've been to see the doctor and it seems that I have inherited my dad's dodgy heart. I'm to go for tests and get it fixed soon."

"You're going to die," wailed Lesley and burst into tears. Molly went around the table and put her arms around Lesley's shoulders.

"No, no, Lesley," she soothed, "your dad is going to be completely fine. The doctor promised." Barbara had stood up and moved to Brendan's side. She dropped a kiss on his head.

"You promise you'll be all right?" she said. He nodded. Michelle reached across the table and took his hand.

"You'd better be," she warned him, "or you'll answer to me."

"When do you go into hospital?" asked Barbara.

"Some time soon," replied Brendan, "I'll get a letter next week, but we need to tell Terry, Sharon and Colin at lunchtime. We wanted you to know first. Now, let's get cleared up and go out for a brisk walk." Lesley was taken into the lounge by Molly and the rest of the family heard much calming and soothing going on while they cleared away the breakfast table and washed and dried the dishes. As they took their traditional Sunday morning walk around the back of the house and onto the hills, Lesley clung to Brendan's hand instead of rushing off to find whatever was out there. Molly strolled with a daughter on each arm and they talked quietly together, her re-assuring them both that everything would be just as it always was.

"I'm going to ask Terry if he can persuade Colin to help out more during his year off," said Molly, "he doesn't have to go to University until next October."

"He'll not want to work early mornings when he's been up all night playing his music," said Michelle.

"Is he any good?" asked Molly.

"Actually, yes, he is," said Michelle, "although he's the star. His singing and guitar playing are as good as I've heard, but the rest of them just want to mess around on stage playing big time and chatting up the groupies." The family completed their circle of the hill behind the house and went back indoors. By the time Terry and Sharon arrived, complete with a still sleepy Colin, the table was set and food was bubbling, boiling and roasting in the kitchen.

"Brendan, will you tell Terry and Sharon the news, while I finish off here," shouted Molly from the kitchen. Lesley descended on Colin and proceeded to pull his hair and exclaim over his latest Joe Cocker T-shirt.

"You're not having twins this time, having missed one five year slot?" laughed Sharon.

"Heaven forbid," Brendan said, rolling his eyes to the ceiling, "I can't afford this lot." The girls gathered around him on the sofa while Terry and Colin stood nursing a bottle of beer each and Sharon took Molly's regular chair.

"Well, spill the beans," said Colin, "Aunt Molly's dinner smells too good to be kept waiting."

"Actually, Colin, this could affect you most of all," said Brendan. Terry's eyes widened with surprise and he looked at his older brother.

"This got anything to do with your going to the doctor this week?" he said, "you've been avoiding the issue ever since."

"Yes," said Brendan, "it has. It seems that Dad left us the business and as an extra he left me the same dodgy ticker he had."

"Oh, my God," said Sharon, "he was only 45 when he died."

Terry hushed her and said, "But you're going to be all right, aren't you? It's nothing serious is it? They can fix it, can't they?"

"Yes, I'm going for tests. The doctor says I can live normally once it is sorted out."

"Thank goodness," said Sharon, "but how does this affect Colin?"

"Because I'd like to ask him if he will help out on the stall two or three days a week until I'm back to normal," said Brendan, "the doctor said avoiding lifting would ease matters." All eyes in the room turned to Colin who looked embarrassed at being the focus of attention. A call came through from the kitchen.

"Lunch is served," shouted Molly, "come and get it while it's hot."

Colin bolted first through the door into the kitchen and Terry put his arm around Brendan after they had ushered the females through.

"Do you think he'll do it?" Terry asked.

"You're his dad, Terry, what do you think?" replied Brendan.

"It'll interfere with his music," said Terry, "so I'm not betting on it."

"He hasn't said 'no'," said Brendan.

"And he hasn't said 'yes' either," said Terry as he propelled Brendan through the door. Colin tried to respond to Lesley's teasing as he always did at these family gatherings. As a ten-year-old girl she set great store at school by talking about her 'pop singer cousin' and she was frequently asked for autographs of the whole band. She extracted them mercilessly from Colin and sulked at him if he forgot to bring them along. Today though, he had to think. For the first time his uncle had asked for his help and while he was not keen on early mornings, the great advantage would be that he might, just might, see Elizabeth again. It was a powerful incentive. He knew, despite his protests to his parents, that the band wasn't going anywhere. His commitment was one hundred percent but the other members were already missing rehearsals, weren't willing to play new songs that he slaved over or were keener on the girls that came flocking to see anyone in black leather with a musical instrument. Maybe when he went up to University he could pursue his music further. He made his decision and by the time the apple pie was handed round and the custard poured over it he declared, to the amazement of his father, that he would join him and Dee on the stall while Brendan had his treatment.

"Thanks, Colin," said Brendan and leaned over to shake his hand.

"Thanks, son," said Terry and he squeezed his arm affectionately, before adding, "we may get some muscles on you yet."

"Does that mean you'll be giving up playing in the band?" said Lesley, seeing her popularity going rapidly downhill.

"For the time being," said Colin, ruffling her fair hair, "but I'll get you stacks of signatures from the others before I tell them, OK?"

"OK," she said happily.

"Well done, Colin," said Michelle, "I knew you wouldn't let dad down."

Chapter 5

"Terry, where are you?" Sharon shouted from the foot of the stairs.

"In the bathroom," Terry shouted back, "can't a man get any peace these days? Is the house on fire? Has someone died?"

"I'm going to be late," said Sharon, "where are the car keys?"

"Hold on just one minute, Sharon," Terry shouted back in increasing exasperation.

"Mum," a voice came from the doorway behind Sharon, "here they are." She turned to see Colin, a bunch of car keys swinging on his little finger.

"Oh, damn," she giggled, "Where were they?"

"Just where dad said they would be, in his inside pocket," Colin replied.

"Oops, I only tried his outside pockets. Are you ready?"

"We are now," replied Colin, "come on, let's get out of here before he comes down."

"Sorry, love, got them," Sharon shouted, "See you later."

"See you, dad," shouted Colin, "I'll not keep her out too late." Sharon giggled.

"Want to drive?" she said to her son.

"Yes, OK," said Colin as he opened the door for her.

"Did you phone Molly and Michelle?" asked Sharon.

"They're waiting for us," said Colin. Ten minutes later Molly and Michelle were in the car.

"Gosh, it's getting cold," said Molly, blowing on her hands, "have you got the file?"

"In my hands," said Michelle, "all organised."

"Right, into the fray," said Molly. Colin drove to town and they made their way to The Crown. The upstairs room was crowded with traders, most of the men at the back with pints in their hands. The women sipped soft drinks or tea.

"I can guess who is doing most of the driving tonight," said Colin.

"I'll drive back if you want a pint or two," offered Sharon.

"Cheers, mum, don't mind if I do," said Colin and shot off before she could change her mind. "Pint of bitter, please," he said to the young barman. Clutching his pint he circulated around the side of the room until he spotted Mrs. Patel, but he couldn't see Elizabeth. He began to edge towards Anne but was interrupted by the sound of 'one, two, three, four, testing,' that echoed around the room. It was his mother, calling the meeting to order and people began to move forward.

"Damn," Colin said under his breath. His mother had been joined at a long trestle table by five other women and four men- jointly known as the Market Traders Christmas Party Organising Committee. Sharon stood up and called the meeting to order.

"I'm not going to keep you long," she said, "As you know this is our 20th annual party and we have to thank the ladies and gentlemen who give so much time every year to making it a success." There was a round of applause from the audience.

"I'm going to hand over to Molly, who will run down the standard list. If people could just put their hands up and tell us everything is under control, then we move on fairly quickly." Molly stood up, file in hand, nodded to the people in front of her and began.

"Musical entertainment?" A hand went up in front of her.

"The same boys as last year, Molly, booked two months ago and at the same price," said a sandy haired man.

"Thanks, Charlie," said Molly, "they were pretty good."

"Tables, chairs, table linen and cutlery?" asked Molly.

"The council are providing everything at the normal fee, Molly, but as it's our twentieth party, they have also agreed to give us twenty pounds towards decorations," said Mrs. Hall.

"Oh, Sally," chuckled Molly, "their generosity knows no bounds." There were a few other chuckles from the assorted traders and a hand shot up.

"Yes, Fred," Molly pointed at him.

"I can get a fair showing for twenty quid from the wholesaler. I'll be going there on Monday," said Fred.

"Any objections to Fred spending the money at the wholesalers?" asked Molly.

"As long as he takes his wife with him," quipped one man, "he's colour blind!" There was a bout of laughter but no dissent.

"Thanks, Fred," said Molly, "go ahead. See me afterwards for the money."

"Now, the major item- food," said Molly.

"Meat and fish taken care of?" she asked. Two hands went up and nods were exchanged.

"Fruit and vegetables we'll take care of," said Molly ticking two items off the list.

"Desserts?" Anne Patel put her hand up.

"Our corner is doing desserts," she said.

"Thanks, Anne," said Molly and ticked off another item.

"Drinks?"

"Here, Molly," said man near to the front, "courtesy of the non-food traders, as usual."

"Last but not least, the room," said Molly.

"The small ballroom in Queen Victoria's Hall, already booked and paid for," said Sally.

"Right, that's it. Hope everything goes as smoothly as in previous years," said Molly, "anybody remember anything I've forgotten or any questions?" A hand went up.

"Yes, Barry?" Molly pointed at the man.

"Have we invited the Mayor and his Lady?" he asked.

"Yes, of course, and they will grace our presence for the usual hour and then go on to another pressing engagement," said Molly with just a touch of sarcasm.

"And Nathaniel?" pressed Barry. Around the room there was some low level muttering.

"Nathaniel has been invited," said Molly, "it is the season of goodwill to *all* men. Anything else?" She scanned the room but no hands went up.

"Then the meeting is closed," she declared, "Thanks again and see you two weeks on Saturday."

She sat down and waited for the usual people to come and check out things with her. For ten years Sharon and Molly had been the main organisers of the Christmas party and they had it down to a fine art. Colin saw his aunt and mother being surrounded by people and stood on tiptoe to try to locate Mrs. Patel. He desperately wanted to speak to her about Elizabeth. He saw her copper hair and began, as courteously as he could, to push his way towards her.

"Mrs Patel," he called out as he saw that she was about to make for the door. Anne Patel turned and saw Colin. A smile broke across her face.

"Is everything all right with you?" she said, "That was some punch up last night."

"You were there?" said Colin, his eyes lighting up, "Elizabeth was there? Oh, I wish I'd known. What a mess it was."

"We didn't stop to see," Anne laughed, "I was worried it might develop into a right scrap, but you've obviously lived to fight another day." Colin held a hand to his side and winced.

"Just a boot print in the ribs," he said, "but don't tell mum, will you?"

"No," replied Anne, "But Elizabeth was pestering me to go to your stall today but by the time we had a minute to spare, you'd gone."

"I was the same today," said Colin, "with Brendan off I had to do the wholesalers and then go back for more. It's weeks before Christmas, but I'm sure people are buying in already."

"What was it all about, Colin, the fight last night?" asked Anne.

"The fight? Earlier in the evening I'd told the rest of the band that this would be my last night playing with them. I asked them to play their hearts out and let it be a night to remember," Colin said, shaking his head.

"Well, it was certainly that!" exclaimed Anne.

"Yeah, well, that's amateurs for you," said Colin, "they decided to play just as they always do. A missed note here, out of step there and I just got fed up with it all. After the third song I turned and gave them a mouthful and that's when it all blew up."

"It's taken Elizabeth and I weeks to find out your band name and then find you actually playing where you were supposed to be, and it turns out to be your swan song," laughed Anne.

"You've been looking for us?" asked Colin, a huge grin on his face.

"At my daughter's insistence," Anne smiled back at him and winked, "you were supposed to be at the Fox and Hounds two Fridays ago," she said counting on one hand. Colin clapped his hand to his forehead.

"That's when the bass player decided he wanted to go away for the weekend," he groaned.

"And The Grapes a week last Wednesday?"

"Flat tyre on the van."

"Good job we made it last night then," smiled Anne, "even if it was only for three songs. Did you write them?"

"Yes, all three," replied Colin.

"You have a talent," said Anne, "why don't you stop messing around and go solo?"

"Because pubs and clubs want bands, simple as that, unless you're Tom Jones," Colin laughed, "but thanks."

"Well, see you Colin," Anne said and turned to go.

"Mrs. Patel," said Colin. She turned to see him standing there with the faintest colour on his face.

"Yes," she said, knowing what was coming.

"Do you think, that is, would you mind, if I asked Elizabeth out sometime?"

"I don't mind, Colin," said Anne, "but you'll have to ask her yourself. Why not call her?"

"I don't know your phone number or where you live," he said. Anne took out a business card and scribbled on the back.

"That's our home number," she said and gave it to him.

"Thanks, Mrs. Patel," said Colin.

"Call me Anne," she said, "and why not ring her now - while I'm out of the way." She winked at him again and turned to leave the room. Colin dashed to the nearest public phone box and rang the number.

"57786," said the voice he knew.

"Elizabeth?" he said nervously, "It's Colin. Colin O'Malley."

"I recognise your voice, Colin. Did Mum give you our phone number? said Elizabeth.

"Yes," replied Colin, "and she said it would be all right for me to ring and ask you out sometime, that is, if you'd like to go out with me."

"You asked her permission!" exclaimed Elizabeth.

"Well, no, that is, yes, but not like you think," stammered Colin.

"How do I think?" said Elizabeth.

"I don't know," replied Colin, "but I'd like to find out."

"OK," said Elizabeth. There was no sound from the other end of the phone.

"Colin, are you there?" asked Elizabeth. Colin was busy punching the air with his fist and mouthing 'yes' to himself.

"Sorry, Elizabeth," he said, "where would you like to go?"

"Well, a gig is out of the question," said Elizabeth, laughing, "after last night."

"I'm really sorry about that," said Colin, "I had no idea you were there otherwise I'd have kept my temper until the end of the night. They were just driving me crazy."

"They certainly let you down," said Elizabeth.

"Would you like to see a film?" said Colin, "Space Odyssey is on."

"I'd rather we sat and talked first," said Elizabeth, "tell you what, there is a brilliant little Indian restaurant near here. Why not take me there?"

"OK. Can I pick you up tomorrow?"

"Make it Friday," Elizabeth said, "but remember I have to be on the market early on Saturday."

"Me too," said Colin, "about eight o'clock be all right?"

"Great, see you then." Elizabeth put the phone down and smiled. Colin did the same.

"There you are," a voice said from behind him, "I thought I'd lost you." Sharon raised an eyebrow at her son's face.

"And who have you been calling?" she teased.

"Elizabeth Patel," Colin beamed, "she's agreed to go out with me on Friday." They walked to the car where Molly was waiting.

"You found him," she said to Sharon.

"Yes, making a date for Friday night with Elizabeth," said Sharon.

"Oh, good," said Molly, "I know Anne but I've only seen Elizabeth once, at last year's party.

She's a stunner if I remember rightly." Colin's face creased into a broad smile.

"She's that all right, aunt Molly," he said.

"Well, have a good time," smiled Molly, "but don't be late for the market on Saturday."

"I won't," replied Colin, "Elizabeth has to work too, you know."

Colin thought that Friday night would never come. He glimpsed Elizabeth twice during the day but they were both kept busy by parents and customers. They had to be content with waving and smiling at each other in passing. Coming out of the bathroom at seven thirty on Friday night, Colin bumped into his father.

"Any chance of a lift to town, Dad?" he pleaded, knowing that Terry was going that way.

"Yes, as long as you stand outside for two minutes first," laughed Terry.

"Why?" asked Colin.

"To let some of that smell blow away. I'm not sure your mother would believe I hadn't had a woman in the car," said Terry, "what on earth is it? Did you have to *pay* for it?"

"It's a new after shave I bought, Dad," said Colin, "is it that bad, shall I wash it off?"

He made to push past Terry but found his arm in a vice like grip.

"Stop panicking," smiled Terry, "it's not bad, just a bit much right now. How much of the bottle is left?" Terry dodged into the bathroom and closed the door. Colin walked down stairs and asked Sharon if the smell was too much.

"It'll be all right, Colin," she said, recoiling away from him, "in about half an hour. Be sure to wrap up warmly, it's going colder by the minute."

"Come on, Colin," his father said from the bottom of the stairs, "I'll take you to the young lady's door, if you like."

"Thanks, dad," said Colin. They got into the car and Terry shivered.

"Your mother's right. It is getting colder."

"I don't feel it," said Colin.

"No, you've got your love to keep you warm," said Terry. He drove for a few minutes before saying casually,

"Your mum and me really appreciate the time you've given on the stall, you know, son."

"Funnily enough, dad, I'm enjoying it," said Colin, "I never thought I'd ever actually like getting up in the mornings. But it's all right - and I never realised how much other stuff you have to do as well as humping sacks of spuds around."

"Nobody realises, Colin," said Terry, "as long as we're there, rain and shine." They drove into the street where Elizabeth lived and found the right house. Colin got out of the car and waved to his dad.

"See you later," Terry said. Elizabeth opened the door before Colin had time to knock.

"Mental telepathy?" said Colin.

"We don't get many cars down this street," said Elizabeth.

"Are you ready?" asked Colin.

"Come in while I get my coat," said Elizabeth. Colin walked down the narrow hallway and into the lounge. He was struck immediately by how crowded the room seemed. There was barely space to move around. Anne was sitting by the gas fire, reading a book and listening to the radio.

"Hello Colin," she said, "is it still as cold out?"

"It is, Mrs. Patel," he replied. Elizabeth came into the room, with her coat on, and crossed it to kiss her mother goodbye. The manoeuvre involved some fancy footwork between her, the furniture and Colin, and she was embarrassed.

"See you later, mum," she said. Colin squeezed against the wall to let her pass and they left the house and walked to the Indian restaurant three streets away. The proprietor greeted Elizabeth warmly and she spoke to him in his own dialect.

"We don't have to order," said Elizabeth, "Mr. Singh will bring us one of his specials."

"Sorry about the clutter in the house," Elizabeth apologised, "but mum won't part with it."

"It's nice stuff," said Colin, "but a bit big for such a small room."

"That's because it was bought for a much bigger room," said Elizabeth, then she looked him straight in the eye before saying,

"You know what happened to my father, don't you?"

"No," he said, "the only thing anyone has ever told me, time and time again, is that he was an Indian. As if I care. Do you want to tell me?" Elizabeth took a deep breath.

"Five years ago, dad went to India to visit his father and brother. I was supposed to be going with him, but I got measles and the doctor said I'd better not go. Dad was supposed to be gone for a month, but we haven't heard a single word from him since."

"I'm sure he'll come back," Colin said lamely.

"Mum and I have tried everything," said Elizabeth, "had letters translated and sent over to his father and brother, but had no reply. We've tried advertisements in Indian newspapers- but had no response. We contacted the police who said they would make enquiries and let us know if they found out anything- we've never heard from them."

"Do you think he's...?" said Colin, nervous of mentioning the word.

"Dead?" said Elizabeth, "I don't know. Mum said once that she thought he might, just might, have found another woman, one of his own race, and fallen in love."

"But he's married to your mum!" exclaimed Colin, "and he's got you."

"I know," said Elizabeth, "but it wasn't easy for them. An Indian marrying a white woman isn't acceptable now, let alone back then. Mum was called some awful names. She told me some women would cross the street when she walked out with Dad."

"We've got a Race Relations Bill now," said Colin emphatically, "all that will stop."

"You might be able to stop the gossip in public," said Elizabeth wearily, "but you can't stop people thinking the way they do. Look how many agreed with Enoch Powell earlier this year."

"It must have been an awful time for you both," said Colin, reaching across the table and squeezing her hand.

"For Mum it was," said Elizabeth, "as soon as word got out that Dad wasn't around, Mum was refused credit and people called in loans. Mum had to sell the house to pay everyone back and only just had enough left to buy the house we're in now. That's why it's so crammed with furniture. She had me to look after as well. I don't know how she managed."

"But you are OK now, aren't you?" said Colin.

"Oh yes," said Elizabeth, "no debts now. Business is picking up. Mum wants to open a little shop sometime, as well as keep the market stall. She's ambitious."

"I'm absolutely sure she'll do it," said Colin, "especially with you to help her."

"Thank you," she said, giving him a huge smile, "It's worse at this time of year, Christmas coming up and all that happy family stuff. Dad always made it such a special time even though he wasn't a Christian." The waiter brought their main course and took away the starter plates. He spoke to Elizabeth, who answered him again, in his own tongue.

"What did he say?" asked Colin.

"He wished us a good appetite," said Elizabeth.

"When did you learn..." Colin started, but then he realised that he didn't know which language she was speaking.

"Hindi," she laughed, "and I learned it at my father's knee. He spoke Hindi to me all the time at home and mother spoke English, so I learned both languages together." They began to eat and continued chatting together easily as dish after dish arrived. The restaurant was filling up and Colin noticed one couple came in laughing, shaking their coats and stamping on the doormat.

"It looks like it's snowing," he said to Elizabeth.

"Well, it's cold enough," she said. An hour later Mr. Singh came over to Elizabeth and spoke rapidly. He looked worried.

"It's snowing very heavily," Elizabeth said to Colin, "and a lorry has just slid down the street where I live and brought down the telephone pole. This area now has no telephones, including here."

"Damn," said Colin, "I was going to phone a taxi to get home."

"Even if we could," said Elizabeth, "there's no way they'd come out this way until the roads have been gritted and that won't be until morning. They'll do all the main roads first."

"I've got to get back home," Colin said, "We need to be at the wholesalers early in the morning and Brendan's been in hospital today having tests. They won't let him out until tomorrow lunchtime. Dad will be on his own at the wholesalers. I could walk into town and maybe the taxis will be running from there."

"It's two miles to town from here," said Elizabeth, "at least come to my house and get some of dad's warm clothing." They left the restaurant and put their heads down against the snow. Anne let them in and protested when Colin said he must try to get home.

"Listen, young man," she said, "I'm a mother and I know Sharon would prefer you to stay here until the morning, rather than risk being on foot in that weather."

"I have to get home, Mrs. Patel," Colin insisted, "Brendan's in hospital having his tests so tomorrow will be bad enough for two of us to manage. Dad can't do the wholesalers on his own."

"It's eleven-thirty, Colin," said Anne, "Look; the snow shifters won't even have done the main roads yet. Compromise and get at least a couple of hours sleep and then set off. We only have two bedrooms, but I can make up the sofa, it's big enough." Elizabeth giggled and Colin coloured.

"No, Mrs Patel, thank you," Colin insisted, "I must get home somehow, but I will borrow a hat and scarf if you've got them."

"What size shoes do you take?" Anne asked him.

"Nines," said Colin.

"Right," Anne was all business now that she knew she couldn't dissuade Colin from getting home, "Mo was the same size and I've got warm long socks and the boots he wore to the market. I'll go and get them." Elizabeth took Colin's hand.

"Are you sure about trying to get home?" said Elizabeth.

"No, not really," he whispered to her, "but I've got to make the effort. Dad used to think me a right wimp and I'd like to prove him wrong."

"Foolish boy," she said, reaching up to kiss him on the cheek. His arms went round her and he was just about to kiss her properly when Anne's cough alerted them to the fact that she was standing at the foot of the stairs, looking into the room.

"Here," she said, "try these on." Colin took the socks and boots and put them on, wrapped a long scarf round his neck and topped it with a hat.

"Will you take Mo's long warm overcoat as well, please?" said Anne.

"Thanks, Mrs. Patel," he said, "now I'd better get off. Wish me luck with a cab in town."

"I'll make time to get to the stall tomorrow to see you," said Elizabeth, "take care." Colin left the house and began the long walk into town

Chapter 6

It took Colin two hours to battle through the snow into the town centre but at least the snow ploughs were out and a few cabs were working. Colin was in luck and got a cab. It crawled precariously all the way. He put his key in the lock, glancing at his watch. It was almost three o'clock and he groaned. Only two hours to get some sleep. Was it worth it? He opened the door and was surprised to see a light on in the kitchen. He went in and saw Terry sitting at the table, his head in his hands.

"Dad," he said, "what are you doing up?"

"It's Brendan," his father raised his head and Colin was horrified by the look on his face.

"Dad, what's happened?" Colin said as he shrugged off the heavy overcoat and walked across the room to his father's side.

"He was having some tests and suddenly his heart failed," said Terry.

"He's not dead!" exclaimed Colin.

"No," said Terry, "but it'll be touch and go for the next twelve hours, they say. We've just left the hospital. Molly's there. She wouldn't leave him. Your mother's with the girls at Molly's."

"God," said Colin, "it's a good job he was in the hospital. Imagine if it had happened on the stall."

"It doesn't bear thinking about," said Terry.

"So, what are we going to do?" asked Colin, "I mean its past three o'clock now. Are we doing the market today?"

"I hadn't even thought about it," said Terry wearily, "but we should. Saturday's our main trading day. But suppose something happens to Brendan?"

"Listen, dad, Dee and I can manage if you'll just help with the wholesalers. Drop the produce and me at the market and get back here. The wholesalers will be open in an hour."

"You've had no sleep, lad," said Terry, "in fact come to think of it, how on earth did you get home in this weather? And where did you get those clothes? Have you walked?"

"Long story, dad," replied Colin, "but it will wait. Let me get into a hot shower and some dry clothes and I'll be ready for work." Terry looked at his son in admiration. Colin was taking charge.

"Right," said Terry, "off you go. I'll get some tea on and a couple of bacon sandwiches."

"Great!" exclaimed Colin and he bounded out of the kitchen and up the stairs two at a time. The tea was brewed and the bacon sizzling under the grill when the phone rang.

"I'll get it," said Colin. Terry strained his ears to hear.

"That was mum," Colin said as he came back into the kitchen, "Molly has phoned to say that Brendan is sleeping. The doctor says things are looking good. Although today will be the test."

"Thank goodness," said Terry. Colin was munching on a sandwich.

"Maybe I could risk working the day," mused Terry.

"No, dad," said Colin emphatically, "we'll do as we planned. You get back here and sort out the girls and Molly. They'll want ferrying to the hospital and mum will probably be cooking for them all day. I can cope as long as Dee is there." Terry came across and ruffled Colin's hair.

"You're OK, son, you know that," he said, "I'm proud of you."

Colin looked embarrassed but pleased.

"Come on, dad," he said, "let's get off." An hour later they were leaving the wholesalers. The roads were just about passable.

"It might be a bit quieter today," said Terry. They collected Dee and told her the news about Brendan.

"Poor man," she said, "but it's a good job you made him see the doctor, Terry."

"Aye," Terry said, "that was a good day's work." Colin and Terry had the stall filled and prepared an hour later and Terry left for home.

"Dee," Colin said, "can you manage for just one minute while I go and see Elizabeth?"

"Go on," she said, "with this snow it'll be a while before customers start streaming in." He ran round to Anne Patel's stall and found her there.

"Hi, Anne," he said, "I've only got a minute." He looked around for Elizabeth but there was no sign of her.

"She's just gone to the ladies," said Anne, "shall I send her to see you? You got home safely then?"

"Yes, thanks to your husband's coat and boots, I was OK," he garbled, "but Brendan's not well. He's in hospital and dad has gone to take care of things at home and Molly's house, so I'm not going to have time to see Elizabeth today."

"I'll give her the message," said Anne, "maybe she'll get over to you instead. Give my regards to all the family and I hope Brendan makes a full recovery."

"Thanks, Anne," he said, "I've got to dash. Sorry." He sprinted back to the stall to find three customers waiting to be served.

"Sorry, folks," he shouted, "right, who's next?" By three o'clock in the afternoon Colin was beginning to feel the effects of his night without sleep. Dee had managed to get a passing trader to bring them some sandwiches and tea at mid day but neither of them had left the stall. He was tired.

"I'm bursting for the ladies," she said, "Colin, I've got to go or we'll have a wet floor."

"Have one for me while you're there," he said, laughing. She had been gone for only two minutes when more customers appeared from nowhere and Colin spotted Elizabeth hovering nearby. He waved and shrugged his shoulders in a gesture of frustration and she nodded, waved back and mouthed, 'I'll come back later.' Elizabeth returned to Anne and shook her head.

"Colin looks shattered," she said, "and there's two hours to go before he can get away."

"Listen, love," Anne said, "why don't you go and help him? I can manage here now."

"But I don't know anything about the fruit and vegetables," protested Elizabeth.

"What's to know?" asked Anne, "you know a banana from a potato. All you have to do is weigh them out, take the money and serve the next person." Elizabeth looked doubtful.

"Do you think he'll think I'm pushing in?" she said.

"Go and ask," said Anne, giving her daughter a push, "he can only say 'no'."

Elizabeth hesitated for a fraction and then said, "All right, I'll go and offer." Back at O'Malley's she found only Dee serving one customer.

"He's gone to the toilet," laughed Dee, "the first time today, poor lad."

"I was wondering," said Elizabeth, "that is, would you mind, the thing is, mum's fairly quiet now and......"

"You're offering to help?" said Dee, a huge smile on her face, "get behind here right now and put on an apron. The next two hours can be busy." Elizabeth dashed behind the counter and found the apron. By the time Colin returned she was busy weighing potatoes and apologising to the customers for being slow. Her youthfulness and bright smile was winning them over.

"Cheers, Elizabeth," he said as he turned to the next customer.

"Thank me when the day is over, Colin," she smiled back, "I'm only learning." There was no time for any more conversation as the three of them weighed, packed and took money for the rest of the trading day. As the huge clock that stood sentry over the building struck five thirty, Colin breathed a sigh of relief and sat down on an empty wooden crate.

"God, I'm so tired," he said. Dee took his takings and Elizabeth handed hers over.

"I'll cash up," Dee said, "You just sit there a minute."

"I should go back and help mum," said Elizabeth. Colin stood up quickly and went over to her.

"I must pay you," he said.

"Colin!" she exclaimed, "please don't insult me. I thought we were friends." She turned away but he caught her arm.

"Elizabeth," he said, "I'm sorry. I wasn't thinking straight. I never meant to insult you." She smiled at him.

"You are exhausted," she said, "I suggest that you sleep for the next twenty four hours." She reached up and touched the side of his face.

"I wish I could," he said, "but I'm not sure what I'm going to face when I get back home."

"Bed for a couple of hours first," a familiar voice came from behind them, "then supper later at Molly's house." They turned round to see Terry.

"Dad," said Colin, "how's Brendan?"

"Over the worst," said Terry, "they'll be keeping him for a week, but he's going to make it. I thought I'd bring you the news and help clear up."

"That's great news, Mr. O'Malley," said Elizabeth, turning to Terry.

"That looks like my apron," said Terry, "but it looks better on you." Elizabeth blushed.

"She's been helping us out, dad," said Colin and he put his arm around her shoulders.

"Well, young lady," said Terry, "I thank you."

"I'd better be off," said Elizabeth, taking the apron off and handing it to Colin, "see you."

"Is your phone back on?" he asked her.

"Not yet," she said, "but they say it'll be back on by Monday." His face fell.

"Listen, Colin," she whispered; "your family need you this weekend. I'll see you here on Monday. We'll talk then." He smiled, leaned over and kissed her very gently.

"Thanks, Elizabeth," he said, "see you Monday." By the time they had closed, taken Dee home and got into the house, Colin was yawning.

"Do you want to grab some shut eye?" asked Terry.

"If you don't mind, I'll get a shower and stay up. But if we go to Molly's, can we come back early?" said Colin plaintively. Terry laughed.

"I never thought I'd hear the day when my son wanted an early night on a Saturday," he chuckled, "but

I promise you, we'll be home as soon as we can. I'm ready for a good night's sleep too." Colin showered and let the warm water soothe his skin. He flexed his body into a state of refreshment, dressed quickly and went back downstairs.

"Ready when you are, dad," he said. They drove to Molly's house and she let them in.

"How are you, Molly?" asked Colin as he dropped a kiss on her cheek.

"Much better than yesterday," she smiled at him.

"Something smells good," said Terry.

"You've your mum to thank for that," said Molly, "she's done all the shopping and made supper. It's chicken, baked potatoes and salad."

"Well," said Colin, "I could eat a horse." He made his way into the kitchen and greeted his mother and the girls who were helping lay the table and cut up salad.

"See ya, Colin," squealed Lesley, dropping her knife and flinging her arms around him.

"Have you been a good girl for your mum?" he teased her.

"Oh, no," she teased back, "I've been rotten and awful."

"Everything normal, then?" he said and raised a smile around the room.

"Come and finish this salad," demanded Michelle of her youngest sister, "then we can eat."

"I'm coming, wicked sister," said Lesley and she dramatically placed the back of her hand across her forehead and wiped away imaginary sweat.

"Anything I can do to help?" Colin said.

"What!" exclaimed Barbara, "after the late night last night, which we want to hear all about, by the way, and the market all day? No, just sit quietly. It's almost ready." Fifteen minutes later Molly and her three girls, Terry, Sharon and Colin sat down at the table and they all began to eat.

"So," said Barbara, between bites, "tell us about the new girl in your life, Colin."

"She's called Elizabeth and works on the market with her mum," he said.

"Which stall?" said Barbara.

"Patel's baby wear," he said, reaching for more salad.

"She's a..." started Lesley, her voice slightly raised but her mother was quicker, anticipating her daughter's remark.

"Elizabeth is half English and half Indian," Molly said, "and she's had a very sad life."

"Why?" asked Lesley.

"We almost lost your dad yesterday," she said, "but Elizabeth hasn't been as lucky as you. She lost her dad five years ago."

"What did he die of?" Lesley said. The adults looked at each other and then at Colin as if expecting him to explain.

"Elizabeth's father went to India for a holiday and to see some relations there. Somehow he got lost and he hasn't found his way back yet," said Colin.

"Is he walking back from India then?" asked Lesley, by now intrigued, "how far is it?"

"Oh. It's a long, long, way," said Colin, looking around for support.

"Well, why doesn't he catch a train or a plane or something?"

"That's enough, Lesley," said Molly, "eat your dinner." Lesley was about to speak again but Molly's eyes warned her off.

"How are the rehearsals going, Barbara," asked Colin, keen to change the subject.

"Last one on Wednesday," she replied, "then first night on Friday."

"Nervous?" he asked her.

"Petrified," she said, "its one thing performing in front of school mates and quite different when friends and relatives are there. I'm sure I'll dry up or something."

"I hope we've all got tickets," said Sharon, "I'm looking forward to it."

"Yes, they're in the drawer," said Molly, "front row, first night. Although there will be a spare one now. Dad will still be in hospital."

"Well, Colin can bring his new girl friend," said Lesley.

"That's a good idea," said Sharon, turning to Colin, "do you think she'd like to join us?"

"I can only ask her," said Colin.

"And she can only say 'yes'," said Lesley. They all laughed.

"Well, Molly," said Terry, "that was lovely, but Colin and I are absolutely exhausted. We neither of us got any sleep last night. Can we call it a day and go home?"

"Of course, Terry I'm sorry," said Molly, "and thank you for your help today, Sharon. I don't know what I'd have done without you." She got up and put her arms around Sharon and hugged her.

"Do you want me to stay tonight?" Sharon said.

"No, I'll be all right now," Molly said, "I'll go up to the hospital with Michelle while these two wash the dishes and we'll have an early night too. I think we all need it." Terry's family were home within minutes.

"I'll hit the sack," said Colin and he yawned.

"We all will," said Terry and Sharon nodded. All the O'Malley's, including Brendan, slept soundly that night.

Chapter 7

"Deep breaths, Barbara, one-two, one-two," said Mrs. Bishop.

"I'll never do it," gasped Barbara, "have you seen the number of people out there."

"Yes, marvellous, isn't it?" said Mrs. Bishop, "and they have come to see you and the rest of the cast sing." Barbara's best friend, Jennifer, came up behind her.

"You all right?" she asked.

"Stage fright," said Mrs. Bishop, "it happens to the best of them."

"Listen, Barbara, Angela's dying to get out there. Shall I go and tell her to get ready," said Jennifer, and she turned as if to go.

"No!" exclaimed Barbara as she straightened her shoulders, "an understudy is for when I'm sick." Mrs. Bishop winked surreptitiously at Jennifer who nodded and smiled back.

"Right," said Mrs. Bishop, peeping through the curtains, "there's the nod from the conductor, and we're ready to go. Break a leg." They heard the conductor tap his rostrum, whisper encouragement to the pupils and then the curtains were pulled back and the show began. The Sharks and the Jets sang, strutted and pouted their way through the first forty-five minutes of the musical and Barbara's voice captivated the audience.

"She's very good," whispered Elizabeth to Colin during another round of applause that greeted the end of one of Barbara's songs.

"She is, isn't she," he replied and turned round to look at the back of the hall.

"He's not coming until the interval," Elizabeth whispered.

"Molly and the girls will die when he arrives," Colin said but he reached over and took her hand.

"I hope not," she whispered back and she kept hold of his hand. When the curtain came down for the interval Colin turned around again.

"I have to go and see," he said and Elizabeth nodded. He made his way to the back of the hall and he could see an ambulance through the glass door. Anne Patel was holding the wheel chair that held Brendan and a tall shaven headed man was lowering a ramp. Anne waved as she spotted Colin and he went up to the door.

"Can I help, mate?" he asked the man

"If you'd just put these ramps back in, I can park up round the back," he said.

"All went well, then, Brendan?" said Colin, unable to find his uncle's hand but patting the blanket in greeting.

"Aye, lad, like a dream," replied Brendan.

"I only hope Barbara isn't struck speechless if she spots you," said Colin.

"Well, we'll stay at the back, and hopefully she won't spot me until the lights go up at the end." He chuckled, "Wouldn't do to spoil my girl's big night, would it?" The driver of the ambulance joined them at the door.

"Have you met Dave?" Brendan said to Colin, "he's the guy who helped Anne persuade the doctors to let me out. Told them he'd bring me back safe and sound."

"Cheers, Dave," said Colin.

They waited for a few moments while people went back to their seats and the curtains twitched. The prompter was checking that everyone was sitting down.

"Now," said Colin, and he pushed the chair into the hall and parked it at the end of the back row.

Colin just managed to get back to his seat as the chorus began to sing.

"Mission accomplished," he whispered to Elizabeth.

"Well done," she whispered back and then turned her attention to the show. By the time the final curtain fell there were more than a few damp eyes among the women. The applause was loud and sustained as the curtain rose for the cast to take their bows. Dave slipped outside and come back carrying the largest bouquet of flowers Brendan could buy. Dave gave them to him then wheeled him forward as Barbara came out on stage with her male lead to take another bow.

"Sorry I can't make it up the steps, love," Brendan called to her, "but these are for you." Dave took the flowers from Brendan and thrust the bouquet into Barbara's hands.

"Dad!" she shouted, "oh, dad, how long have you been there?" She almost pushed Dave out of the way in her haste to throw herself on her father's neck. Molly and the other girls had also made their way forward as they spotted Brendan and he was threatened with suffocation as four women surrounded him. Dave came to his rescue.

"Ladies," he chided softly, "give the man some air. I have to get him back, and preferably alive." The rest of the audience joined the cast who had broken into applause at this unscheduled scene-"Oh," Molly blushed, "we're in the spotlight, I think." She mouthed a 'sorry' to the cast.

"Can you come home with us, Dad?" asked Lesley, clinging to her father's leg.

"No, love," Brendan said, "Dave's got strict instructions to get me back tonight."

"Oh, dad..." Lesley began to say but Molly shushed her.

"You want him to get better, don't you?" she said. Lesley pouted a little but nodded. Dave was looking anxiously around the room.

"Mrs. O'Malley," he said to Molly, who was clutching Brendan's hand, "I'd better get Brendan back. Can you do me a favour?"

"Anything," she said.

"Would you get a taxi for Mrs. Patel?" he asked, "she came to the hospital on the bus to help me but I can get him back to the ward by myself and then I'm on a late shift so I can't run her home."

"Anne?" Molly queried, "I hadn't seen her." She looked around the room and spotted Anne talking to Elizabeth and Colin.

"Of course, leave it with me," she said, "I'll get her home. Don't you worry."

"Thanks, Mrs. O'Malley."

"Thank *you*," she said emphatically, "that was a lovely surprise for Barbara, and all of us."

"If he behaves himself you can have him home in time for the Christmas party," said Dave as he wheeled Brendan back towards the rear of the room. Molly walked behind him and gathered her three daughters, Colin, Sharon, Elizabeth and Anne together.

"Shall we all go back to our place for a drink?" she said.

"Thank you, Molly," said Anne, "but we'd better be getting the bus home."

"Nonsense!" exclaimed Molly, "you'll come back and let us say thank you properly and then we'll get Colin to run both of you home." Anne looked at Elizabeth's face and caught the small pleading smile."That's very kind of you, Molly, we'd be delighted," she said. Ten minutes later they were sitting around the lounge.

"Well, that was wonderful," said Molly, beaming around the room.

"I hope you mean my performance," said Barbara with a broad smile.

"Of course, darling," said Molly, "you were superb. Not a flat note all the way through."

"Hear, hear," said Colin, "if I'd known you could sing like that, I'd have had you as lead singer in the band." They toasted Barbara and she blushed.

"Whose idea was the surprise visit from dad?" asked Michelle. Colin pointed at Elizabeth.

"It was a conspiracy between Anne, Elizabeth and Dave," he said.

"Dave?" queried Michelle.

"The ambulance guy," said Colin, "he's Anne's, er, well..." He looked embarrassed and Anne laughed out loud.

"He's a friend, Colin," she said, "we only met recently."

Elizabeth regaled the family with the tale of how Dave had rescued Anne in the park and from then on had called round regularly for a chat. Anne had taken the opportunity at the first of those visits to apologise profusely for her misconceptions of Dave.

"I only saw the bald head, the black clothes, the studded collar and the dog. And with Elizabeth's colouring I thought we were in trouble," she'd said to him.

"The shaven head is purely practical," Dave had said, "and the collar covers an old scar. It's fading, but I'm still a bit conscious of it."

"How did you manage to cut your throat?" Anne had asked and then she clapped her hands to her mouth as she realised what she'd said. Dave laughed so hard she had to join in with him.

"It was a broken windscreen," he'd said, "I was trying to get a woman free. I should have waited for the fire brigade. That's what you get when you interfere with someone else's job." He touched the side of his neck gently.

"You can't see it with a shirt on, can you?" Anne shook her head. During one of their conversations they had talked about Brendan being in hospital and missing Barbara's big night.

"I can have a word with the ward sister and see if she'll let me spirit him away," Dave had said and the two women had colluded with him in organising the event.

"I had to tell Colin," said Elizabeth, "I just couldn't keep it to myself."

"You must bring Dave to the Christmas party," Sharon said to Anne.

"Yes," said Molly, "join us, I can organise a bigger table." Anne smiled and nodded. Elizabeth and Colin beamed at one another.

"Can we sneak Dad out again for the party?" asked Lesley.

"I hope he'll be out of hospital by then," said Molly, "but he must be quieter than normal."

"Oh, fat chance," said Michelle, "you know Dad. He'll be the one wanting to get up for the first dance and drink every one under the table." They all laughed but Molly held up her hands.

"I'm relying on each and every one of you to help me keep him under control this year," she said, "next year will be stressful enough for all of the traders, moving into the new Hall and getting business up and running without a hitch."

"Oh, crumbs," said Sharon, "I'd forgotten about that. Terry's taken Brendan's place at the council meeting tonight. He'll be home soon. I'd better get off." She rose and waved Molly back to her seat.

"I'll let myself out," she said, "good night all and Barbara, once again, you were wonderful." She left the room and they heard the door close.

"We'd better be going too," said Anne, nodding at Elizabeth, half an hour later.

"I'll take you home," said Colin, "can I borrow your car, aunt Molly?"

"What a lovely thing to do," said Barbara, "it made a perfect end to the performance."

"Yes," said Molly, "lovely people. Now, Lesley, come on, it is time you were in bed." Lesley protested only slightly.

Chapter 8

Nathaniel Sharpe winced as the after shave hit his face. His pores contracted away from the onslaught of a highly scented but very cheap preparation. Tonight was the trader's Christmas party. Nathaniel knew that he was tolerated at the party each year but he never missed going. Tonight he could watch the poor fools drag out their Christmas spirit and pretend they loved each other. Tonight he would accept, graciously, a half-pint of beer from one or two of his victims. Tonight he would slide around the room and gloat inwardly at their mundane lives. He adjusted his tie until the knot was perfect then stretched his neck so that his Adam's apple was comfortable. He combed his hair just one more time before going to the full-length swivel mirror to check his appearance.

"Nathaniel." The high thin voice came from the bedroom across the landing.

"Coming, mother," said Nathaniel. His mother was propped up in bed; the pillows arranged like the Alps behind her head, one snowy peak after another. Her pale lashed eyes were closed. The skin on her face was papery and white as only skin that has not seen the sun can be. Her hands were as soft as a baby and the fingernails trimmed neatly. The faint smell of Yardley's Lavender Water hung in the air. She wore a night gown, buttoned up to the neck, one of three dozen that Nathaniel had bought years before. He made sure she changed them every second day.

It hadn't taken Nathaniel long to persuade her to give up the stall, then the housework. He knew his mother was a selfish, lazy, scheming woman. Over a period of months, he had come in from work and told her how tired she looked and she had nodded wearily and wiped nonexistent moisture from her forehead.

"Go and rest, mother," he had said, "I'll get dinner ready and bring it up on a tray."

"Thank you, Nathaniel," she would say, "I really am feeling a little peaky." She would undress and luxuriate in her bed, wriggling until its comfort cocooned her completely. Then he had started calling in to her bedroom in the mornings with a cup of tea and fresh toast.

"Stay in bed, mother, you look tired," he would say and she would nod. Before long she was willingly hooked to her bed like an addict and only ventured to the bathroom. In her bed Mrs. Sharpe would read and listen to music, imagining herself to be a Victorian lady. She manicured her perfect nails. As long as Nathaniel coddled and cosseted her, she worried not one iota about tomorrow. Today was enough for her. Nathaniel was content too, she was out of his way while he listened to the radio downstairs and planned his great escape.

"Yes, mother?" he asked the woman propped up in the bed where he had been born. She opened her eyes and smiled weakly at him.

"Will you bring me fresh water before you go?" she asked him.

"Of course, mother," he replied. She continued to smile at him.

"You're looking very dapper, Nathaniel," she said.

"Thank you, mother," he replied and he turned around to let her see all aspects of his appearance. As he turned he plucked at a non-existent speck on his sleeve and carefully smoothed the fabric.

"Are you sure you'll be all right while I go out, mother," he asked solicitously, "because I can always stay at home with you."

"No, Nathaniel," she said, "you go and enjoy yourself. It's only once a year. You really should go out more, you know."

"I don't enjoy it, mother," he said with a sigh of patient resignation, "but I'm compelled to go. The Mayor and his lady will be there and, as Market Superintendent, I must show my face."

"Of course, of course," his mother replied, "such a trial for you."

"One has to do these things, mother," he replied, "Now, I'll go and get that water." He left the room and went downstairs, taking her water jug. Carefully he emptied the jug, rinsed it, wiped it dry and then refilled it. He carried it upstairs and placed it by his mother's bed. Leaning over he kissed her gently on the cheek and said goodbye.

"See you later," he said, "I'll pop in to see that you're asleep."

"Take care, Nathaniel," she replied, "don't get cold." She switched on her portable radio and the sounds of light music filled the room.

"Lovely," she murmured.

Nathaniel left the house. Half an hour later he was handing his apparel to a cloakroom attendant and taking his ticket. He strolled casually into the room where the trader's Christmas party would take place. He was early. In fact he was the only one there. The band had set up their instruments on the stage earlier. He wandered around the room, and stopped to check which table belonged to whom. The O'Malleys had two tables together and he could see it was a setting for twelve people. Mentally he counted the family, plus Dee, and wondered who the other three places were for. He shrugged. He'd find out soon enough. Molly O'Malley and her tribe were always among the first to arrive. He wandered some more and noted the familiar family names- the Browns, Fitzgeralds, Entwhistles, Green the fishmonger, Chadwick- whose family had bought his mother's stall all those years ago. He noted that the tenants who had been on the market the longest were the nearest to the stage and dance floor.

"Hierarchies even here," he sniggered to himself. There were sounds coming from the back of the hall and he positioned himself by the wall.

"Who would have thought it?" a voice came through the doors.

"Let's hope it doesn't get worse," replied another voice. Nathaniel recognised the voices as belonging to Terry O'Malley and his wife Sharon. They came into the room and Terry immediately spotted Nathaniel.

"Nathaniel," he called across the room, "can I buy you the first drink tonight?" Nathaniel moved forward and raised the edges of his mouth in what passed for a smile.

"Very kind of you, Mr. O'Malley," he said, "just a half, please. May I say that your good wife is looking extremely chic this evening?" He took Sharon's hand and bowed over it, planting a dry kiss on the surface. Then he turned and shook Terry's hand.

"Have you been here long?" Sharon said.

"Only a matter of minutes," Nathaniel replied.

"So you haven't seen the snow?" she said, "it's coming down fast and furious again."

"Oh, dear," said Nathaniel, "let's hope everyone gets here safely." More noise heralded the arrival of other guests and within fifteen minutes the hall was resounding to the chatter of more than half the traders and their wives. The talk was of the weather and the hopes that it would not spoil the evening. At eight o'clock the catering manager rapped his gavel on a table and announced that the meal was about to be served.

"Enjoy your meal!" the manager shouted and motioned the waiting servers forward.

"I'm worried that the band haven't arrived yet," whispered Molly to Sharon.

"They aren't due on until nine thirty," Sharon said.

"Yes, I know," replied Molly, "but they're normally here before we eat. Pre-something checks they call it."

"Anyone got Graham's phone number?" asked Colin, who had been listening.

"In my bag," said Molly.

"Let me go and ring them," said Colin.

"But wouldn't they ring here if there was a problem?" said Molly.

"I'll ring them just to be on the safe side," said Colin, "then you can enjoy the soup."

"Won't be a moment, love," he said, to Elizabeth by his side, "just got to make a call." He left the room, went to the foyer and dialled the number Molly had given him.

"Hello," a woman's voice answered on the first ring.

"Hello," said Colin, "is that Graham's house?"

"Yes," the voice sounded agitated, "do you know where he is?"

"No," replied Colin, "But his band is supposed to be performing for us tonight."

"Oh, no," the woman sounded distressed, "I told him it was too risky going out in this weather. It's been snowing here for two hours but he said he couldn't let you down."

"What time did he leave?" asked Colin.

"More than an hour ago," the woman replied. Colin did a quick calculation. If Graham and the band had left more than an hour ago they should have been at the hall, even allowing for the snow.

"Listen," he said, "I'm sure they are just stuck in the snow somewhere. I'll ring again in another hour. Maybe they will have got to a phone box by then."

"Will you let me know if they get through to you?" she said.

"Of course," replied Colin, "now don't worry, they're all sensible lads."

"Thanks," said the woman, "and I hope they make it to the party."

"So do I," laughed Colin, "or it will be my dad at the mike all night." He replaced the receiver and sprinted across the foyer to the door. Opening it he glanced outside and saw that the snow was now six inches deep. He shook his head. It was unlikely that the band would get through but he decided not to worry anyone until they had finished eating. No good spoiling the meal. He made his way back to the table. Molly looked at him and he made a calculated effort to look nonchalant.

"They're on their way, Molly," he said, "they left in plenty of time. I'm sure they've just had to take it slower than normal because of the snow." Molly looked relieved and went back to eating her meal.

"They took your soup away," said Elizabeth, "it was cold."

"It doesn't look like the band is going to make it," he whispered to her, "but let's at least enjoy the meal before we tell anyone else."

"Oh, that's bad news, Colin," replied Elizabeth, "but you're right. Bon appétit." There was much good-humoured bantering between tables during the different courses of the meal and toasts proposed from one table to another. When the desserts had been finished, Colin slipped out again. He phoned Graham's house once more and the same woman answered the phone.

"Hello," he said, "I'm calling from Victoria Hall again. Have you heard from Graham yet?"

"Yes," replied the woman, "and not good news I'm afraid. The van went off the road. The boys aren't hurt but they can't get there tonight. They need the van to carry the entire equipment home after the session. I'm ever so sorry."

"That's a blow," said Colin, "but as long as no one has been hurt, that's the main thing. Tell Graham not to worry about his equipment, I'll make sure it's locked away somewhere for the night."

"Oh, thanks ever so much," replied the woman, "he was worried about that."

"No problem," said Colin, then he had a brainwave; "I don't suppose Graham would mind if we used one guitar, would he? I can play a bit and it will be better than nothing."

"I'm sure he won't," said the woman, laughing, "but no smashing it up at the end, mind you."

"Promise," said Colin, "thanks." He got back to the hall just behind the Lord Mayor and his wife and sidled back to the table where he grabbed Barbara and dragged her to the side of the room.

"Barbara," he said urgently, "the band can't get here tonight. The van's broken down. I've asked Graham's wife if I can use the guitar and she agreed. Now, will you join me on stage and sing like you've never sung before and make the evening complete? Otherwise it is going to be a fiasco."

"Oh, I don't know," said Barbara, "I mean, I know songs from West Side Story, but not much else."

"You know loads of songs from the Top Ten and you know all my songs, don't you?" said Colin.

"Well, yes," said Barbara hesitantly.

"And the music is all set up," added Colin, "we could tackle some of them too."

"Colin!" Barbara exclaimed, "I'm not a blooming cabaret singer."

"Please," he urged, "our mums spend ages on this night every year. We can ask for volunteers to sing too and it might be a giggle. What do you say?" She hesitated.

"Your dad's been looking forward to it too," added Colin, "after his spell in hospital."

"Blackmailer," she said and punched him on the arm.

"You'll do it?" he said. She nodded and he threw his arms around her and hugged her.

"Come on, then, let's go and break the news," he said. He led Barbara into the room and they went and stood behind Molly.

"Colin has some news for you, mum," said Barbara.

"Good or bad?" laughed Molly.

"Both," replied Barbara.

"The band can't make it," Molly wailed, "I knew this would happen. Our anniversary dinner too."

"That's the bad news," said Barbara.

"So what's the good news?" said Brendan.

"The O'Malley kids, plus volunteers, are going to do their best to make music for everyone," said Colin, "but first of all I'm going to ask their permission."

"You'd better ask Elizabeth if she minds too," said Sharon, "she came here expecting to dance with you not watch you play all night." Elizabeth shrugged her shoulders and held her hands wide, palm upwards, in an expression they all understood.

"Once a musician, always a musician, I guess," she said but she was smiling.

"Thanks, Elizabeth," said Colin. He grabbed Barbara before she could change her mind and dragged her up onto the stage. Taking the microphone he tapped it. The room hushed and he began to speak.

"Sorry, ladies and gentlemen," he said, "the band has run their van off the road and can't make it." There was a groan of disappointment but Colin waved his hands.

"We know this is your 20th anniversary Christmas party and that all of you have worked very hard to make it happen so we, that is my cousin Barbara and I, would like to kick off the music with a few numbers." There was a round of applause but he quietened them and added,

"And then we want volunteers to come up and do their own party pieces." The audience began laughing and one man shouted,

"Don't let your dad near the microphone until the end, I've heard Danny Boy murdered by professionals- and that he ain't." Colin laughed.

"I promise you *he* won't do Danny Boy if all of *you* are up here stopping him, fair enough?"

"Fair enough," the man replied and everyone applauded. Colin turned to Barbara and picked up a guitar.

"Shall we start with a Beatles number to get them going?" he said. She nodded.

"You know 'Can't buy me Love?"

"Doesn't everyone?" she said.

"I hope so," he replied, "okay, one two three." At the table Molly grabbed Terry and hauled him to his feet.

"Come on," she said urgently, "if they have the guts to sing the least we can do is find partners and get the rest of them dancing." She led him to the dance floor and left him to find a partner while she took the hand of the nearest man and asked him to dance. Soon there were five or six couples dancing and the evening was saved. It had turned midnight before Brendan was allowed to sing his version of Danny Boy to close the evening.. On the last note applause broke out and he bowed and smiled.

"A big hand, please, ladies and gentlemen, for Colin and Barbara," he shouted. The market people clapped and whistled.

"Take a bow," said Brendan, beckoning the blushing pair to the stage. As they basked in the limelight no one noticed Nathaniel Sharpe leaving the hall. He was determined to get one of the first taxis home. With all the contrariness of a spoilt child, the snow, which had covered the town not two hours before, had all but disappeared. The taxi rank outside the hall was full of cars and their drivers, stamping feet and blowing white plumes into the air. Nathaniel went to the front of the queue, gave the driver his address and climbed in.

"Good night?" asked the driver pleasantly.

"A duty,' replied Nathaniel blandly, "one that I won't repeat until next year." The driver raised his eyebrows, put the car in gear and drove off. If he had known that his mother was still up and about at home, Nathaniel would have told the man to step on the gas. As it was she was looking at the clock and making preparations to get into bed. It was important that when Nathaniel looked in on her later, she appeared to be asleep. It had been a most interesting night for her. One that she looked forward to as much as Nathaniel said he hated it. This was the one night of the year that Nathaniel brought home all his pocket books and ledgers as the market was closed for two days. The first year of her supposed confinement to bed, she had got up, a little shakily, and gone into Nathaniel's bedroom. The room had all the hallmarks of a confirmed bachelor.

Bed made up with sheets and two dark blankets, bobbling with age. Curtains of a dark material, pulled tightly across to keep out even the friendliest chink of light. The linoleum, boasted one square of carpet. Nathaniel had, grudgingly, allowed carpet to be put in her bedroom, and the off-cut was here, by his bed, in all its fraying glory. But she was not here to admire the furnishings. She knew her son better than any other person on earth. If ever there was a replica of a scheming man, it was Nathaniel. She had known Nathaniel's father, Herbert Walker well - very well. She knew his scams and was convinced that Nathaniel would have been taught them. She began to search systematically, through cupboards and drawers, making sure that clothes and shoes were put back in the same place. She lifted the rug, peered under the bed, heaved the mattress up at each corner and spent valuable time smoothing and straightening the corners. She dragged a stand chair from her room and climbed to inspect the top of the wardrobe. Nothing was to be found.

"Damn you, Nathaniel," she said, "where is your hiding place?" She tapped her foot, the bare skin leaving moist toe prints on the linoleum.

"Think, woman, think," she muttered and then it came to her. The only other place Nathaniel used upstairs was the bathroom. Holding on to the walls, she made her way there.

"No time to waste," she thought and dropped to her knees, pulling the nightdress under her for a scrap of warmth. The bath panel showed signs of being removed but she needed a screwdriver. She looked at the wristwatch her husband had bought her. Nathaniel should be a couple of hours yet. Laboriously she went downstairs, found a screwdriver and returned to the bathroom.

"You're going to have to get a bit fitter than this, old girl," she chuckled, "if you're going to go around snooping even once a year." Back on her knees she gently unscrewed the panel and eased it forwards. Peering into the recess she saw a battered leather briefcase and she hauled it out. For the next hour and a half, oblivious to her body going slowly more numb, she sifted carefully through the note books inside, digesting some contents instantly, memorising figures, and puzzling over others.

"What are all these initials and what do they stand for?" she said. Tracing her finger down one page she tried to make sense of the initials. A.H.-d.i.s; B.T.-f.h. L.B.-u.c. At the other side of the page was a sum with a gloriously florid pound sign in front. Small amounts, yet checking back over the year, they amounted to over 350 pounds.

"Nearly a pound a day," she said, closing the book and replacing it, "and all tax free."

Beginning the following February, so as not to arouse any suspicions, she began to question Nathaniel in an innocent way.

"Any new stall holders this year yet, son?" she asked.

"One that stayed after Christmas," he replied, "Les Burton, Does fancy goods."

"Good tenant, is he?" she asked.

"Good enough," said Nathaniel, shaking his evening newspaper open, "once we'd sorted out his underage child working." Over the course of twelve months Nathaniel's mother had worked out that the initials were stall holders and had innocently gleaned from Nathaniel that d.i.s. was dirt in scales and f.h. meant fire hazard. Once she had these meanings it was irrelevant what the others meant. She knew that Nathaniel was extorting money illegally from the market people. Every year after that she had almost leapt out of bed as soon as the door had been closed behind her son and copied the updated figures onto tiny scraps of paper. These she dated and filed away between the back cover of her large old bible and the brown paper that protected it. She also began exercising for half an hour every morning and afternoon. Each Christmas she could barely contain her excitement. She knew how much money Nathaniel had and where it was lodged. It became the focus of her life from November onwards.

"What sort of a year have we had this year?" she would say to herself. She heard Nathaniel's key in the lock. Turning her head and shifting her body sideways, face away from the door, she began the regular, slow breathing of one completely at peace. Only when her son had opened the door, peered in, and closed it behind him did she open her eyes and whisper.

"A good year, son, well done."

The Thursday night after the Christmas party, Colin and Elizabeth were on the sofa, babysitting Lesley. They were watching Top of the Pops, in common with half the young people in Britain.

"I'd still rather have Cathy McGowan on Ready Steady Go," said Elizabeth, "her hair is just fabulous." She tugged at her naturally curly hair, trying to straighten it.

"You're my Queen of the Mods," said Colin, pulling her hand away and kissing it.

"Do you miss your music?" asked Elizabeth.

"Yeah," said Colin, and he sighed, "but I've got you, haven't I?" She sat upright, moving away from the comfort of his shoulder.

"Did you ever make any demo tapes?" she asked him.

"Of course," said Colin, "half a dozen, they're in my drawer at home."

"And what did you ever *do* with them," went on Elizabeth, "apart from making them?"

"Well, I looked up some agent's in the music papers….." he said lamely.

"But you never got round to sending them?" she said.

"No," he replied.

"Then why don't you try?" Elizabeth said excitedly, "Send them and see what happens. If nothing does, well, you've not lost anything, have you?"

"And what happens if I get the call to go to London to see one of them?" said Colin,

"Would you come with me?"

"Ooooh," said Elizabeth, "I don't know. I've Mum to help. I've never been to London."

"Well, neither have I," said Colin, "but it can't be much different to Manchester. Bigger maybe, but that's all. We could go and see 'Hair' while it's still on."

"We'll see," said Elizabeth non-commitally, "but in the meantime, get those tapes out and send them off before they become last year's music."

Two days later Colin had posted six tapes to music agents down in London.

Chapter 9

From the warmth of his twelfth storey office, Stewart McIntosh, Chief Executive of Burnside Borough Council, watched with mounting satisfaction the activity on the building site less than half a mile away. He lifted the binoculars and trained them on the bulldozer. He watched as it flattened the last three terraced houses. The occupants of the houses, built for mine workers, had been removed only twenty four hours before, baffled and bewildered by the legal jargon about compulsory purchase yet mollified by the compensation. One elderly miner had gone to his daughter, and a widow woman had gone into a council home five weeks ago, protesting feebly. McIntosh had feared that the occupant of the third house, an old woman and her cats would never leave and one journalist on the local paper seemed intent on causing trouble. McIntosh shook his head as he remembered how she had cornered him one evening, after a council meeting, and harangued him about "poor Mrs. Shaw and her cats, how can you force her to move out when she's lived there all her married life?" He had promised, emphatically, to look into the matter and report back to her. The young, naive journalist had gone away happy. A word down at the golf club to the Editor had solved that little problem. Once she was on her own, the woman and her mangy cats had agreed to move to the ground floor of a soulless tower block. She moved one week ago. The telephone rang and reluctantly McIntosh put his binoculars down on the windowsill.

"McIntosh," he said brusquely.

"Jim Wilson," came the reply, "do you have a minute, Stewart?"

"Now?" McIntosh asked, irritated. He wanted to watch the bricks and mortar moved away.

"This is crucially important," Wilson said.

"Then you'd better come up," replied McIntosh. He didn't like the sound of his Planning Officer's voice. McIntosh spread around some papers on his desk. Wouldn't do to look as if he had been slacking. He shrugged off his jacket, loosened his tie and rolled up his sleeves. He frowned as he felt perspiration under his armpits. His shirt was damp already. The veins on his nose bore testament to a love affair with a good whisky bottle. His hands were his best feature, having never done a day's graft in their lives. They were soft, smooth and the nails perfectly manicured. He rubbed his nails on his shirt front and was gratified to see that they were smooth and shiny.

"Come," he said, hearing the knock on the door. Jim Wilson came in with a large roll of plans under his arm.

"You need to see these," he said without any preamble, "where can I spread them?"

"Here," said McIntosh, scooping all the carefully pre-arranged papers to one side. Wilson spread the old plans out on the desk. McIntosh recognised them immediately.

"It's the site for the new Market Hall," he said, "What on earth have you uncovered?"

"Nothing physical or geological to hamper the building, Stewart," replied Wilson.

"Thank goodness for that," said McIntosh with a huge sigh, "I thought for one awful moment you were going to tell me old mine workings were under the terraces."

"There are," replied Wilson, "but they were clearly mapped out and rubble from the buildings will fill them in and we can cap them. No, what is important is this note glued to the side. You can see that as the plan was rolled the note folded itself to the back. Brought forward," he demonstrated by flipping a piece of paper forward, "you can read it." McIntosh peered intently at the scrap of paper but could barely make out what it said.

"OK, cut the dramatics," said McIntosh, "you have obviously taken the time to decipher it. What does it say?"

"The bottom line is that this paper proves that the land we are building on is not council owned land," said Wilson, "when the mines were nationalised the government compulsorily purchased land from mine owners, houses and all. In some obscure cases, where owners were vehemently opposed to selling their mines, the government gave minimal compensation at the time, with a cast iron guarantee that if the mines closed and the properties were demolished the land reverted back to the family members. I've checked sources and records before I came to you. So far, only three instances have occurred. But in each case, the family descendants have claimed back the land. The precedent has been set."

"So what!" blustered McIntosh, "we're talking the Shuttleworth family here? They didn't have any descendants. Old man Shuttleworth died, his daughter died. There isn't anyone. Our lawyers checked."

"I grant you, none of the Shuttleworths are still alive. I've also checked. But then I checked the family papers lodged in the public archive. Shuttleworth did pass on the right, along with the government guarantee, about the time..." He paused. He knew McIntosh was not going to like this.

"Spit it out man," McIntosh said impatiently.

"Brendan and Terry O'Malley's grandfather came over from Ireland."

"The gambling grandfather?" said McIntosh, who knew the story of the O'Malley family.

"The very same. Patrick O'Malley's son, Sean O'Malley, for some reason, became the owner of the land," said Wilson quietly, "and a copy of the solicitor's record of the transaction is in the Shuttleworth papers. The O'Malley brothers, as Sean's direct descendants, own the land and the government guarantee." McIntosh sat heavily in his swivel chair. Jim Wilson watched him carefully, saying nothing, as McIntosh's face turned from its usual ruddy glow to white, then beads of perspiration formed on his brow. Wilson could almost see his boss's brain churning under the skin. At last McIntosh spoke.

"We did all the usual checks before going ahead with the building, didn't we?"

"Sure," replied Wilson, "we advertised in one national and two local papers asking anyone with an interest in the land to come forward. No one did. But having found this information, we're on a hiding to nothing if it goes to court."

"Of all the ironies life can throw at you, it turns out that O'Malleys, who actually suggested this new market hall, owns the land we're building on," said McIntosh.

"They obviously don't know this?" he went on carefully.

"The O'Malley family?" replied Wilson.

"Who else," spat out McIntosh, "the bloody Lord Mayor?"

"Calm down, Stewart. As far as I know, you and I are the only ones who have this information," replied Wilson, "although, as I said, it is only a copy of the solicitor's agreement that is in the archives. The original is probably gathering dust in a file."

"Do we know which firm of solicitors handled the transaction?" asked McIntosh.

"Wheeler and Blackstone," replied Wilson, "they were taken over by Grey Brothers after old man Wheeler died. Blackstone took the money and retired to Jersey."

"And the Grey firm, if I remember rightly," mused McIntosh, "moved out of Water Street after a fire and took over new offices in Preston Road about ten years ago."

"That's right," said Wilson.

"It would have been reported in the papers," said McIntosh, "can you find out what was said in the back issues of the Evening Telegraph without arousing any suspicions?"

"I don't need to," replied Wilson, "I only need to access records of the business rates paid in Preston Road. They start the day a firm moves in."

"Do we have any idea which solicitors the O'Malley brothers use?" asked McIntosh.

"No," said Wilson, "but again, that's not difficult to find out. We know where they live and an official call to the Land Registry will tell us who registered the title on their behalf."

"Anything else we need to cover?" said McIntosh.

"I take it from that," said Wilson carefully, "that you're keeping this just between us two."

"Yes," replied McIntosh firmly, "the project is too far advanced now to cancel it. We'd look like fools, all of us." Jim Wilson nodded but said nothing. McIntosh pointed at the plans on the desk.

"Those have to go back, I take it?" he said.

"Yes," replied Wilson, "I had to sign them out- I'll have to sign them back."

"But, we can dispense with this tatty piece of taped on paper, can't we?" McIntosh leaned over and removed the piece of paper with care.

"As you wish, Stewart," said Wilson with a nervous smile, "I don't remember seeing it." McIntosh took the paper and tore it into tiny scraps which he let flutter into his waste bin.

"Let me know when you've got that other information," said McIntosh. Wilson carefully rolled up the plans and left the room. Stewart McIntosh hit the intercom on his desk.

"Mary?" he queried. No one replied. He strode to the door just as his secretary entered the outer office.

"Sorry, Mr. McIntosh," she said, "I just nipped out to get some water. Do you want coffee?"

"Yes, and make it strong today," he said. He walked back into the office, frowning. The last thing he needed was for this project to be jeopardised in any way. The firm of architects, into which he had sunk a large amount of money, was not performing as well as he had been led to believe it would. The managing director, who had courted McIntosh assiduously for more than a year, until he had extracted his money, seemed to be all mouth and no substance.......

.......Only last month McIntosh had challenged him at the golf club.

"Eric,' he had said, cornering the man in the changing room, "we've got the market hall project in the bag, but what else are you looking at?"

"Oh," Eric had replied breezily, "don't you fret, Stewart, there are four or five projects we're working on, should be raking it in soon."

"Four or five projects where exactly?" McIntosh had replied sharply.

"Erm, one in the suburbs of Preston," said Eric.

"And what project is that?" demanded McIntosh.

"Oh, it's a good size," said Eric, bending down to tie his laces.

"Supermarket? Housing?" insisted McIntosh.

"Well, actually, it's a barn conversion," replied Eric meekly.

"Duckworth and Co.," McIntosh snapped, "more like blooming Jobsworth and Co. You're going to have to do better than wait for me to hand projects on a plate to you. When I advance money to people I expect a damned better return than I get from a bank. Every substantial project your firm has had over the last two years has come from me."

"And you've had a hefty annual divvy, Stewart," Eric replied.

"So far, Duckworth,' McIntosh replied harshly, 'but I worry that plans are not coming into the council for approval from *your* firm. I see plenty coming in from other people. Why are *you* not winning those contracts?" The changing room door opened, banging noisily against the wall. Eric Duckworth breathed a sigh of relief and the sound was not lost on Stewart McIntosh.

"Pull your socks up, Eric," he said quietly, "or we become ex-business colleagues. And your company wouldn't last long if I was against you."

"Is that a threat?" Eric said, equally quietly.

"No, it's a promise," McIntosh replied before walking out of the room.......

"Coffee?" said Mary, as she put the cup and saucer down in front of the Chief Executive, "I did knock but you weren't answering."

"Sorry, Mary," McIntosh managed a half smile, "I was miles away."

"Is it all right if I go for lunch early today, Mr. McIntosh? You remember I have a dental appointment at twelve."

"Yes, yes, off you go, whenever you want," McIntosh replied. She was about to say something but decided against it. Her boss had one of those faces that showed all was not well in his world. Returning to her desk she looked for her handbag then realised that she must have left it in the ladies, after she had filled the kettle.

"Blast," she whispered then decided to make a dash to retrieve it. Rushing out of the office she almost collided with Jim Wilson.

"Sorry, Mr Wilson," she gasped, "left my handbag in the ladies."

"Is there anyone with him?" Wilson asked as he moved to one side to let her pass.

"No," she said, "go right in." Forty seconds later she was back at her desk, breathless, but clutching her handbag.

'I don't believe it!' she heard McIntosh's voice shouting through the intercom, *'damn Brendan O'Malley. Of all the solicitors in town he has to be using Grey brothers.'* His voice was heavy with sarcasm and bitterness and Mary winced to hear the tone of it. She leaned forward to listen more closely at the intercom.

'But that's not bad news about the Shuttleworth documents. Where are they?' Mary heard her boss ask.

'Stored in sealed, air proof, fire proof, water proof containers in a security firm's lock up. The paper said that only recent stuff had been destroyed. All the old papers were in the basement and little damage was caused to them,' replied Wilson.

'So, the papers are not in Preston Road?' she heard McIntosh say.

'No,' replied Wilson, *'it seems to me that they are out of harm's way. O'Malley has no way of finding out he owns the land.'*

'We could make sure,' she heard McIntosh say.

'What,' replied Wilson, *'you mean...'*

'Not today, not even this month,' McIntosh said, *'but some day the papers could disappear.'*

'But how on earth are you going to locate the right ones?' said Wilson.

'How many containers can Grey brothers have in that store?' said McIntosh.

'I don't like this, Stewart,' said Wilson, *'Why not leave well alone?'*

'Come on, Jim,' Mary heard McIntosh wheedle, *'it's not as if I'm going to burgle the place myself.'*

Mary's phone rang.

'Christ,' she heard her boss say, *'I've left the bloody intercom on.'*

Mary grabbed her bag, glanced at the clock and was out of the door before McIntosh had time to get round his desk and stride across the room to reach the connecting door. She knew he would probably look in the corridor so she opened the first door on her left and walked in. The telephonists were surprised to see Mary enter.

"Lost my internal phone list again," she said to the nearest girl, "would you have a copy?"

With one ear on the corridor she heard her own door open and then close again. The girl handed Mary a copy.

"Thanks," Mary said and made her way out into the corridor. Stuffing the list into her bag she left the building by the stairs. Ten minutes later she was bracing herself for the anaesthetic needle poised inches away from her gum.

"Are you all right, Miss Clarkson?" the dentist said to her. She nodded.

"Here we go then," he said and pushed the needle gently. Mary shut her eyes and tried to remember exactly what she had heard. It was not official council business that much she was sure of.

"You can go now," she heard the dentist say, "just rinse out first for me." Mary dragged her thoughts back to the immediate present.

"Thank you," she said. She walked out of the surgery and wandered towards the old market hall. Without realising it she found herself in front of the O'Malley brother's stall. Brendan was serving an old woman with potatoes and he nodded to her to let her know he'd be with her soon.

'Yes, love?' he said, startling her.

'Oh, a pound of bananas, please,' she said. He wrapped them and she handed him a note.

'Nothing less?' he said.

'No, sorry,' she said. He handed her the change and asked if she was all right.

'Don't I look it?' she said.

'Well, a bit far away,' said Brendan, 'as if you've got a lot on your plate.'

"Oh, house moving," she said, thinking quickly and crossing her fingers at the impending lie, "my mother. She wants to move in with me and sell her house. I don't know any good firms of solicitors to deal with though."

"Grey Brothers," said Brendan cheerfully, "on Preston Road. We've used them for years. They're reliable and they don't cost the earth."

"Thanks," she muttered but Brendan had already moved away to serve someone else. Mary made her way outside, clutching the paper bag of bananas. She sat down on a bench and unconsciously took one of the fruits from the bag and began to eat it. Her mind was whirling. The words she had overheard kept coming back time and again:

'Damn Brendan O'Malley ....is using Grey brothers.'

'No way of finding out he owns the land'

'The Shuttleworth documents.'

'It's not as if I'm going to burgle the place myself.'

What on earth did it all mean? How could she make sense of it? It had to be something to do with the building site. That much she was sure of. The new development had become an obsession with Stewart McIntosh. He thought about nothing else these days. She could easily check with the archivist which plans Jim Wilson had taken out just to be sure. The town clock began to strike and Mary jumped up. Glancing down, she saw that she had almost shredded the paper bag, but she could still make out the letters that made it distinctively one of O'Malley's bags. She threw it and the contents into a nearby waste bin and ran to the building where she worked. McIntosh was not at his desk. The connecting door to his room was wide open which was a sure sign that he had gone for lunch. Mary breathed a sigh of relief. She looked at the calendar. Stewart McIntosh was due at a conference in three days time. He would be away for two days. If she could clear her desk of things she would normally do in that time, she would have time to delve around within the building. Maybe even get into McIntosh's filing cabinets. He was not a careless man but she knew where he kept the spare key. Having made the decision she attacked her in tray with gusto and by the time McIntosh came back from lunch she was rosy cheeked and smiling.

'How was the dentist?' he threw the question at her on the way to his office.

'Fine,' she replied, 'thank you for asking.'

"Oh," he paused and turned to her, "I've had a word with maintenance about the intercom."

"Is there a problem with it?" she asked, looking at the machine on her desk.

"No, just a bit un-necessary," he said looking at her closely, "on the grounds of cost, I've decided to have it removed."

"Fine, Mr McIntosh," she replied. He went into his office and closed the door.

"Cost," thought Mary, 'what blooming cost?" But she knew instantly that what she had heard was more important than ever. She bent her head to her work and all was quiet for the rest of the day. On the bus home and walking through the dark streets she began to have doubts. What did it matter that the site did not appear to be legitimately available to build on? The O'Malley brothers had a good living. She had a good job and she'd worked hard to get from the typing pool to McIntosh's office. If he was caught doing something illegal and was sacked, a new boss might not want her. He'd probably have his own secretary. She needed her £1500 a year salary. She had only ten years work before she got her council pension, but she wanted more than that to live on comfortably. But, she couldn't get those words out of her head. Three sleepless nights followed before she walked to her office on auto pilot. McIntosh was not due in for two days and in that time she was going to snoop as much as she could. It was a role she found distasteful, but necessary. Mary Clarkson was small and, if you wanted to be generous you'd call her dumpy. Since childhood she'd fought a losing battle with chocolate, cakes and biscuits. They were such insignificant, but comforting, items and one always led to another. Her teenage years had been miserable and her early twenties mortifying. As her friends got married she was never asked to be a bridesmaid and never caught the bouquet. But she was a demon at work. From the typing pool to secretary to Stewart McIntosh had taken her less than ten years and she ran his office meticulously. Never a piece of paper out of place. Never the smallest detail overlooked. Four rings adorned her hands, but none on her wedding finger. She patted the dark brown, severely pinned bun and hung her coat and scarf on the hanger. She had called in at the archive Department before going up to her office and checked the plans that Jim Wilson had shown McIntosh. They were of the site for the new market hall. Locking the office door behind her she found the spare key to his filing cabinet and began rifling through files, working systematically and methodically. At the end of the first day she had found absolutely nothing and her head was pounding. Everything was perfectly legitimate council business. Most of the documents she had typed herself.

"Damn," she said. She put on her coat and scarf and left the building, unsure what else she could do except confront the O'Malley brothers with a wild piece of hearsay. And maybe lose her job.

"Enough, you stupid girl," she whispered, "let it go." For weeks she watched the new Market Hall foundations being laid and she also began to buy her fruit and vegetables at O'Malleys. A small article in the evening paper caught her eye one night.

"Break in at storage depot."

There was a forced entry at Safe Store last night, thwarted by a security guard on patrol with his dog. Nothing was taken and the intruder ran away as soon as the dog barked. The intruder was out of the premises before the guard could even unleash his faithful companion.

"I don't understand it," said the owner, called out by the police, "the container he was trying to gain access to hasn't been used for over twenty years. There is nothing in there except old papers belonging to a local firm of solicitors."

Mary's heart skipped a beat and her throat went dry. She felt sick and just made it to the bathroom before heaving over the basin.

"Dear Lord," she prayed, while wiping her face and eyes, "what do I do now?" She went into her bedroom, sat heavily on the bed and looked at the wall. A crude print of "The Light of the World" was the only thing she saw. Two minutes later she was striding down the street towards her local church. It was confessional night and there were ten minutes to go. Only two people were waiting and she was thankful no one came into the church behind her. The person before her came out and she walked into the tiny, scented box.

"Bless me father, for I have sinned, it is five weeks since my last confession..." She began to recite the words that had been etched into her mind at the age of seven. Then she stopped. What sin had she committed that she could confess to? Seconds went by and then she heard a small cough from the other side of the grill.

"Yes, my child," the priest said quietly. Mary took all her courage in both hands and blurted out,

"Father Rigby, I have to tell someone, but it has to be in confidence."

"Yes, Mary," he replied, "you know that whatever you say will not be repeated to a soul." She was not surprised at the use of her name. Father Rigby had been hearing her sins for over twenty years.

"Well, Father," she went on, "it's a complicated story."

"Was there anyone else in the church when you came in?" he asked her.

"No one waiting," she replied.

"Just pop out and have a quick look for me. If the coast is clear then we can go into the presbytery and have a cup of tea. I'm gasping." She chuckled and left the confessional. There was no one else in the church.

"All clear," she whispered into the box.

Father Rigby came out, kissed his stole, and, linking arms with Mary, escorted her to the back of the church and locked up.

They walked to his tiny house by the church and he let her in.

"Put the kettle on, there's a good girl," he said, "while I get this stuff off." He re-appeared as Mary was setting two cups of tea on the small table by the fire.

"Right," he said, "you'd better tell me what's bothering you." Mary told him the whole story and he listened carefully, nodding and sipping his tea. When she had finished and sat back he said,

"Well, Mary, that's a tale and a half, isn't it?"

"You *do* believe me?" Mary said fearfully.

"Of course I do," he soothed her, "it's too far-fetched to be anything but the truth. And anyway, how long have I known you. You are not one of life's liars."

"So what can I do?" she said, "I'm just so sorry I was too afraid of losing my job to say anything before. That was my sin, Father."

"Perfectly understandable," he said, before continuing, "leave this with me. I can do some digging around without looking suspicious. I also have a few contacts in Ireland that might be able to get some information about the O'Malley clan before Patrick O'Malley came over with his bundle of money. We'll see what that turns up."

"I didn't think you were Irish, Father," said Mary.

"I'm not," he replied, "but I trained in Ireland and we old boys from the seminary still keep in touch. In fact, I'm due there soon to a retreat. I love that country, even if it does rain more than here." They both laughed together.

"Am I forgiven?" Mary said as she rose to go.

"Completely," he said, "now go home with a clear conscience and just say a couple of Hail Marys and a Glory Be before you go to sleep."

"Thank you, Father," she replied, "I think I will sleep tonight."

"I'll be in touch," he said.

When Mary had left, Father Rigby sat musing in his chair.

"Patrick O'Malley," he said to the fireplace, "I don't pretend to know how you got hold of a piece of land in this county, and maybe I don't want to know. But, I'll not see your grandsons cheated. No, that *would* be a sin."

Chapter 10

Nathaniel Sharpe was having a bad day. A letter had arrived at his office two days before, and he had stared at the envelope bearing the town's crest for two minutes before opening it. Once he had digested the request, for him to meet with Stewart McIntosh, he had sat in a reverie, biting the side of one finger, for half an hour. This was not the way McIntosh operated. Normally Nathaniel would have received a phone call from Mary, McIntosh's secretary, asking him to pop in and see McIntosh and they'd have arranged a mutually convenient time. McIntosh had never written to him before.

The day of the appointment he made his way across town, having carefully locked his office and set his latest junior to some meaningless task, and approached the reception area of the Town Hall.

"I have an appointment to see Mr. McIntosh," Nathaniel said to the receptionist. The girl smiled, rang Mary and nodded at Nathaniel.

"You are to go up to Mr. McIntosh's office in five minutes," she said.

"Thank you, young lady," Nathaniel said and returned to his seat. Exactly five minutes later, to the second, Nathaniel rose and walked across to the lift. Nathaniel needed to go into Mary's tiny office to gain access to McIntosh. He knocked twice and entered.

"Good morning, Mary," he said.

"Good morning, Mr. Sharpe," she replied, "please go through. Mr. McIntosh is waiting for you."

Nathaniel took a deep breath, walked across the room, knocked once and entered.

"Nathaniel," said McIntosh, "good of you to come. Tea? Coffee?" McIntosh's tone was far too boisterous for Nathaniel's liking. Nathaniel shook his head before saying:

"I received your letter, Mr. McIntosh, I had no choice."

"Ah," said McIntosh, "well, it had to be official."

"Is there a problem?" replied Nathaniel."

"Sit down, sit down," said McIntosh. Nathaniel took the seat in front of McIntosh's desk and waited. McIntosh bent forward on his desk and leaned on his elbows with his hands clasped. It seemed to Nathaniel to be ages before he spoke.

"How long have you been Market Superintendent, Nathaniel?" Before Nathaniel could reply McIntosh went on.

"It must be coming up for thirty years, give or take a year or two." Nathaniel nodded.

"And in that time, you've had how many assistants?" McIntosh went on. Nathaniel opened his mouth but was stopped by a wave of McIntosh's hand.

"According to Personnel," McIntosh went on, looking at a sheaf of papers, "more than we've had bus drivers and conductors combined in the town's history."

"Mr. McIntosh, I can explain..." began Nathaniel.

"No, no, no," McIntosh stopped him once more, "I have all the records. The reasons why most of them left are perfectly adequate, from a Council point of view." He began leafing through the papers, reading out loud: "wanted something more challenging", "did not feel that this was a good career move", "could not fit in to the way the Market runs", "lazy and unwilling to learn" and here's the favourite "unable to adapt to a disciplined way of working." Nathaniel nodded at each statement. All were valid and could not be challenged.

"You have forgotten the ones who were dishonest and bad time keepers," Nathaniel interjected, "and the ones who just left one day and never came back."

"Even so, Nathaniel, you go through assistants like a dose of salts," McIntosh replied and he smiled at his own weak joke.

"Can I ask why this is suddenly such an issue?" Nathaniel asked. McIntosh closed the sheaf of documents and put them away in his drawer, sighed deeply and leaned right back in his chair.

"Politics, Nathaniel, pure and simple," he said quietly. Nathaniel sat there saying nothing.

"I'll be honest with you Nathaniel," McIntosh began, "I've never doubted that you run the market hall well."

"Thank you," replied Nathaniel, "I do the best I can."

"But," went on McIntosh, "things are changing. Damn it, the whole bloody world seems to be going mad. We don't operate in a vacuum. Government pokes its sticky fingers into things it should leave well alone. As you know, in a few months time the new market hall is due to be completed. There will be a grand civic reception and the local M.P. will attend. Well, he's bringing along some big wig from London to see the building in all its glory and there is the chance of some award that our local M.P. is keen to get..."

"I don't understand what that has to do with my assistants, Mr. McIntosh," interjected Nathaniel.

"You will, you will," McIntosh waved him quiet. "Our beloved M.P. has a daughter doing a degree in some high-faluting social subject. She's writing her dissertation on the development of the town over the last fifty years. It seems she's decided to study changes in the way people shop and spend money, particularly in council owned and run properties, as her special project. She has been bothering people all over the town hall with wanting this information and that information and, being who she is, I've had to co-operate. It was she who brought these papers," he pointed to folder, "to my attention and asked what I was doing about finding a replacement for you when you retire, as you seem unable to keep an assistant for more than a few months. Her exact words to me were 'what is it with this man? Does he eat boys for breakfast?"' Nathaniel turned pale and it was his turn to reach for his handkerchief. He mopped his brow.

"Retire?" he almost choked on the word.

"Well, you'll have to one day, Nathaniel, we all have to retire," McIntosh said quite sharply, "and anyway, suppose you dropped dead tomorrow? Who would be able to take over from you? Your last boy has been with you four months, the one before lasted three months. It is a valid point." Nathaniel's mind raced but he could think of nothing to say. This was not the way it was supposed to go. *He* was the one who was to choose the day he drew all his money and left, not some slip of a girl poking around asking questions and precipitating events.

"Mr. McIntosh," he said eventually, "I am so sorry that you have been bothered by such trivia. I promise you that you will have a month by month report on my latest assistant. I feel I can lick him into shape. He's perhaps one of the brightest boys I've had."

"Right, good, Nathaniel," replied McIntosh, glancing at his watch, "do that." He stood up, terminating the interview.

"Thank you, Mr. McIntosh," Nathaniel said as he left the room. Outside he nodded to Mary and closed her door behind him. He leaned on the wall and exhaled deeply. Things might have to move before he really wanted them to but he could see no other way.

"Time to put plans into action," he said. Nathaniel returned to his office in the Market Hall.

"Entwhistle," he called out and his latest victim came running in.

"I'm going out for an hour," he said, "on business. I want you to make yourself busy in that time."

"Doing what?" the boy asked with a blank look on his face.

"Anything useful," snapped Nathaniel, "and tell me, when I come back, what you found to do, so that I can put it into a report."

"A report!" exclaimed the boy.

"Yes, you numb skull," Nathaniel said more smoothly, "the Chief Executive wants to know just what you get up to, on a monthly basis, to earn your nine pounds a week."

"I only do what you tell me to," said the boy and his voice quavered.

"Then let's see if you actually have any initiative," replied Nathaniel.

"Any what?" said Entwhistle as a frown appeared on his forehead.

"Just go," said Nathaniel, shaking his head. The boy left the room and Nathaniel followed him, closed the door and locked it. Nathaniel stroked Marmalade's head.

"You've more sense in one paw than that boy has in his whole head," he said. Marmalade purred assent. Nathaniel turned to the safe in the corner and dialled the combination. Only Nathaniel knew this six digit number and he chuckled every time he dialled it. The Chief Executive *thought* he had the number. McIntosh was given it when the safe was installed and one of his annual tasks was to meet with Nathaniel and together they were supposed to change the number. After the first two years McIntosh found this small task too onerous.

"Just change the number and send me a memo," McIntosh had said the third year.

Nathaniel changed the number alone, sent the memo with a completely different number, sat back and waited, and no one ever queried it. The fifth year he had sent a memo with exactly the same numbers as the previous year. No one queried it. The seventh year he hadn't even bothered to send the memo. He heard nothing from the Town Hall. Carefully he reached behind a stack of files and extracted two building society books. He put them in his pocket, locked the safe and the office, leaving Marmalade outside, and left. He walked to the bus station and caught a bus to the town ten miles away. He took out one of the books, and went into the office of the Society named in the front.

"Good afternoon," said the teller, as he approached, "how may I help you?"

"I wish to close this account," Nathaniel replied as he slid the book towards her. The girl opened the book and looked at the amount. There was over £900 deposited-more than she earned in a year.

"Do you have any identification with you, sir?" she asked.

"You don't ask for identification when I'm depositing money," replied Nathaniel, "what sort of identification do you want?"

"A driving licence?" she said.

"I don't drive," said Nathaniel.

"Passport?" she tried.

"I do not have one," replied Nathaniel, "and even if I had I wouldn't carry it with me."

"Well," said the girl, "will you wait one moment while I see the manager? Please take a seat."

Nathaniel walked away from the counter and took a seat. He was irritated.

This was his money and he wanted it. Five minutes went by and then a tall, thin, young man came out of a door and walked up to him.

"Mr. Sharpe?" Nathaniel rose and took the extended hand.

"My apologies for the delay, Mr. Sharpe," he said, "I am Mr Smith, the manager. I believe you wish to close your account with us?"

"I do," said Nathaniel.

"I hope there have not been any problems with our service?" said Mr. Smith.

"None whatsoever," said Nathaniel, "I just want my money - in cash."

"It is rather a large sum," replied Mr. Smith, "to take away."

"So, how much can I take today," said Nathaniel sarcastically, "without identification?"

"A hundred pounds?" queried Mr. Smith.

"And tomorrow," replied Nathaniel, "with identification?"

"All the rest, sir," said Mr. Smith.

"What do you consider to be proper identification, Mr. Smith?" said Nathaniel.

"Oh, an electricity or rates bill, perhaps," said Mr. Smith airily.

"And your statements of interest for ten years," said Nathaniel, "would you like to see those too?"

Mr. Smith gulped.

"Not necessary, Mr. Sharpe," he replied and a slight flush warmed his cheeks.

"I shall see you in three days," said Nathaniel, "be sure you have enough money."

"Will you be wanting your hundred pounds, sir," Mr. Smith queried.

"No, thank you," said Nathaniel, "all or nothing. I bid you good day." He turned away and left the office. He was furious that these Societies had taken his money, month after month, year after year, and now that he wanted his money, they were being difficult. He stowed away the book and extracted the second book. Walking across the road he entered the second building society office.

"How much of this," he asked the teller, pushing the book across the counter, "can I take out, in cash, today?"

"Possibly a hundred pounds, if you have..." she began to say.

"Some identification," Nathaniel chipped in.

"That's correct, sir," she smiled at him.

"And to withdraw all the money in one day?" said Nathaniel.

"Identification and two days notice, Mr. Sharpe," she said, glancing at his name on the book.

"Right," said Nathaniel, "I'm giving you two days notice and I want to collect all of it in three days." He turned to go and was stopped by the teller.

"Mr. Sharpe," she called out, "may I just ask for a sample signature that is up to date and then there won't be any problems."

"I've been putting money into this account for years, young lady," he said tersely, "and your company has been taking it for years, without an up to date signature."

"Sorry, sir," she said, sliding a form over the counter. He signed.

"Three days," he repeated as he turned and walked away. Travelling back to his home town on the bus, Nathaniel was troubled. It should have been easy to take his money and go home. Instead he was being met by rules and regulations. Being a man who lived by rules and regulations he appreciated their existence, but he did not want them applied to him.

"Jobsworths," he muttered to himself and his teeth chattered causing the woman sat next to him to take a sideways glance at Nathaniel. He got off the bus and walked briskly into the market hall.

"Call your lad off," said an irritated stall holder near to the door.

"What?" said Nathaniel, startled.

"He's been rushing around like a blue bottle checking we've no blooming fire hazards lying around," shouted the man, "but damn it all, it's nearly five o'clock. We're packing up, for goodness sake."

"Sorry," said Nathaniel, "I told him to keep busy, not be a nuisance." He rushed up to his office, missing the final comment of "aye, one blooming nuisance is enough." His boy was sat on an upturned box outside the locked door, a cup of tea in one hand.

"Out of the way," Nathaniel snapped at him, "and get rid of that box. I've heard already about your little escapades this afternoon."

"You told me..." the boy started to say, as he jumped to his feet, but Nathaniel cut him short.

"Get that box moved, now," Nathaniel spat, "then go home."

"Yes, sir," the boy replied, picking up his box, spilling the last drops of tea on the floor and turning crimson all at the same time.

"Leave it," said Nathaniel, tutting at the slopped tea, "the cleaners can do it."

The boy slunk away and Nathaniel opened the office door and then carefully locked it behind him. Going to the safe he opened it and placed the two savings books back in exactly the same place.

"I need to think about this," he said to himself, "in peace and quiet." His ears were tuned in to the sounds of traders clearing up downstairs.

"I'll get off home," he thought, glancing at his watch, "there's a first time for everything." He glanced at his desk and everything was in order. Leaving the building he nodded once or twice to acknowledge farewells called out. Mrs. Black from fancy goods turned to her husband in amazement.

"Did you see that," she said, "Nat Sharpe leaving before us? I never thought I'd see the day."

Nathaniel was home fifteen minutes early. Silently he slid the key into the door and opened it. He paused as he heard a sound coming from upstairs. Carefully he stepped into the hallway and closed the door without a sound. Two strides took him to the bottom of the stairs. The noise persisted. A rhythmic beat and the faint squeak of the bed. He waited. After two minutes the noise stopped and he heard his mother's bedroom door open. He ducked away from the foot of the stairs and then peered around the wall. He was in time to see his mother vanish into the bathroom and close the door. Two things struck Nathaniel immediately. One, his mother was humming a tune and two, she was not shuffling around in the expected manner. Her movements had been almost sprightly. He glanced at his watch. She would be expecting him home in twelve minutes. He sidled back towards the front door and, with even more care, opened it, stepped outside and closed it with the key. He began to walk down the street, hugging the wall. McIntosh talking about Nathaniel retiring, not being able to access his money and now his mother bounding around the bedroom and the bathroom. It seemed to Nathaniel that, unlike the Americans, about to land a man on the moon – his whole world was turning upside down. The bathroom! Had she discovered anything in the bathroom? There was nothing there now, of course. Only once a year was there anything she could find. That is - if she knew what Nathaniel hid there every Christmas and had seen it. He wracked his brain, trying to remember conversations he had had with his mother. They talked about so little. A piece in the local paper, trivia about the market, nothing about the outside world. He doubted whether she even knew, let alone cared, who was the current Prime Minister of England. If World War Three broke out Mrs. Sharpe would probably comment for at least a minute or two, and that would be dealt with. He glanced at his watch. He was due home in one minute precisely. He walked back along the street, and entered the house with more noise than normal.

"I'm back, mother," he called up the stairs, "be up in a minute." Following his usual routine, he shrugged off his overcoat, and hung it in the hall. He put the kettle on and changed his shoes for slippers. He bent forward and lit the tiny gas fire, hearing the comforting whoosh of gas and the 'pop' as it lit. Preparing two cups of tea and putting them on a tray he then climbed the stairs to his mother's room. He pushed the door with one elbow and entered. The tray placed by her bed, he leaned over and kissed his mother's papery cheek. Was there a faint flush to her cheeks? A sign of moisture on her brow? He could detect nothing.

"How was your day, mother?" he asked, as usual.

"The same, dear," she replied, "except that today they started a new book reading on the radio."

"Anything good?" he said.

"Yes, they're doing Great Expectations," she replied. He looked up quickly but her eyes and her face remained impassive. She accepted a cup of tea from him.

"And your day, Nathaniel?" she asked before taking a sip.

"Oh, a meeting with McIntosh about market business then a trip out to the bank to deposit the rents," Nathaniel said casually. She did not even blink, just carried on sipping her tea.

"How are you feeling these days, mother?" Nathaniel smoothed a wrinkle in the bedspread, "it has been a long winter."

"Not much different, son," she replied, "The tiredness comes and goes. I'm very lucky to have you." He merely nodded.

"I'll get dinner started then," he said.

"Liver and bacon tonight?" she said.

"It's Wednesday, mother," he replied, "of course it's liver and bacon."

"That'll be nice, son," she said, "Did you bring the evening paper?" Nathaniel stopped dead. For the first time in his working life he had forgotten the evening paper.

"Oh," he blustered, "I must have left it on the bus, or dropped it. Give me four minutes and I'll pop out and get one from the corner shop."

"There's no need, Nathaniel," his mother protested, "I can live without one tonight."

"No, no," Nathaniel said, "we always have an evening paper. I'll go and get one." He left the room, carrying the tray, went downstairs, and abandoned the tray on the sofa in the lounge before changing his slippers, putting on his coat and leaving the house.

"What's happening to me?" he thought as he almost trotted to the corner shop, "Am I going mad?" The whole basis on which he worked and lived was by everything happening according to a plan. He rose at exactly the same hour each morning. He was always the first non-trader in the market hall each day, the last to leave. His routines were now ruts and his life travelled down those ruts towards his goals. One wheel, or maybe two, was out of those ruts today. McIntosh and those Building Societies were to blame. He reached the shop, collected a paper from the pile in the doorway, paid for it without a word and left the shop.

"I'm back, mother," he called and he climbed the stairs without removing his coat.

"Thank you, Nathaniel," she said, "but you shouldn't have."

"No trouble, mother," he said, "Now, let's get dinner on." Mrs. Sharpe opened the paper and went straight to the obituary columns. Folding the paper in half, she paused for a moment or two. Her son had never, ever, forgotten to buy a paper before. And she was sure he had forgotten to buy one because he would never pay for two. So, his excuses did not ring true. If that had been the case he would have acquiesced and not gone out for another. She would have to try to find out what was going on. Half an hour later she had her tray in front of her on the bed. Nathaniel was sitting on an upright chair, knees almost touching the underneath of a table placed in the alcove of the room.

"Lovely liver," she murmured, "and the bacon is done to perfection." Nathaniel nodded as he ate another mouthful.

"Anything special Mr. McIntosh wanted to see you about?" she asked, dropping her eyelids and intently cutting another piece of liver.

"No, just the usual things," Nathaniel replied, "I won't bore you."

"Oh, Nathaniel," she said, "it doesn't bore me. I was a market trader once, you know." Nathaniel looked at her. Then he made a decision.

"He talked about my retirement, actually," he said.

"He did what?" Mrs. Sharpe almost shouted and the tray slid down the bed awkwardly as a knee jerked under the bedclothes. A knife slid off her plate, and landed on the bedspread.

"Mother, mother," Nathaniel rose from his place and lifted the tray expertly off the bed. Mrs. Sharpe leaned forward and retrieved the knife.

"Your back seems better," said Nathaniel quietly. Mrs. Sharpe grimaced as she leaned back.

"I didn't want you to have to wash the bedspread," she said, a pained expression on her face. He pulled the bedclothes back towards her chest and replaced the tray.

"No damage done," he said examining the bedspread. He returned to his seat and began eating again. After Mrs. Sharpe had swallowed another mouthful of food she said calmly,

"You gave me such a turn, Nathaniel, telling me Mr. McIntosh was talking about your retirement."

"We all have to retire sometime, mother," he said.

"Yes, but not yet, son," she said, "you've years of work in front of you."

"Yes," said Nathaniel, "and then what?"

"Whatever you want, son," said Mrs. Sharpe, "travel, a car, maybe even a bungalow by the sea."

"On a council pension?" said Nathaniel casually.

"Oh, come on, Nathaniel," his mother retorted, "we don't exactly live extravagantly, do we? You can't spend what you earn and there's my pension from your dad going in the bank every week." Mrs. Sharpe flushed slightly as she said the words "your dad." She had never told Nathaniel that he was not Mr. Sharpe's biological son, but the likeness between the two of them was non-existent. Nathaniel glanced and saw the flush. He'd heard enough sly remarks to piece two and two together. He knew whose son he was. Suddenly he hated the woman in front of him. She had betrayed his father. She had willingly taken to her sick bed without protest. She was not doing the decent thing and dying on him. She was a thorn in his side. And now she was up to something.

"You are right, mother," he said, "*we*," and he stressed the word, "have lived frugally for years and we are quite well off. Maybe we could travel a bit. A cruise around the Mediterranean or the Greek Islands, America even." He stopped then and clapped his bony hand to his mouth.

"Oh, what am I saying?" he said apologetically, "I'm dreaming of things that are impossible. With you so poorly and unable to..." He stopped. Now was the moment. Mrs. Sharpe's eyes had begun to shine. She saw herself swanning around a ship, dining at the Captain's table, flirting with the young men who would serve her.

"Maybe I could try, Nathaniel," she said, "to get up a bit. I'm sure I could if I had something to look forward to. We've never had a holiday. The only time you go out is at Christmas for one night."

He was alert. She knew. She would have to be dealt with. No one was sharing his money, especially not his mother. He smiled lovingly at her.

"Wonderful," he said, "let's get you on your feet again and then, when I retire, we'll go off and see the world."

CHAPTER 11

Elizabeth watched as her mother sorted coins and notes. Piles of pennies, sixpences, florins and half crowns were shuffled onto pieces of paper marked house, gas, water, rates, electricity, food and the Fund. She saw that once the first six papers had coins on there was very little left.

"Whew," she exhaled noisily, "I thought we'd had a fairly good month, considering it's February. After Christmas is usually quiet but there seem to be plenty of new babies around this year."

"Um," said Anne, as she put the last, smallest pile on the paper marked Fund, "I thought so too."

"Still," Elizabeth said, "we must have a tidy sum put away by now."

"We have," Anne said, "but the problem is that inflation keeps nibbling away at it. The price of travelling to India has gone up since we started saving. But, we're not making bad interest on it."

There was a knock at the door and Elizabeth looked nervously at her mother.

There was quite a lot of money on the table.

"That'll be Dave," said Anne, "he said he'd come round and take me to the bank."

"Then I'll let him in," Elizabeth smiled. She went to the door and opened it.

"Hello, Elizabeth," Dave smiled broadly at her, "is Anne ready for the bank job?"

"I wish we were going on a bank job," laughed Elizabeth, beckoning him to follow her.

"Hi, Anne," he said as he entered the room, "your daughter has turned criminal today. Things aren't that bad are they?" Anne rose and greeted Dave with a kiss on the cheek.

"It's this," she pointed to the Fund paper with its meagre pile, "not growing fast enough."

She sighed. Dave looked puzzled.

"It's a fund we started three years ago," explained Elizabeth, "in the hopes that one day we would have enough money to go to India to look for father. But it never seems to be enough. We have enough for plane tickets but not for accommodation, food or the right type of clothes to wear. I think we'd probably both collapse with exhaustion if we went in our English clothes. Not exactly made for hot climates are they?"

"No, you're right there," Dave said with a smile, "but how long were you thinking of going for?"

"The maximum time would be two weeks, during the Wakes, when the Market closes," said Anne.

"July," said Dave, "what's the weather like in India in July?"

"I've no idea," replied Anne, "but we can easily find out. We've plenty of Indian friends."

"Another thing," mused Dave, "I'm sure I heard that once the new market hall opens, there was talk that it wouldn't close for Wake's weeks any more.

They say it will be open all year, excepting maybe Christmas and Easter Monday."

"Well, that would make sense," said Elizabeth, "the whole idea of towns closing for two weeks is a bit outdated, isn't it?"

"So we shut the stall and miss two week's money?" Anne said rather sharply.

"Mum," Elizabeth replied calmly, "don't get upset about what is not likely to happen for ages yet. By the time the fund is ready, we may well be out of the market and into the shop you want. Then we can get help and they can look after it when we're away."

"Sorry, love," Anne said, contritely, "you are right. It may be years before we can go."

"Go and get your coat on," said Elizabeth, "while I put the money into bags." Anne left the room and Elizabeth heard her take her coat from its hanger. She grimaced at Dave and whispered,

"She gets very upset sometimes."

Dave nodded, whispered back, "I understand," and reached over to help Elizabeth with the bags.

"What are you doing with your half day?" he asked, "its lovely outside, for February that is."

"I'm meeting Colin," she smiled, and we're going to Brendan and Molly's house for dinner."

"A family gathering, eh?" said Dave.

"Sort of," she said, with the faintest of blushes coming to her cheeks, "but first we're meeting some friends in town for coffee."

"Well, have fun," said Dave as Anne came back in, complete with outdoor clothes.

"Shall we be off?" said Anne.

"Yes, and, if your daughter doesn't mind, as she won't be in for dinner," said Dave, "how would you like a trip out to Greenwood Park this afternoon? I hear the daffodil displays are magnificent. We could do our Wordsworth bit, and then have dinner at a little bistro that's opened. My treat."

"That sounds lovely," replied Anne.

"Shall we drop you in town?" Anne said to Elizabeth.

"No, thanks, mum, I'm washing my hair first," replied her daughter.

"Again!" exclaimed Anne.

"Take her away, will you Dave?" Elizabeth said, pointing at the door. Anne picked up the money bags and left, tutting as she went.

"Be sure to dry it properly," Dave said cheekily as he turned to go. On the road into town Anne turned to Dave.

"You were very good back at the house," she said.

"I try to be good all the time," he laughed and changed down a gear.

"No, I mean, about the Fund money," she said.

"What did you expect?" said Dave.

"Well, we have been seeing each other for quite some time now," she began.

"Since last year," he quipped.

"Gosh, so it is," she said, "and you know that I'm getting very attached to having you around."

"Glad to hear it," he said.

"And, well, Elizabeth has set her heart on going to India one day to find her father or at least search herself. I'm at a very strange stage right now when I'm not sure I want to go anymore." Dave indicated, pulled over and stopped the car.

"Are you saying what I think you're saying?" he asked gently.

"What am I saying?" she said and tears glistened in her eyes.

"Maybe, that is I hope, that finding out about Mo isn't the most important thing in your life," said Dave, "that after, well, more than five years, you may be ready to move on."

"Maybe," said Anne, "but how in God's name do I tell Elizabeth that you have become more important to me than her absent father, whom she worships?" He put his arm around her and drew her close.

"We'll find a way," he said, "the right time will come. Not soon, maybe not this year, but if I can live in hope, then that's good enough for me."

"You really are a very special person, Dave," said Anne, "I never thought I would find another man I could feel so strongly about."

"Thank you," Dave replied, "you've just made me the happiest man alive. Now, dry your eyes and let's get off to the bank before it closes."

Elizabeth stood by the statue of William Gladstone in the town centre and shook her freshly washed hair. It really was a lovely day and she could see Colin ambling towards her from the direction of the bus station. His hair was almost as long as hers and she smiled.

"You washed your hair, too," she said, leaning into his open arms and kissing him,

"Have you had any replies to the tape demos you sent off?"

"Not yet," said Colin, "but I live in hope. They probably get thousands a week."

"Let's go and meet the others," Elizabeth said.

"Sure," Colin said. They walked across the square towards the coffee bar. Their friends were mostly other trader's youngsters and Wednesday afternoon was half day for them all.

"See you," called out one of the boys at the counter, "shall I get coffees for you?"

"Please," said Elizabeth, "two whites." They settled themselves down, discarding coats on the backs of chairs and waited for their coffees. Colin put sixpence in the jukebox, pressed one button and turned to Elizabeth.

"Your choice," he said.

"The Move, Blackberry Way," said Elizabeth.

"Mm, yeah," said Christine, "love that one." The door opened and they all glanced up to see who was coming in.

"Crumbs," said Colin, "not Susan Evans."

"Shush," said Elizabeth, elbowing him in the ribs, "she's not that bad."

"Oh yes, she is," muttered Colin, "the worst gossip and rumour monger in town." There were a few titters from the crowd with them.

"Am I missing something?" Susan approached the table, making it obvious she wanted to join them. Too polite to tell her she was not wanted, they shuffled their chairs and made space for her. She turned to Elizabeth.

"I've just seen your mother, outside the bank," Susan said.

"Oh, yeah," replied Elizabeth.

"Very lovey dovey with a bloke, she was," Susan said, "it was quite embarrassing to see actually." Susan sniffed before continuing.

"Not your dad though, is he?" she said, "but then this bloke today was white." Elizabeth sprang to her feet.

"What do you mean by that?" she demanded. Colin also got up and took hold of Elizabeth's arm.

"Come on, we're going," he said quietly, then seeing Elizabeth's face added, "Not another word." He grabbed their coats and almost dragged Elizabeth out of the coffee bar.

"Well, what did I say?" they heard Susan question her audience as the door closed.

"Come on, Elizabeth," said Colin, as he pulled her along and into her coat, "she just loves attention and doesn't mind in the slightest how she gets it." He turned to button up her coat and saw the tears in her eyes.

"Oh, love," he said, "don't take it to heart. Those who love you don't care. You are Elizabeth Patel and I for one am proud as Punch to be seen with you."

"Colin," she cried, "it's not the race thing. We learned to live with that years ago. It's mum."

"I don't understand," he said.

"Oh," she sighed, "if you knew how much mum and I have tried to save up for years now so that we can go to India. Now I hear that she and Dave are 'lovey dovey' all over town. Suppose she doesn't want to go anymore?"

"Do you still want to go?" asked Colin.

"Well, yes," replied Elizabeth, "I feel I owe it to dad to try and find out something. But, I don't want to go on my own and I don't think mum will want to go if she's fallen in love with someone else. But then, if I find dad and she doesn't want him back, oh, it's just a mess, isn't it?"

"Are you bothered that your mum might have fallen in love again?" he asked her.

"No, not really," she said quietly, "I'm actually surprised it has taken her more than five years. It didn't take me that long." Elizabeth's face began to turn pink.

"To fall in love again," said Colin, initially puzzled.

"No, you comic," she said, punching him on the arm, "to fall in love."

"Ah, now I'm beginning to understand," he grinned broadly, "and who might be the lucky man in your life?".

"Oh, it might be a budding rock star," she teased, "or it might be a humble potato seller, I haven't quite decided yet."

"I think the rock star left town," said Colin with a touch of regret, "but the potato man loves you too."

"Well, music can't fill an empty stomach," she laughed, "so I'll have to take the potato man."

"He's all yours," Colin said and they stood in the street kissing, oblivious to people around them.

They arrived at Brendan and Molly's house around six o'clock. Lesley opened the door.

"Colin," she squealed, "have you decided to go back to being a rock star yet?"

"You'll be the first to know," he said, picking her up and hugging her.

"Let the poor people in, Lesley," said Molly, coming to the door, wiping her hands on her apron.

"They aren't poor," protested Lesley, "well, maybe Elizabeth is, but Colin isn't."

"Where do you get these ideas from?" Molly said, shaking her head.

"Last time we talked about Elizabeth, when dad was ill," Lesley went on, while drawing the bemused young people into the lounge, "you said poor Elizabeth had lost her father and maybe he was walking home and I said...."

"That's enough, Lesley," Brendan approached her and clapped one very large hand over her mouth.

"I'm sorry, Elizabeth," Brendan said, "We weren't talking about you behind your back. It was just the way the conversation went."

"That's all right, Mr. O'Malley," Elizabeth said, "no harm done. In fact, she's probably done me a favour.

I was going to mention my father later, maybe when Lesley is off doing her homework."

"Little ears, eh?" Brendan grinned at her.

"And a mouth as big as Mick Jaggers," added Colin.

"I do not have a big mouth," said Lesley, "do I?" She ran up to the mirror and peered intently at her face, pulling her lips this way and that. Molly went up to her and hugged her close.

"A figure of speech," she said, "you'll be learning all about them one day, but right now, dinner is ready. Will you all come through?" They filed into the kitchen and sat around the table.

"Where are Barbara and Michelle tonight?" Elizabeth asked politely.

"Gone off to the cinema somewhere," said Brendan, "escorted by one of Michelle's police colleagues so they should be safe."

"A new boyfriend colleague?" asked Colin.

"Maybe," said Molly, "we'll see." They chatted about the market and the new hall which was nearing completion.

"Have you heard anything about the rents, Mr. O'Malley?" Elizabeth asked.

"Nothing concrete," he replied, "but I'm certain the council will be asking for more. I don't know if it'll affect your mother, as you don't store stock, but they are adding better storage for perishables, walk in deep freezers for meat and cold slabs for the fish mongers. And the stalls will be permanent with the council responsible for repairs. And the parking will be under bays. No more rain dripping down your collar as you unload."

"Sounds like it will be a lot more comfortable," said Colin.

"Yes, for us and the customers," said Brendan.

"When will we find out about the rents?" asked Elizabeth.

"Quite soon," said Brendan, "the Trader's Association meets with McIntosh a week on Wednesday."

"All finished?" asked Molly, before adding, "and that's enough about work. Can no one in this family talk about anything other than the market these days?"

"Yes, thank you, that was delicious," said Elizabeth and Colin added his thanks.

"Help me with the washing up, Lesley?" Colin asked, "While they have a cup of tea in the lounge."

"Yes," said Lesley, "I'll wash, you dry and put away."

"Slave driver," laughed Colin.

"And then, Lesley," said Molly, "straight upstairs and finish your book. You've a test on it tomorrow."

"Okay, mum," said Lesley.

"She's ever so sweet," said Elizabeth going into the lounge with Brendan and Molly.

"At the moment," said Molly, "she may change with adolescence."

"We've been lucky with our three," said Brendan, "touch wood, they haven't been much trouble."

He looked around to find a piece of wood to touch, found none within reach, so tapped his head.

Elizabeth and Molly smiled.

"So, Elizabeth," said Molly directly, "do you want to talk about your dad now, or wait for Colin."

"No, now is a good time. Colin and I have been talking all afternoon about it," replied Elizabeth and she took a deep breath.

"Is there any news about him?" asked Brendan.

"No," said Elizabeth, "but, it seems mum and Dave, you remember the ambulance driver she met?" They both nodded.

"Well, it seems they are getting quite fond of each other. Maybe mum will get to a stage when she isn't bothered any more whether dad comes back to England or not. I don't know the implications of that. I mean, can they get married? Without any proof that dad is dead?" she asked.

"That's a tricky one, Elizabeth," said Brendan, "but I've a feeling that after seven years you can ask the courts to declare him deceased. I'm not sure, but a good solicitor will be able to tell you."

"But, how do you feel, Elizabeth?" asked Molly gently.

"I'm mixed up," replied Elizabeth, "I'm actually happy for mum. She's had such a hard time and put up with such a lot of uncertainty. If she really wanted to marry Dave, I'd be happy for her. As for me, well, I've always dreamed of going to India, finding dad somewhere, somehow, and bringing him home. But, after five years or more, it has to be just that, a dream."

"Do you have any relatives in India on your father's side?" asked Molly.

"Yes," said Elizabeth, "dad has, or had, one brother and a father. His mother we know is dead. They live in a village outside Delhi. Mum wrote to the address dad left but we never had a reply. She contacted the High Commissioner but the reply was vague. He said he would make inquiries and let her know. We've heard nothing since. We've never had word from my uncle or grandfather either."

"And what do you think might have happened?" said Brendan.

"I think dad met someone in India," Elizabeth replied, "fell instantly in love, forgot about mum and me, married her and they are living there, probably with a new family."

"So if you found him," said Brendan, "it could be heartbreak all round?" Elizabeth nodded.

"He might have had an accident and lost his memory," said Molly, without much conviction.

"Yes," said Elizabeth, "we thought that and mum got a friend to write to the newspapers in Delhi asking if they would write a piece about our mystery missing man. Nothing came from that either."

"It really does sound a bit hopeless, doesn't it?" said Molly.

"What's hopeless?" said Colin, coming in from the kitchen.

"Finding my dad," said Elizabeth and she burst into tears.

"Come on, love," Colin said, instantly by her side, "if you really, really, want to go and look for him, we'll move heaven and earth to do it. It may take us a long time to get the money together, but we'll do it. I promise you. It will be a lot easier once we start saving up together." Elizabeth looked up and smiled at him. He held her close and smoothed her hair.

"You'll be all right, you two," said Brendan, "just stick together." Molly nodded.

Chapter 12

"If I had the guts, I'd take that bitch to the highest mountain in India and pin her out for the vultures," Basil Whicker muttered, as he woke from yet another disturbed night's sleep. He swiped at a mosquito and drifted back into a fitful, non-refreshing, doze for half an hour. When he finally roused himself he sat up, swung his pale legs over the edge of the bed, and the dizziness and nausea caught up with him. He fell back. The room swam around him and he wished that he was dead.

"This cursed country," he mumbled to the wall, the door and the wardrobe, "why have you done this to me? I'm not a bad man. I was trying to do my best, as God is my witness, I was trying."

Half an hour later- and an hour since Basil should have been at his desk dealing with matters pertaining to England, his man servant crept nervously into the bedroom and tentatively opened one curtain and shutter. Sunlight flooded the room and fell onto the empty side of Basil's bed. The pillow was crisp, white linen and had not a crease in it. The other side of the bed looked as if a wrestling match had been taking place. The man servant did not bat an eyelid. He knew, as did all of Delhi, where Mrs. Whicker was. Basil groaned and turned from the light. It hurt his eyes, his head, his very being.

"What time is it?" he said hoarsely.

"Nine forty five," his man servant replied.

"Oh, Lord," Basil said, "I'd better get up."

"I think so, sir," his servant replied, pulling back the second curtain, "for my sources tell me there is an English gentleman waiting already for one hour at your office. He is, apparently, showing signs of impatience."

"Oh, God," Basil groaned, "not another ex-patriot idiot wanting special favours and invitations."

"Apparently, sir," answered his servant with a sly smile, "this gentleman arrived from England only last night. My sources think he is something to do with your Queen."

"What," shouted Basil, then held his head in his hands as the pain of a drink-fuelled night hit him, "why, in the name of all you hold sacred, didn't you waken me?"

"But, sir," his servant whispered, "you have told me time and time again never to waken you. That you are a grown up man who can get out of bed without being woken."

"Oh, shut up and prepare my clothes," Basil snapped, unable to argue as these had indeed been his instructions. He staggered across the room and into the bathroom, stubbing his toe on the chair as he passed.

"Curses," he screamed and hopped towards the shower, trying to clutch one foot while maintaining his balance. Blood began to drip from a small gash. He watched it drip across the tiled floor and almost wept. He showered under cold water, the better to refresh himself and watched as the soap and blood- stained water drained away.

"Bring me a sticking plaster or a small bandage, or something," he shouted through to the bedroom. He had wrapped a towel around his midriff and was shaving by the time he heard a small cough behind him. He jumped and nicked his chin.

"Can anything go right today?" he asked the face in the mirror. The face looked back and Basil was almost surprised. It was not the face that had left England. That face had been young and full of high hopes. This face was pale, drawn and the eyes were dull with drink and grief. His hair, which had always been neatly trimmed, was now curling around his neck.

"You need a haircut, you scruff," he said to the face in the mirror. The servant came into the bathroom. Basil turned round, grabbed the plaster from his servant and attempted to apply it to his toe, while gripping onto the towel slipping around him. He could feel a warm drop of blood dripping from his chin.

"Another very small plaster," he moaned, "and make it fast." Half an hour later he was running up the stairs to his office, two by two and feeling every step jar his head. His crisp white shirt was wet through and his linen trousers were crumpled and creased. He opened the door and was met by a blast of cold air. The air conditioning was on full. He paused, allowed his eyes to become accustomed to the semi darkness, then shivered. He became aware of a tall, distinguished, white haired man, sitting at the far side of the room. The man rose.

"Mr. Basil Whicker, I presume?" the man said. Basil nodded.

"Jonathan Smythe, special envoy from England," the man continued but, Basil noticed immediately, he did not extend his hand in greeting.

"Won't you come through to my office, Mr. Smythe, I wish I'd have known you were coming," Basil said, hoping that the mess he had left there had somehow miraculously gone away.

"The idea was that I came unannounced," replied Smythe pointedly. Basil opened the door wide, allowing Mr. Smythe to precede him, and followed him in.. Basil Whicker groaned.The office looked as if a whirlwind had swept through it.Metal filing cabinets had papers dripping out of them.The desk seemed to have been wall papered. Not one of the three chairs around the room could be sat on, piled high as they were with boxes spewing more paper. Even the floor had files on it.To crown it all, a large, half full bottle of whisky stood four square on top of the papers right in the middle of the desk. Basil Whicker exhaled the longest, deepest, sigh.

"Not a pretty sight," remarked Jonathon Smythe, "but as I'm here, you may as well clear one of those chairs and let me sit down." Basil moved sheepishly to the nearest chair and grabbed the papers from it. They seemed to come alive in his hands, sliding and slithering their inevitable path to the floor. Smythe raised one eyebrow, extracted a handkerchief from his pocket, dusted the chair and sat down. Basil crept around the other side of the desk, tried to remove the bottle of whisky, knocked it over and burst into tears. Smythe sat impassively for exactly one minute before barking at Basil.

"Pull yourself together, man. You are representing Her Majesty. Where is your backbone? What happened to the stiff upper lip? Did we run Empires on snivelling? No, we did not. Get a grip."

Basil reached into his pocket for a handkerchief but found none. Smythe threw his rather dusty one over the desk top.

"Here," he said, "use mine. And I do not want it back." Basil blew his nose, wiped his eyes and stuffed the handkerchief in his pocket.

"Right, Whicker," Smythe said, "start right at the beginning and tell me everything. And I mean, everything."

"We were all right, at the beginning," Basil began hesitantly, "my wife and I were really excited to be coming to India to represent England in administration. She bought lots of new dresses in London before we left. A veritable mountain of luggage came over after us. The house provided was cool and comfortable and the servants marvellous. They made us so welcome. We began to invite local dignitaries and businessmen and their wives over to dinner or for Sunday lunch at the Club." He extracted the handkerchief and wiped his forehead.

"She shone, you know, sir," Basil continued, "like a star."

"I've been told she is a very pretty woman," said Smythe, "so, she must have been a credit to you."

"Oh, yes," said Basil "for eight months we were the talk of the town and feted everywhere we went. I had my work of course, which kept me away during the day,"

"Don't tell me," said Smythe with a sigh, "she got lonely and fed up of the Club every day and found someone else to console her." Basil looked up sharply.

"How do you know that?" he asked.

"Because it happens all the time with foreign postings. If they would listen to older, wiser, people, like me, and send out single men we could save all the problems that bored, lonely, wives cause."

"I say," protested Basil, "the attention started the first day of our ninth month here. She only....."

"You, Whicker," retorted Smythe, interrupting him, "should have seen that the first day and either warned him off or sent her packing back to England." Basil's face went white, then red, then white again.

"And, then," Smythe went on, "let me see. You began to neglect your duties, taking time off work to try to win her back. That didn't work so you began to drink. She put up with it for a while and then she left you and, presumably, has moved in with this other man." Basil's jaw dropped.

"Yes or no?" asked Smythe.

"Almost, exactly, yes," replied Basil slowly.

"What have I missed out then?" said Smythe sharply.

"It's not a man," said Basil, "she left me for another woman." It was Jonathon Smythe's turn to blanch.

"Another woman?" he asked eventually, and then quickly he added, "European or Indian?"

"What does that matter?" Basil asked tersely.

"It could matter a great deal if, and I only say if, you are both shipped back to England. If your wife won't play the game, we can arrange for the Indian lady to escort her as a companion. Given sufficient time your wife can get over this infatuation and then we can simply ship the other woman back here to India," Smythe said thoughtfully, " A European, on the other hand, would not take kindly to being told what to do, unless she is one of those who likes the limelight. That would be removed once you were back in England and she would probably disappear." Smythe was pleased with his analysis and his problem solving answers.

"What makes you think this woman, who is Indian by the way, will take kindly to any of the above suggestions?" asked Basil.

"I don't understand," said Smythe, puzzled, "who is she?"

"She is Dr. Rampal, a senior paediatrician at The Imperial Hospital," Whicker replied.

"A career woman, eh?" said Smythe, shaking his head, "well, that complicates matters, and I'll have to think about that, but, let's cross that bridge later. In the meantime, what about all this mess?" He waved his arms around and surveyed the office.

"What's going to happen to me?" Basil asked, "I'm truly sorry. Things just sort of got out of hand and then the mountain defeated me."

"That depends on what we find here," Smythe replied, "but we're going to need some good, discreet, help. If we can sort out this mess and get you up and running again, maybe I can report back that the last half year has been a temporary blip. Although some of the complaints that filtered back to London were damning. If we find any major disasters here, then I'm sorry, old chap, you get shipped back to a desk job buried in Whitehall, from which you will not emerge until you are sixty five. But at least you'll have a pension." Basil groaned.

"You get started here," Smythe said, "while I go to the Club and see if I can find help." Smythe left the office and went outside into the sweltering, humid heat of Delhi. A cab took him to the Club, where he swiftly and diplomatically used his position to find a young woman very pleased to be called upon to help such a distinguished visitor.

"You know about Whicker's situation, I presume?" Smythe said on the way back to the office.

"Everybody knows, Mr. Smythe," she replied, "It was the talk of Delhi when it first happened, but now, well, there is always something new to talk about."

"We're here," Smythe said as the cab pulled up, "I hope you are ready for this, Miss Fitzpatrick."

He took her arm and led her up the steps to the office.

"Right, let's enter the fray," he said. Miss Fitzpatrick smiled to herself. This was going to be a lot more diverting than the tennis club.

"Miss Fitzpatrick is here to help us," Smythe said, as he led the young woman into the office, "I suggest we clear the desk, take a pile of files or papers each and try to make stacks relating to similar topics. Once we have a stack, then you, Basil, can begin reading and attaching notes for action or filing. As soon as that is prioritised then Miss Fitzpatrick can begin typing letters for you to sign. Got that?" Basil stared at Miss Fitzpatrick. He vaguely recognised her from functions that he had been to. She was tall, auburn haired, and green eyed. The pale complexion had neither a blemish nor a hint of sun on it. He guessed she was in her middle twenties. She smiled at him and he smiled tentatively back.

"Got that?" Smythe repeated loudly.

"Got it," Basil replied as he carefully took papers from the desk until it was clear.

"Right," Smythe said, "let's get on." It was not until the fifth day that Miss Fitzpatrick unearthed a envelope, still sealed, dated two years previously, containing a battered passport and a letter. She read the letter carefully and frowned.

"Mr. Smythe," she said, "I think you should see this." Jonathon Smythe took the letter from her and read:

Dear Sir,

I enclose a passport for Mohammed Patel, showing him to be a British citizen. We have been able to ascertain

that he entered the country about three years ago for the intention of visiting relatives. At some point during that journey, and before he arrived at his family home, he fell, or was pushed, from the train. We have checked with left and lost luggage at his destination and, after a search, we have found his suitcase. Because of the nature of the railways, running as they do through very sparsely populated areas, his remains were only discovered when a piece of track nearby had to be cleared because a cow had expired on it. But for that dead cow we may well have remained in total ignorance of Mr. Patel's body for ever. When he fell, or was pushed, from the train, he landed on his chest and his passport was taped to his body. Scavengers have, of course, taken the best part of Mr. Patel. The remaining portion has been interred. We managed to locate the village where his relatives lived. It would appear that Mr. Patel had a brother and a father. Both of them had succumbed, along with most of their village, to the influenza epidemic the year that Mr. Patel was due and have been interred locally. We are sure that your records in England will give you much more information and if he has relatives there, perhaps you could let them know of the tragic events that have befallen all three of the Patel family. Please also let us know what to do with his belongings.

I remain,
Yours faithfully,

The letter was signed by the police officer in charge of the district where the tragedy had happened.

"Good God Almighty," said Smythe, shaking his head, "this is serious, really serious." Basil looked up from the desk where he had commandeered one corner to read and mark papers, saw the expression on Smythe's face and he turned as pale as the paper he was reading. He had been almost cheerful the last few days, having his mind occupied with work and the companionship of Smythe and Miss Fitzpatrick. He had gone home each evening tired out but mentally satisfied. He had not touched a drop of alcohol. He had slept like a baby and had no bad dreams to waken him.

"What is it?" said Basil.

"A dead British subject," replied Smythe, "which is a worst case scenario, I'm afraid. To cap it all he may have family in England- who do not yet know he is dead."

"Oh, bloody hell," said Basil, fearing the worst, "how long has he been dead?"

"Well," replied Smythe, "no one is certain. The authorities found him by the side of the railway. They think he died before he got to his destination five years ago. This letter was dated two years ago. That means if he has relatives in England they won't have heard from him for more than five years."

"Then I'm finished," said Basil, dropping his head into his hands in despair. There was complete silence in the room. Only the clock ticked relentlessly on and on.

"Not necessarily," replied Smythe carefully, after an interval. He had, over the last days, seen Basil throw himself into work wholeheartedly. Smythe knew that if he could redeem the situation it would look very good back home for him personally.

"Apart from the belongings," he mused, "which even now we could probably get hold of, does it really matter that they found him two years ago? This letter could have been written a week ago. The remains, such as they were, have been interred so, even if the relatives in England wanted them, all they would get would be a box. Wouldn't it actually be a kindness to change the date forward two years and let them think Mr. Patel had only just been found? Anyone see a flaw in that scenario?"

"The district records?" queried Miss Fitzpatrick.

"Um," said Smythe, "you're right. Better take one step at a time. Let's telegram the Home Office and see what, if anything, they know about this particular passport holder."

"And I could write to the police chief and ask if his remains and belongings could be transferred to Delhi," said Miss Fitzpatrick, "if Basil could dictate to me the right form of diplomatic words."

"I'll do it now," said Basil. Smythe nodded.

Ten days later the three of them were together when the post arrived at the office. Miss Fitzpatrick seemed loathe to give up her new adventure, and there was still plenty to do. Basil had shyly asked her out to dinner and she had agreed.

"I've had a reply," said Basil, opening and scanning a letter, "we can have the belongings and remains sent to Delhi."

"I've got an express delivery from London," said Smythe, "and Mr. Patel has a wife named Anne and a daughter, Elizabeth, both living, in the north of England, and running the family business."

"I'll organise the remains and belongings to be brought to Delhi," said Miss Fitzpatrick.

"Yes," said Smythe, "do that. If they do want to come over, we'll deal with it, but if they are happy to have Mr. Patel, and his suitcase, returned to England, admin. in Delhi will deal with it."

"Should we tell them about the other two deaths in the family?" said Basil.

"Let's find out first if they were even aware of the deaths. Someone in the village may have written to them in England but I think it very unlikely," said Smythe.

"Poor Anne," said Miss Fitzpatrick, "she's lost her husband, father in law and brother in law and she probably doesn't know about any of it."

"India can be a cruel country," said Basil ruefully, "and full of unexpected happenings." Smythe looked across at him.

"Yes, but it is also a wonderfully surprising country," he said.

Chapter 13

It was the first day of Father Rigby's Irish retreat. He had risen at first bell, thrown open his window, sniffed the air, and then withdrawn as the rain hit his face. After prayers he had gone to the refectory. He looked around and was satisfied that the monastery was full. At least thirty priests had assembled for a period of meditation and reflection. After breakfast, they would be allocated tasks until lunchtime. Father Rigby hoped that he would be given gardening to do, despite the rain. He wanted a change from the dull, grimy air of his parish in the North of England. The afternoon would be spent in meditation, and then there would be a good, plain dinner. Father Rigby had his tracts of St. Augustine to re-read and he was looking forward to doing so. There never seemed to be time in Lancashire for quiet contemplation. He always chuckled inwardly when people made remarks about a one-day-a-week- job. After dinner all the guests would go to the library and they could mingle to their heart's content.

"Father Rigby?" a voice called out.

"Here, brother," he replied, startled out of his reverie.

"Would you care to do gardening this morning?" the brother asked politely.

"Delighted to, thank you, brother," replied Father Rigby. He almost ran to the shed in the large garden. Inside he found wellington boots, brown coveralls and all the tools he would need. The rain had stopped and the sun was shining. Father Rigby's heart soared and he sent a small 'Thank you' heavenwards. Another priest joined him, and then the resident gardener appeared.

"Shall we start on weeding and hoeing the vegetable garden?" said the resident gardener. Half an hour before lunch Father Rigby was beginning to know muscles he hadn't felt in a long time.

"A good morning's work," said the gardener, winking at them, "thank you. You'd better get in and bathe now, before all the hot water has gone."

"Thank you," said Father Rigby. They dashed to disrobe and get to the bathrooms first. That afternoon he settled himself onto his bed in his cell with the works of St. Augustine and promptly fell asleep. A bell ringing through the building woke him. It was the ten minute warning bell. By the time the second bell had rung, he had washed his hands and face and was ready. Sedately he joined the other visitors coming out of their cells, nodding and smiling to each other. Old friends waved discreetly and fell into step together. They walked in double file the length of the corridor to the chapel. Father Rigby noted the new visitors gazing at the rather lurid statues set into niches along the way. Father Rigby knew them all. A gory Sacred Heart, complete with crown of thorns, the stigmata on his hands and feet, dripping the reddest blood ever found in a paint pot. A pale and sickly Our Lady of Sorrows, her exposed heart pierced with daggers - and the inevitable St. Patrick standing on a vicious snake, clutching a shamrock of luminescent green. He smiled at the naive plasterwork and the almost childish use of bright, unreal colours. After prayers they all filed out into the dining room and enjoyed steak pie, boiled potatoes and fresh vegetables, lashed with homemade butter, followed by apple pie and clotted cream. Taking water or tea with them from the table, they adjourned to the library. This was the moment Father Rigby had been waiting for. He sat right in the middle of the chairs and sofas. Soon all the other seats were taken and pleasantries were being exchanged.

"I wish my house keeper could cook like that."

"You could always ask one of the brothers to come and visit- indefinitely."

"Where are you from?"

"Is this your first time here?"

"When were you ordained?"

"Where is your parish?" Before anyone could begin a long, usually tedious, theological discussion, Father Rigby drew attention to those around him by saying quietly,

"A situation has arisen in my parish and I would like to ask your help, brothers." Half a dozen heads inclined in his direction. He began to tell the story that Mary had related to him. By the time he had finished more than half the room were listening avidly to his every word. He spread his upturned hands in front of him.

"So, I need the help of any of you that have parishes in Ireland," he said, "Can you help me to track down the O'Malley family that I seek? All the information I have is that it was a Patrick O'Malley that went over to England. There is a connection with a family named Shuttleworth. I know Patrick's son was Sean, and his sons are Brendan and Terence. But no one over here may even know them. Am I looking for a needle in a haystack? It is surely a common name over here in Ireland?" One or two heads nodded.

"Families that didn't emigrate tended to stay put though," said one young priest.

"Wild horses wouldn't make a lot move," said another, older priest, "even if they were scraping a living from the soil."

"True," added yet another, "but the younger ones are moving to the cities more and more now."

"The Shuttleworth connection might bring something forward. Maybe they owned land over here too," said Father Rigby.

"Why not check the library here?" a voice said from the back of the crowd. Father Rigby turned..

"Brother Andrew," said an olive-skinned monk, "monastery librarian and archivist." He held out his hand and Father Rigby shook it warmly.

"You'd be surprised," went on Brother Andrew, "at the number of libraries that have been left to the monasteries in Ireland. As the big old families left, or were driven out, they often handed over hundreds of books to us, some of them quite valuable, rather than see them burned. We've been cataloguing for the last fifty years and there are still plenty to go at."

"How many other monasteries hold old collections?" said Father Rigby.

"Well, there are another four major centres, and I have friends in all of them. We pool information on a quarterly basis. If we have a half-set or a rogue issue, we try to match them. A set of books is worth far more than a single issue. I could send out a message for help tomorrow."

"Would your superior mind you doing this?" asked Father Rigby.

"We are righting a wrong. That's God's work, isn't it?" replied Brother Andrew with a smile.

Father Rigby saw many heads, old and young, nodding around him.

"Then, let's do it," he said decisively. The bell for evening prayers tolled. Then they would retire for the night. Father Rigby chanted his responses automatically. His mind was elsewhere.

Each morning after that meeting, Father Rigby made a point of looking out for Brother Andrew.

"Any news yet?" he would ask.

"Patience, Father, is the greatest of the virtues, and yes, I agree with you, the hardest one of all," would come the reply. On the day before he was due to leave, a knock came on his cell door.

"Father Rigby," said the animated voice of Brother Andrew, "we have a success, of sorts." He opened the door and Brother Andrew came in, waving a piece of paper.

"We've located the Shuttleworth family land and some of their history," said Brother Andrew, "and it is fascinating."

"Tell me," said Father Rigby, "quickly."

"Well," replied Brother Andrew, "the Shuttleworth family owned land in Ireland and England. Sir Charles Albert Shuttleworth, to give him his full name, farmed over here and owned coal mines over there. His wife died soon after giving birth to their only child, also named Isabel. She grew up, probably a little on the wild side, and at the age of seventeen, about 1900 or so, there was some scandal concerning her and one of the estate workers. Guess what his name was?"

"Not Patrick O'Malley?" asked Father Rigby breathlessly.

"The very same," said Brother Andrew excitedly, "and there is a bit more."

"Go on," said Father Rigby.

"This Patrick O'Malley was bought off by Sir Charles and went to America. Isabel was packed off to Switzerland and from there to London. We have no idea what happened after that. Although we know where the Shuttleworth family estate and house lie and which parish it was in. It may be worth a trip there to see if the Parish has any other records."

"I leave here tomorrow," mused father Rigby, "where is the Parish?"

"Kilkenny," replied Brother Andrew, "and you are in luck. Father O'Driscoll is on retreat here and his Parish is right next door. He could take you all the way by car."

"I think God is on our side, Brother Andrew," said Father Rigby.

"He is supposed to be," replied Brother Andrew. They smiled at each other.

"Thank you, Brother," said Father Rigby.

"Good hunting," replied Brother Andrew, "and let me know how you go on. If I get any more information I'll send it to you in England. Be sure to leave an address for me at the desk."

The next day saw Father Rigby and Father O'Driscoll driving along narrow unmarked roads bounded by lush green meadows and then onwards through hills. In the distance they could see streams meandering their haphazard way. Sheep and cows grazed nonchalantly and ignored them completely.

"It's a beautiful country," sighed Father Rigby, "such peace, such tranquillity." They stopped once for lunch at a roadside and ate homemade bread, creamy cheese and pickles to take the breath away.

"Will you stay with me tonight at the presbytery, Father Rigby?" asked Father O'Driscoll, "we'll be arriving late. I've phoned the housekeeper to expect you. The bed will be made up and supper ready. I can run you over to St. Bernadette's Parish first thing in the morning."

"Yes, thank you," said Father Rigby.

The following morning, after breakfast, the two priests set off for St. Bernadette's Parish Church.

"Where did you find that cook?" asked Father Rigby.

"She came with the territory," laughed Father O'Driscoll, "no one knows her age, but rumour has it she cooked for St. Patrick himself and he made her immortal, the better to serve all the priests who would come after him." They were still laughing when they pulled up in front of St. Bernadette's. Here was a compulsory grotto with the Virgin in blue and white, looking heavenward and Bernadette Soubirous gazing up at her. A tiny man-made stream ran between the two statues.

"No mistaking which Parish this is?" said Father Rigby.

"They love their statues," said Father O'Driscoll a trifle wryly.

"Let's see if there is anyone about," said Father Rigby. As they walked up the path the church doors opened.

"You must be Father Rigby," a tiny, rotund priest called out, "I had a call from Brother Andrew. He gave me the gist of your quest. Very exciting, isn't it? I'm Father James." Father Rigby went forward and shook his hand.

"This is Father O'Driscoll from St. John the Baptist," he said.

"Oh, we know each other, in passing," replied Father James, "but unfortunately our working days always fall on the same day."

"I'll be back for you later," said Father O'Driscoll, having shook hands. He turned to leave.

"Make it dinner time and we can eat together," invited Father James.

"Thank you, I will," said Father O'Driscoll. Father James led Father Rigby into the cool of the church. They dipped fingers into icy cold water and crossed themselves, genuflected as they passed the host and then disappeared into the sacristy. It was surprisingly large and one wall was covered with old volumes of Parish Records.

"Any idea of dates?" Father James asked.

"Only that Isabel was seventeen around 1900 - we think," replied Father Rigby.

"But we have no idea when she died, or if she got married, or even if she ever set foot in Ireland again?" asked Father James.

"No," sighed Father Rigby, "all those records may be somewhere else. Possibly they are in Somerset House in London. It's also possible that she went abroad, stayed abroad, and died abroad for all we know. Are we sensible even trying to find anything here?" He looked at the rows of volumes and his heart sank.

"Courage, Father," replied Father James, "we will find some of the O'Malley family here. We still have O'Malleys in the village. It won't take long, once we get a system going. We'll take alternate books from 1900 and work our way through them. Make a note of anything relating to the O'Malley family and we'll look at them together tonight." By five o'clock that evening the two priests were covered in dust and their fingers were blackened. Father James' housekeeper had come across at intervals during the day with warm drinks and a sandwich and now she called them into dinner.

"Fifteen minutes and no longer," she said sharply, "Father O'Driscoll is here already, and waiting for you both."

"We'd better go," said Father James, "it doesn't do to keep Mrs. Edwards waiting." They gathered their notes together. As they entered the presbytery Mrs. Edwards called from the kitchen.

"You have time to wash and change. It's stew and dumplings tonight." They took turns to wash and they did it quickly, like schoolboys late for a lesson. When the three priests were sat around the table, Mrs. Edwards came in with the stew.

"Will I put these notebooks on the side table," she said, nodding at the papers, "so that I can find room for the potatoes and vegetables?"

"No, oh, sorry, Mrs. Edwards," said Father James, jumping up, "I'll do it." She put the stew centre stage and lifted the lid. The aroma of beef and onions filled the room. They all peered forward and saw fluffy dumplings floating in rich, dark gravy. Mrs. Edwards brought the rest of the food from the kitchen.

"Help yourselves," she said. The three clerics soon finished the meal and had seated themselves round the fire when Mrs. Edwards came back in. Father James was telling Father O'Driscoll about all the O'Malleys they had found, and there were many of them. They were trying to make sense of the dates and names, trying to link births, marriages and deaths.

"May I be interrupting you, fathers," said Mrs. Edwards.

"By all means," said Father James and the two other priests nodded.

"If you are trying to trace the O'Malley clan, why not go to the Carmelite Convent?" she said, "Sister Marie Julie is an O'Malley by birth and she has a family bible with all the O'Malley family in it going back generations. It was the only thing she was allowed to take in with her. Although I'm not sure she'll be allowed to actually use such a fine piece." She sniffed before continuing,

"The O'Malleys always did their duty by the Church and gave either a son or a daughter to God's service. Although some say it was a way of making sure one member of poor families got food. The Convent is only twenty five miles away, give or take a hill or two." The three priests smiled.

"Mrs. Edwards," said Father Rigby, "you are very kind, and knowledgeable, if I may say."

"Those of us that have lived here for generations don't miss much," she said, with yet another sniff, "It's the priests that come and go, not us."

"But that's because we are not allowed to have families," said Father O'Driscoll.

"Have you actually seen this family Bible?" asked Father Rigby.

"Oh, yes," replied Mrs. Edwards, "once a year the treasures are put on display and the faithful can go and view them, and attend a Mass given by a visiting Bishop. It's a way of letting us offer a little contribution to the upkeep of the Convent."

"Do you know the Mother Superior?" asked Father James.

"Only slightly, I was in a year below her at school. She went off to do her missionary stuff and once she came back she entered the closed, silent branch. So there was no talking to her after that. She did well though, becoming Mother Superior within twenty years. She used to be Sister Joseph," said Mrs. Edwards, "now, I'll be off. Breakfast will be at eight in the morning, on the dot, Father James. Good night."

"God be with you," they said, almost as one. When they heard the front door close behind her they all burst out laughing.

"To think we spent all day in the dust and grime of old records," said Father Rigby, wiping his eyes.

"Do you think she actually knew what you were looking for?" asked Father O'Driscoll.

"The Lord knows," smiled Father James, "but it would not surprise me if she did too. She likes to keep me on my toes."

"Then I suggest we go and see Mother Superior tomorrow, Father Rigby," said Father O'Driscoll.

"How about a nightcap before you leave?" asked Father James, "but we'll have to wash the glasses before Mrs. Edwards gets back in the morning."

The next day Father Rigby pulled on a rope hanging outside the Convent. He heard the toll echo across the courtyard. A few seconds later came the unmistakable sound of rosary beads; click, click, clicking as someone walked towards the door. A section of the door, no more than a foot square, opened. The nun behind said not a word but inclined her head as she saw his dog collar.

"God be with you," said Father Rigby, "I don't have an appointment but would like to see your Mother Superior. I have another priest with me, Father O'Driscoll. He is from a Parish in Kilkenny."

The nun raised her index finger to him, closed the partition and he heard the beads clicking away. Father

O'Driscoll, who had parked the car on the main road, joined him.

"Can we get in?" he asked.

"I hope so," replied Father Rigby, "a sister has just come and gone. Hopefully to get someone allowed to speak today."

"I don't know how they do it," mused Father O'Driscoll, "although I could wish silence on some of my more vocal parishioners." The tiny section opened again. This time they had missed the clicking of the rosary beads.

"We do it for the love of God," said a soft Irish voice, "please, do come in." The nun who greeted them was over six feet tall. Her brown and yellow habit was immaculate. She wore nothing on her feet. She saw that Father Rigby had noticed this.

"Not compulsory, Father," she smiled, "but it keeps me humble. I'm Sister Joseph, Mother Superior of the Convent, how may I help you?"

"It's a long story, Mother," said Father Rigby, "and it is probably not necessary that you know all of it. But we seek a family bible belonging to Sister Marie Julie that was an O'Malley by birth." Sister Joseph's eyes widened.

"Oh, a story," she said, smiling, "there is nothing we Irish like more than a story. Indulge me with all of it, please. I'll do the penance later." She turned and led them into the Convent.

"Will I organise lunch for you both?" she asked, "today is vegetable soup and dry bread," her eyes twinkled as she went on, "But it's homemade soup and freshly baked bread."

"Most kind of you," replied Father O'Driscoll.

"Please take a seat," said Sister Joseph, "I'll ask Sister Marie Julie to bring her family bible to you. She won't speak, but I'll tell her all she needs to know in due course." They settled themselves on two large, lumpy, armchairs, while Sister Joseph left the room.

"She seems a happy sort," said Father O'Driscoll.

"Yes," replied Father Rigby, "not like some I've met."

"Poor Sister Marie Julie is going to be bursting to know what is going on," said Father O'Driscoll.

"Maybe," replied Father Rigby, "maybe not. Nuns can be terribly unworldly. But I'm glad we found her, and her Bible." The door opened and a tiny nun came in, wheeling a huge book on a trolley. Following behind was Sister Joseph.

"Thank you, Sister Marie Julie," she said, "you may return to your duties."

"This," said Sister Joseph, pointing at the book, "is the O'Malley Bible. And before you ask, no, there wasn't a poor Irish family alive who could afford such a book, far too costly. It came into the family by way of Isabel Shuttleworth." Father Rigby jumped to his feet.

"The one who was sent off to Switzerland by her father?" he asked.

"The very same," said Sister Joseph, "and you will find in the back of the bible a sealed letter, marked for the attention of her son, Sean O'Malley. Who may or may not still be alive." She said it in such a matter of fact tone that Father O'Driscoll gasped.

"No one has ever opened it?" he said amazed, "not even Sister Marie Julie?"

"No one has tried to find Sean O'Malley to give it to him?" asked Father Rigby.

"It is not addressed to her, nor to me," she said calmly, "we feel that only Sean O'Malley, if he is alive, can claim it. If he is dead then it belongs to a direct descendant. On the second point, Father Rigby, forgive me, but I must remind you that we are a closed order. No one leaves these walls, except in a dire emergency. Most of the sisters here will be buried in these grounds where they have lived their adult lives. It is our way."

"It may be no more than a mother's letter to her son," said Father O'Driscoll pragmatically.

"Or it may contain more," replied Father Rigby, "it is time to tell you what we know, Sister Joseph."

Father Rigby told the whole story to the Mother Superior who listened intently, asking the odd pertinent question now and then. As he finished a bell rang.

"Lunch time, fathers," said Sister Joseph, "will you remain here to eat. A sister will leave your lunch outside the door and knock twice. I will return after lunch. Twenty minutes will suffice. "What an incredible story. You have given me a lot to think about." Twenty five minutes later she returned. The two priests had eaten and returned the dishes outside.

"Delicious," said Father O'Driscoll, "our thanks to you."

"I have given much thought to this letter," she said to Father Rigby, with a smile, "and will have to confess my unseemly interest in worldly matters the next time my confessor calls."

"Would you entrust it to my care, Sister Joseph," asked Father Rigby eagerly, "for I live in the town where Sean's sons, Terence and Brendan live. If it contains anything useful to Brendan O'Malley, you could be helping to right what I believe to be a great wrong."

"Rights and wrongs that happen in the world are not usually our concern, Father," she replied, "but in this case I do think the O'Malley family should have what is rightfully theirs. Yes, take the letter. Will you tell me of the outcome so that I can let Sister Marie Julie know? Once a year she is allowed to write a letter. Maybe she could write to the O'Malley family in England."

"Thank you, Sister Joseph," said Father Rigby.

"I'll show you the way out," she replied. Five minutes later they were driving away from the Carmelite Convent, Father Rigby holding the letter in his hand.

"We never even looked at the family tree," said Father O'Driscoll.

"We may not have to," replied Father Rigby, "this letter may tell us all we need to know. Oh, Lord, the temptation to open it is over whelming."

"Get thee behind him, Satan," said Father O'Driscoll in a mock stern voice.

Two days later Father Rigby was back in his presbytery and the letter stood on his mantelpiece. He picked up the evening paper and read that the town was in turmoil.

Chapter 14

Brendan was bored and restless. He was in yet another council meeting about the market. Normally Brendan would take an interest in every aspect of the new hall but right now he was fed up and twitchy. He looked up from the paper he was doodling on. The meeting had gone on far too long. Other faces were looking just as uncomfortable as they tried to listen and comprehend. Tom Blackledge, the town council's finance controller, was wading through rows of figures and making them as interesting as watching paint dry. Brendan glanced at his watch. An hour already gone. Blackledge droned on for another five minutes.

"And that is why, gentlemen," said Blackledge, eventually, and he glanced up, caught the eye of Stuart McIntosh, saw the slight nod of the head, "rents for the new hall will have to increase." Brendan and all the traders had expected it. They had suggested and welcomed the new facilities that had been built and knew that nothing came without a price.

"Thank you for your attention," said Blackledge, "I'll now pass you to Mr. McIntosh." Brendan looked up sharply. He raised his hand. Alice Boothroyd, who was in the chair, glanced his way.

"Mr. O'Malley?" she queried. Having been given the floor Brendan spoke.

"Are we, the traders, to know exactly how much the rent is to rise by?"

"Mr. Blackledge," said Mrs. Boothroyd, "can you answer the point?"

"Mr. McIntosh will give the figure at the end of his report," said Blackledge smoothly. Brendan looked puzzled but acquiesced. McIntosh took the floor and proceeded with his report. Snags had emerged during the Tenant's Association's visit to the site and they were being corrected. He dragged out the reports on these minor problems interminably. Brendan sighed and glanced at his watch. Another half hour.

"The council proposes, therefore, to increase the rents paid by the tenants... by twenty per cent," said McIntosh, "That concludes my report which I hope you will accept." Brendan was on his feet immediately.

"Twenty per cent," shouted Brendan, "you must be joking."

"Through the chair, Mr. O'Malley," said Mrs. Boothroyd sharply. Brendan raised his hand.

"Mr. O'Malley," she said calmly, "you have a point to raise?"

"Madam Chairman," said Brendan, red faced, "my apologies." He stood again and faced McIntosh across the table.

"Twenty per cent," he repeated, looking McIntosh straight in the eye, "you must be joking. Where do you think I'm going to find another ten quid a week from?" McIntosh said absolutely nothing. Mrs. Boothroyd waited for a minute, during which time not a sound was heard in the room.

"Mr. McIntosh," she said eventually, "will you reply to Mr. O'Malley?"

"There is nothing to add, Madam Chairman," replied McIntosh calmly, "we have all heard the figures explained by Mr. Blackledge. Twenty per cent is the figure we came to." Mrs. Boothroyd looked across at Brendan.

"He says '*we came to*'," Brendan said with disbelief, "and just where does he think the tenants are going to find that kind of money?" McIntosh remained silent although he loosened his collar with one finger.

"He knows," Brendan continued, pointing at McIntosh, "that the only way we can pay those sort of increases is to pass it on to our customers in higher prices. They are not going to like it and they will blame us. They'll think we're racketeering."

"Would you like to comment, Mr. McIntosh?" said Mrs. Boothroyd. McIntosh shook his head.

"You can't just shake your head," Brendan said sternly across the room, "you may think you and Blackledge have justified the figures, but we'll see what the town has to say about it."

"May I remind Mr. O'Malley that matters arising concerning council finance are confidential to this room," said Blackledge.

"But this isn't council finance we're talking about," replied Brendan, "we're talking about how much Mrs. Brown, or Mrs. Boothroyd for that matter, pays for her potatoes, cabbages and carrots next month. She has a right to know why she'll be paying more," he thumped the table before continuing, "This deal was supposed to be self financing. You get the site of the old market hall and sell it for a vast amount of money and the new market hall gets built for almost peanuts. The banks lend you the money to build on the promise that they get a good crack later."

"A rather simplistic view, Mr O'Malley," sneered Blackledge.

"Simple or not," retorted Brendan, "no one ever imagined you lot could get your sums so wrong. What's gone wrong? Are the market traders, and the people of this town, getting value for money from this council or not?"

"What exactly are you implying, O'Malley?" said McIntosh, half rising out of his chair.

"Gentlemen, gentlemen," said Mrs. Boothroyd, "let's not let tempers get out of hand. Can I suggest a further meeting?"

"We're supposed to be moving into the new hall in thirteen days, Madam Chairman," said Brendan, "and my members need to know what they are getting themselves into. The council will want new contracts. Not everyone has a high cash take every week. I'm going to have to talk to them as soon as possible."

"Not possible," said Blackledge, looking directly at Brendan, "the market traders will be informed by letter in due course. Until then this subject remains within these four walls." Brendan shook his head, screwed up the piece of paper he was doodling on and tossed it onto the floor in despair.

"Can I declare this meeting adjourned?" said Mrs. Boothroyd. Heads nodded around the room. Brendan was the last to rise to leave the room, having scrambled on the floor to retrieve his paper. He walked to the waste bin to drop it in.

"Excuse me, Mr. O'Malley," he heard a voice coming from nearby. Looking up he saw a young girl with a sweeping brush and dust pan hovering a yard away.

"I'm sorry," said Brendan, "I was miles away."

"I'm not surprised," the young girl replied, "after news like that." Brendan looked up sharply.

"What do you mean?" he asked her.

"Well, the rents going up a fifth," she said, "that's going to hit the traders, like you said, shoppers in the market are going to think it's you and not the council to blame, if prices have to go up."

"You're right," said Brendan, "but I'm damned if I know how to let the town people into the secret. Blackledge was right in one respect, when we talk about council finances, it's strictly confidential. We sign letters to that effect."

"I've not signed any letter," said the girl with a cheeky grin, "and I've a next door neighbour who's a journalist on the local paper. We like a gossip over the garden fence. I think he fancies my mum."Brendan's eyebrows shot up into his forehead.

"She's a widow, Mr. O'Malley," said the girl, "and that's why I'm here, cleaning council offices, trying to make a bit more for those extras in life."

"I can't ask you to talk about what happened here tonight to a reporter," Brendan said.

"Then don't," the girl replied, "I'll tell him myself. Now, go home. We don't know each other."

"I'd better not ask your name then?" Brendan queried.

"No," the girl replied, "no one ever notices the cleaners." Brendan smiled at her.

"Goodnight," he said as he pushed open the door to the chamber and made to leave.

"See you," she said and she winked at him. Brendan was home half an hour later and telling Molly all about the meeting. After he had finished she sat back in her chair.

"That's outrageous," she said, "can they really get away with it?"

"If they present the figures as given to us tonight, I'm sure they can," Brendan replied, "how many people do you know who can understand council information even without rows of figures?"

"Nobody," Molly said with a small smile, "has ever been able to fathom what they are on about. That's probably why they feel so confident. They can blind us with science. This is an absolute nightmare, Brendan, what on earth are we going to do?" Her face looked drawn and tired. Brendan moved across the room, sat beside her and put one huge hand over hers.

"We have one very slim chance," he said, leaning across and kissing her cheek, "in the guise of a cleaning girl. She heard everything that happened."

"So?" Molly said, looking puzzled.

"Well, maybe she'll do something like going to the paper and spilling the beans on our behalf," Brendan said. Molly drew back from him and looked him straight in the eye.

"Did you prompt her, Brendan O'Malley?" Molly said.

"Emphatically not," Brendan replied.

"What makes you think she'll go the press?" Molly asked him.

"Well," Brendan said quietly, "she just happened to mention..." Molly threw her hands up in the air.

"No more, Brendan," she said, "You've already said too much about council business." Brendan smiled too.

"Keep your fingers crossed," he said, "that she will be as true to her word as I hope she'll be." They didn't have to wait for long.

Two days later, after lunch, as the first edition hit the streets, market traders began to gather around Brendan's fruit and vegetables, waving papers.

"What's all this about the rents, Brendan?" shouted Bert.

"Had you any idea what was going on, O'Malley," shouted another trader, "because if you had we'll skin you alive."

"Hold on lads," Brendan shouted to his fellow traders, "we've customers to deal with. Come back at five thirty and we'll have a meeting here."

"Leave us a copy of the paper, will you," shouted Dee to one of the men, "we haven't seen it yet."

"You'll maybe not want to when you have," was the parting shot as a copy was dumped on the tomatoes. Dee retrieved the paper, pushed it under the counter and continued to serve her customer. Five agonizing minutes went by before Dee, Brendan, Terry and Colin could gather round the paper.

"Can YOU afford to shop in the new Market Hall?"

the headline on the front page ran.

"Oh, my giddy aunt," exclaimed Dee, "what's going on?"

"Read it out to us, Brendan," Terry said, "before we crack our heads open trying to read one paper between four. What are they talking about? How did they find out? Is it about you?"

Brendan took the paper and read:

"News has leaked out, from a member of the town hall staff, that the Council has proposed a rise in rents for the hard working market traders of twenty per cent. Yes, twenty per cent! Imagine what that means to you, the town's people! Even if the market traders can absorb half this massive increase, and we doubt that they can, it means a rise in price of everything you buy there. A new pair of sandals? Ten per cent extra please! A serving of

fish for four on Friday? Ten per cent more please! Fruit and veg for the weekend? Cough up a fifth more or let the kids go hungry!

Dee chuckled. "Sounds like someone at the paper is on our side," she said.

"Someone needs to be if this is true," Colin added. Brendan continued to read,

"This local paper, for local people, has tried to gain access to a senior representative of the Finance Department at the Town Hall. Our reporter was met by a stone wall. "Not for discussion" was one phrase used. "Confidential information" was thrown out as well.

Well, we say that this matter IS up for discussion. We say that anything which affects the livelihood of our market traders, who are also town's people, has to be made public. We say that YOU, the people of this town, should know how this figure was arrived at, and we remind the town hall bureaucrats that their positions are not for life. They can be challenged and they will be challenged. You can let us know what you think by phone or by letter. We demand answers!

"Phew," Colin whistled, "strong stuff."

"Hi," a voice came from over the counter.

"Hello, Elizabeth," said Dee, "Have you and your mum seen this?"

"Yes," Elizabeth replied, "it's all a bit worrying, isn't it?"

"Nothing to fret about, love," Colin said, putting his arm around Elizabeth.

"Will you do me a favour, Elizabeth?" Brendan said.

"Yes," she replied.

"We need to have a meeting, here, after the market closes tonight. I've told some of the traders who have seen the paper. Knowing how news travels around, I'm sure no one is unaware of the news but can you just make sure some of the traders on your side of the market can attend." Elizabeth nodded.

"Colin, can you do our side of the market?" Brendan turned to his nephew, "we don't want anyone saying they weren't told." Colin nodded. He and Elizabeth left the stall and went off in separate directions.

"Right," Brendan said, looking at his watch, "an hour to go. Let's sell some produce." By six o'clock almost all the traders were finished and packed away. They began to drift over towards the O'Malley stall. As soon as Dee had handed Brendan the takings for the day, it started.

"Well, O'Malley, what have you got to say for yourself?" shouted Eddie Bulcock, waving the front page above his head.

"Hang on, Eddie," Brendan replied, not raising his voice, "do you honestly think that I colluded with this ludicrous rent rise?"

"You must have known something about it," Bulcock replied, "you've been in all the meetings."

"True," Brendan said, "and many more of you could have been in those same meetings, if you'd been interested enough." Three or four of the men had the grace to look embarrassed. Brendan had asked repeatedly for the tenant's association to give a time to the dozens of meetings about the new market hall, but one excuse after another was always forthcoming.

"That's as may be," said Fred Barcroft, "but did you know?"

"The first time I heard about it was two nights ago, and," he raised both hands to quell the instant mutterings that arose, "and I was informed by Blackledge that

I couldn't tell anyone as it was confidential information. I was effectively gagged."

"But you told the paper," Keith Dobson shouted.

"Actually, he didn't," Terry replied, "and if you read it properly, you'll see it says that it was a town hall employee who went to them."

"This new market hall was your bloody idea in the first place, Brendan O'Malley," shouted back a red faced butcher, "you should have kept your mouth shut."

"Don't be stupid," a woman called out, "we all needed a new market hall, but no one said we'd end up with such a whacking rent increase. That's not Brendan's fault. The council set the rent."

"And what's their justification for asking for that much?" the butcher shouted back, "the market tenant's association was supposed to be looking after our interests during all this time. How come we only find out days before we're due to move in that the increase is so high?" Voice after voice cut in with complaints. Brendan, Dee, Terry and Colin stood there listening. There was a lot of anger. After a few minutes, a voice piped up.

"Can I say a few words?" Heads turned and Brendan recognised Anne Patel's voice.

"It's all very well standing here muttering and shouting among ourselves," she began, "but we're not getting to the heart of the matter. Let's try and be calm about this situation." There was some nodding of heads and Anne found herself being pushed forward until she was facing the traders. She took a deep breath.

"We have to stand together on this," she started, and was gratified to see many heads nodding.

"We all agree the council have increased the rents to an unacceptable level." More nodding.

"The local paper seems to be on our side and with their help we could get the town's people on our side as well," she said.

"What are you suggesting?" said Eddie Bulcock.

"What about a sit-in, right here in the old market hall?" she said.

"What !"

"Like a bunch of students?"

"Is that a joke?"

"Damned silly idea!" Anne held up her hands when the comments stopped.

"I'm serious," she said, "no one has signed contracts yet. But we do have contracts here. The council can keep their new market hall, and keep it empty. We stay put until they see sense. Just carry on until the costs of the white elephant they have built becomes too much for them. I'm sure the public will support us." There was an immediate buzz through the crowd.

"There's only one small problem with that idea," Brendan said, "and I think it's a good one, Anne."

"What's the problem?" Fred Barcroft shouted.

"The demolition contractors have been booked to start work two days after we move out," said Brendan, "and two weeks later the foundations are due to go in for the new shopping centre the council wants to build."

"Even better," Terry shouted, "they can't demolish a place that's full of shoppers and traders, can they?"

"And the council's costs will soar," added Elizabeth, "They will have to re-think pretty quickly."

"It would mean some of us having to stay in here at night," said Dee, "or they will just move in when we've left at the end of the day."

"So, we get some camp beds and portable heaters," said Tom Entwhistle.

"And we've got running water and toilets already," Brendan added.

"And we can cook," said Mrs. Brown, "I can open the kiosk, do bacon, eggs, you name it."

"We'll have to organise a rota," said Eddie Bulcock, "at least four of us, two asleep and two on watch. Make sure they know we are here." The whole place was buzzing with animated voices. Brendan banged on the counter to restore order.

"Let's have a vote," he said, "make it democratic, all in favour." Hands went up across the crowd.

"Against?" he said. Not a hand was raised.

"Right," he said, "let's do it. But, and this is important, we keep this to ourselves. Not a word must get out until we are organised. We need someone to talk to the press and keep them on our side. Let them get the public on our side. I know I'll be called in to the Town Hall first thing tomorrow. They'll be sure to think I've leaked this to the Press. I can honestly deny that but they may take some convincing, any volunteers to talk to the paper?"

"Anne should do it," said Tom Entwhistle, "it was her idea.

"Do you mind?" Brendan asked her.

"No, I'll do it," Anne replied.

"Good," Brendan said, "now let's get home before our families think we've got lost."

As Brendan had predicted he was summoned to the Town Hall the following morning. No less a person than Mary, personal assistant to Stewart McIntosh had walked up to his stall at 8.30am and coughed nervously.

"Mr. O'Malley?" she had said quietly, "Mr. Brendan O'Malley?"

"At your service, madam," he had said, grabbing a paper bag.

"Oh, I'm not buying, Mr. O'Malley," she said quickly, "I've come from Mr. McIntosh. He requests that you present yourself at his office as soon as possible."

"Oh, he does, does he?" Brendan said with a grin, "would lunchtime be convenient?"

"Oh, no, Mr. O'Malley," Mary said and she began to colour, "I rather think he meant immediately. In fact I know he meant immediately."

"Then immediately is what he will get," said Brendan, "I'll walk back with you." Brendan threw a jacket over his apron, passed his money bag to Dee and walked round the counter.

"I'll not be long," he shouted over his shoulder. Side by side Mary and Brendan walked out of the market hall and into the street. The Town Hall loomed to the left of them. Another huge, decorated monument to Victorian affluence. This two storey building was, however, only an entrance hall to the twelve storey block that had been unsympathetically added to the rear two years before. The town's people hated the modernity of the addition. The men folk of the town had a nickname for the column projecting upwards from a squat base. This name was not repeatable in female company.

"How are your family, Mr. O'Malley?" Mary asked as they walked across the road.

"They're fine, thank you," Brendan said, casting a puzzled sidelong glance at the woman by his side.

"Your family has been trading here a while, I believe," Mary said.

"Indeed," replied Brendan, "for generations. But, excuse me for asking; has McIntosh anything to do with your asking?"

"Oh, no, Mr. O'Malley," Mary added hastily, "I'm not asking anything for that man. He may be my boss, but I'm on your side in all this."

"In all what?" he asked her gently.

"Oh, the rent rises and..." her voice trailed off. Brendan remained silent but Mary did not speak again and within seconds they were entering the lift and ascending to the twelfth floor. Mary knocked on the door leading from her reception area and she felt, as much as heard, McIntosh bellow, "Come."

Brendan took Mary's arm and gently moved her to one side and marched through the door with an opening shout of:

"What the bloody hell do you want, McIntosh. Some of us have got businesses to run." The wind taken out of his sails, McIntosh blustered for a second but recovered himself enough to also go on the attack.

"If I find out *you* told the Press about private and confidential council financial information, you are in serious trouble, O'Malley."

"Can't you read, McIntosh," Brendan shouted back, "it was a council employee who made your little shenanigans public. Not me. I'll bid you a good day." Brendan turned around, walked out of the room, slammed the door deafeningly behind him and winked at Mary on his way out.

Chapter 15

Nathaniel was, for the first time in his life, having trouble getting to sleep at night. It seemed that he had only just fallen asleep when he was waking in a cold sweat. Twice, since that fateful evening that he had discussed 'the future' with his mother, he had left the market hall half an hour early and sneaked into the house, silent as a cat. Twice he had stood silently at the bottom of the stairs and heard sounds that he thought he would not hear again, the sounds of his mother exercising in her bedroom. He could only imagine what she was doing, but it certainly was not lying in bed like the invalid he had spent so long persuading her to be. She was plotting. She was planning. Well, Nathaniel thought, two could play at that particular game. Fortunately for Nathaniel, their local doctor was a pedantic old man. Three times a year he called round to the house and examined Mrs. Sharpe. He chatted about her various ailments, both real and imaginary, prescribed a bitter tonic, and always left with the same words.

"I'll see you in four months, Mrs. Sharpe." Medically speaking, Mrs. Sharpe was housebound, if not bed bound. Nathaniel had already decided that a fall down the stairs would be an appropriate ending for his long-suffering mother. Now she was exercising, maybe she would not fall as planned. Maybe she would be strong enough to fight him off. Maybe she would survive and get out of the house. That was the nightmare that was waking Nathaniel - Mrs. Sharpe running down the street, her night gown clinging to her white, strong, legs. Nathaniel giving chase but never catching her. Her hair coming down, streaming and trailing on the floor, catching his ankles, tripping him. He tries grabbing it but it slips through his fingers. Mrs. Sharpe is laughing hysterically as she reaches the local police station and screams 'Murder'. Two burly policemen come out of the station and stand there saying,

"Hello, hello, hello, what's going on here..." At this point Nathaniel wakens. As if this wasn't enough to keep him awake at night, he was also agitated about what was happening, or, more to the point, what might not be happening, to the market hall? He had carefully extracted from the banks and building societies written guarantees that he could withdraw all his money on demand. He had signed all the forms and warned them, if casually, that he might decide to take off on holiday at any time. He had their assurances that this would not be any problem. He had decided that three days before the bulldozers moved in, he would withdraw all his money, take a train to Manchester and deposit all the cash in a safety deposit box. Then he would return to the new market hall, oversee the installation of his office and return home to find his mother, dead at the bottom of the stairs. This entire plan was being jeopardised by the antics of the traders. They had no consideration at all. Nathaniel had, as Market Superintendent, an inventory of the complete contents of his office. It was part of his duty to oversee the safe transfer of the said items to the new market hall. He had discussed the plan with the demolition contractor. The contractor had agreed that Nathaniel's office contents would be moved and installed first. Nathaniel had asked if his presence would be necessary once his office had been moved. The contractor assured him he would be better off out of the way. Now the stupid people were refusing to move out! For three days he, along with members of the Town Council, had been barred from the market hall. He had strolled towards the market to be confronted by Fred Barcroft, who took two paces and blocked his path.

"You are not allowed in here today," Barcroft had snarled at him, "nor any other day until this problem is resolved."

"Mr. Barcroft," Nathaniel had insisted, "I have a job to do just like everyone else in here."

"You're council staff as far as we are concerned," replied Barcroft, "and probably a spy as well."

Nathaniel made as if to push the man aside and a huge hand gripped the back of his collar.

"You heard, Nathaniel," a voice said from behind, "now clear off." The hand almost lifted Nathaniel from the floor and he felt a push as he was twisted round and sent staggering into the road.

"You can't do this," cried Nathaniel, turning round, "I'll have you arrested for assault."

"Anyone see me assault this man?" asked Eddie Bulcock, grinning. Many heads around them shook.

"No, he stumbled into the road by himself," a woman said, "at least, that's what I saw."

"And I saw nothing untoward," Fred Barcroft added.

"Oh," Nathaniel almost squealed, "Oh, you liars."

"We'll have none of that, Nat Sharpe," Brendan said as he walked out of the market hall.

"I suppose this was all your idea?" Nathaniel said to the burly man in front of him.

"Not my idea at all, Nat," Brendan replied, "but it is proving to be effective. It's early days. We've a long way to go."

"Won't you at least let me get my books," Nathaniel wheedled, "I can do some of my work outside."

Brendan looked around at the other traders and was met by shaking heads and mumbled "No-s"

"Sorry, Nat," Brendan replied with a smile, "it seems you are not wanted here."

"But I have to get my books," Nathaniel shouted, "There are very important documents in there. If anything happened to them I'm, I'm," he paused to draw breath, "I must have them."

"Nothing in your office will come to any harm," Brendan shouted back, "I'll give my personal guarantee on that. We don't even have the keys." He waited for a few seconds and allowed his voice to drop to normal. Nathaniel looked as if he was going to have a heart attack.

"Nothing will be touched. We're keeping records of anything you need to know. We've been in the business long enough. All it means is that when we've resolved this situation, you'll have a bit more copying up to do in your ledgers," Brendan added. Nathaniel turned away and began to walk towards the Town Hall. The traders watched him.

"I've never seen him so agitated," said Eddie Bulcock.

"Makes you wonder what he's got in his office," added Fred Barcroft.

"Well, he's not likely to have whisky," laughed Brendan, "he's too mean for that." They all laughed and resumed positions, some working, some guarding the entrance. Nathaniel entered the town hall, went straight to the lift and pressed the button for the twelfth floor.

"Have you got an appointment?" the girl on reception shouted. Nathaniel ignored her completely and got into the doors as they slid silently open. He turned to the left and walked towards Stewart McIntosh's office. Mary was busy typing at her desk as he knocked briefly and walked in.

"Mr. Sharpe," Mary said, "Was Mr. McIntosh expecting you?" Nathaniel shook his head.

"Only he isn't here at the moment," Mary added, "he's had to go and see the demolition contractor. They are not happy about the delay in beginning their work. They have another job planned and not being able to..." She stopped in mid sentence. Nathaniel had sat down on the hard plastic chair by her desk and dropped his head into his hands.

"Are you all right, Mr. Sharpe," she said, moving round the desk towards him "would you like a coffee, or water?" Nathaniel raised his head and she was horrified to see his eyes were watery with tears. He reached into his pocket and pulled out a pristine white handkerchief. He blew his nose hard. Mary was sure she heard his teeth rattle. He said not a word but rose, gave her the weakest of smiles, and left the room. Mary returned to her chair.

"I wonder what that was all about?" she thought, then recommenced her typing. Nathaniel had never felt quite so bereft. All his careful plans, all his daily routines, everything was turning upside down.

"I can't believe this is happening," he muttered under his breath, "what have I done to deserve this?" He wandered blindly around the town, staring into shop windows but seeing nothing. Then he walked slowly towards the park. He sat on a park bench, ignoring the curious stares of people passing by and the more determined glare of the park warden, who was in two minds to report him after he had passed Nathaniel the fourth time. His body told him when it was time to go home and he had jolted himself back into his routine, walked briskly back down the road to the town centre. Buy an evening paper, catch the bus, go into the house, and prepare the meal. He stopped dead. No food. Every day he bought the food for dinner. Today was, oh, goodness, what day was it? He glanced at the paper- it was Wednesday, liver and bacon day. He clutched his head, disturbing the carefully combed bits of hair that were left there.

"Are you all right, dear?" said a woman waiting behind him in the bus shelter.

"Hum," choked Nathaniel, "Ah, yes." During the bus ride he formulated his plan. He was ten minutes late getting into the house. Without waiting to discard his coat he ran upstairs.

"Sorry I'm late, mother," he said, "what a day we've had down in the town."

"Nathaniel!" Mrs. Sharpe exclaimed, "you haven't taken your coat off nor changed your shoes. And what on earth is that parcel under your arm?"

"Fish and chips, mother," he replied, "I'll get them ready and tell you everything." He almost ran out of the room and down the stairs. Mrs. Sharpe sat up in her bed, bemused by the whirlwind appearance, and subsequent disappearance, of her son. A few minutes later Nathaniel appeared with her tray, put it carefully down on the bed and returned to the kitchen for his own tray and food.

"We'll probably have to leave the window open to let the smell out," Nathaniel said, "but this was an emergency. I hope you enjoy them." He proceeded to eat his food without another word. Mrs. Sharpe had no option but to do the same. She thoroughly enjoyed the fish and chips; such comforting food. It had been more years than she cared to remember since such an extravagant treat had been put in front of her. Nathaniel begrudged paying anyone to prepare his food when he "could do it just as well himself".

"That was lovely," she said appreciatively, "not that your fish and mash aren't wonderful."

"Let me take your tray, mother," Nathaniel said, "and maybe another cup of tea is called for?"

"Two cups of tea," said Mrs. Sharpe, "now that is what I call luxury." She almost purred.

"Well, we'll treat tonight as a special case," Nathaniel said, as he left the room. Minutes later, back in her room, he set the cup and saucer, and the evening paper, by her bed and sat down. She waited until he had composed himself. It didn't do to rush him.

"You'll see from the paper, mother, that there is trouble in the town," he began, "The market hall traders are objecting to the new rents imposed by the Council and they have staged a sit in at the old market hall." She was about to interject but he waved his hand to quieten her.

"Obviously, they are trying their damnedest to keep council staff out of the building in case they sabotage the trader's plan in some way. And obviously, as a council employee, I would, under normal circumstances, be kept out too. But, because of my long standing relationship with the traders, they came to a compromise. As long as I didn't actually go into the market hall, I was allowed to join their picket line outside. It was a day and a half, mother, and most of the people in the town are fully supportive of the traders. We kept getting congratulations from them. The press came to take photographs, at which stage I, of course, had to move to one side. But I'm invited back tomorrow and every day from now on until the council and the traders come to some agreement." He took a deep breath. His mother lay there dumbfounded. That was probably the longest speech she had ever heard come out of her son's mouth. And she didn't believe a word of it. Well, not his part in it, at any rate.

"Well, Nathaniel, you have had a day of it," Mrs. Sharpe said, reaching to pick up the paper.

"Have you read this yet?" she added.

"I skimmed over it on the bus," Nathaniel replied, "but I haven't digested it yet."

"Let's have a look at it then," said his mother. She unfolded the paper and began to read out loud.

LOCK IN or LOCK OUT?

The traders of the old Market Hall have locked themselves into the premises over a dispute about new rent increases. While operating their businesses as normal for you, the people of the town, they are not allowing known council employees onto the premises. Husbands, wives and neighbours of these employees can, of course, shop as normal. But the traders are afraid that some misguided employees of the council may try to hide away or infiltrate the building. The traders are sleeping inside the cold, dark, cavernous old hall to prevent demolition. Mr. Brendan O'Malley, a trader whose family has been selling fruit and veg. for three generations said:

"We all feel betrayed by the council. The deal to build the new market hall was supposed to pay for itself. We don't pretend to understand all the financial information that the council puts out but they must have made a packet out of selling the land we are occupying. They got the new site for the cost of a few miserable bits of compensation. The old folks there were re-located into council flats. They didn't have to build anything for them. Where's all the money gone?" Serious questions indeed, readers and we will leave no stone unturned until we get the answers on your behalf. We approached the council for a statement but no one was prepared to talk to us. Read into that what you will! Below is a picture of some of the traders picketing the outside of the market hall.

Mrs. Sharpe peered intently at the black and white photo. She recognised Brendan O'Malley, Eddie Bulcock and Fred Barcroft. They had been young men in the market when she was there.

"Who is the young girl at the front?" she asked Nathaniel.

"That's Elizabeth Patel," replied her son, "she's going out with O'Malley's nephew. Her mother is Anne Patel, who married the Indian man who went missing five years back."

"Oh, yes," said Mrs. Sharpe, "I remember reading about that. Did they ever find out what happened to him?"

"Not that I know of, but then I don't pry into business that isn't mine," he replied. The remark was made with such an air of self-righteousness that Mrs. Sharpe looked up.

"I thought everything that happened to the traders was your business, Nathaniel," she said softly.

Nathaniel looked at her.

"Everything *inside* the market hall, mother," he replied, "you know I have no interest in their personal lives."

"No," she said, "you've always been satisfied with work and looking after your poor old mother. Christmas is the only time you ever go out socially." He looked directly at her. Was there a hidden meaning in her words or not?

"It's a duty, mother, as I've told you many times before," he replied, "please do not think I enjoy it." Her next words took him completely by surprise.

"What *do* you enjoy, Nathaniel?" He sat there. Not a word came out of him.

"Let me put it another way, son," she said, "What enjoyment is there in your life? There has to be more than work and looking after me. You're a man after all. Don't you ever feel the need to go out for a drink? Go to the pictures? Perhaps meet a woman?" She sighed deeply before adding,

"When I was young your father and I had some wonderful trips out to the country and the seaside. We even went off one holiday week in a caravan. It rained three of the six days but we didn't care. We enjoyed it." She was smiling at the memory and about to add more happy reminiscences when he interrupted her - and this time it was her turn to be shocked speechless.

"And which father of mine would that be, mother" he said very deliberately, "the one on my birth certificate or the real one?" She felt a deep blush begin to spread on her cheeks and tears sprang to her eyes. Her hands flew to her face to cover it. Nathaniel opened a drawer and extracted a clean white handkerchief. He stood with his arm outstretched, the handkerchief dangling by one lace corner in front of her. She reached out and took it. Carefully she dabbed at her eyes but Nathaniel knew that she was buying time. He resumed his seat, sitting bolt upright and with legs uncrossed so as not to crease his trousers. He examined one fingernail and could find no fault with it. He heard her inhale deeply before she spoke.

"So you know?" was all she said.

"Of course I know, mother," he said bitterly, "you know the traders as well as I do. They live in a hotbed of rumour and innuendo. They made sure, with a word here and a sly remark there that I heard enough years ago to put two and two together. Herbert Walker was my father, wasn't he?" She nodded.

"And you deceived me for all these years?" he questioned. She nodded.

"And you never once thought it right and proper to tell me?" he went on. She looked up and there was genuine anguish on her face, which suddenly looked old and worn.

"There never seemed to be a right moment, Nathaniel," she said, "and what good would it have done for you to know?"

"It would have made me able to go out with my head held high, mother. After the scandal had blown over, I might," he paused before going on, "but what does it matter? It's too late now. They all know I'm Herbert Walker's son. I know it and I know they know. But *you* didn't know that I'd found out, mother. You carried on cheating and lying by your silence." There wasn't a sound as Nathaniel sat there, stony faced and his mother lay dabbing her eyes. The lace handkerchief was damp with her tears.

"Can you ever forgive me, Nathaniel?" his mother said eventually and held out one hand to him. He shook his head.

"No, mother," he replied and his voice was cold, "you robbed me of my dignity when you kept quiet. You should have told me when your husband died that I was not his son. Instead you handed me over to Walker and I'm just a duplicate of him. He got you and I got his job. I guess you got some enjoyment out of your end of the bargain. What did I get?"

"You got his job, Nathaniel," she said with a sly smile, "and the best training a Market Superintendent could have. I hope that you learned well from your father." He stared hard at her. In that one sentence she had revealed that she knew what he had been doing. Nathaniel had no idea how she could prove anything but he knew that she would have not one penny of his money, legal or otherwise. His stare turned into a look of naked hatred. She backed into her pillows and was afraid, very afraid.

Chapter 16

Rain was streaming down the windows, the wind howling enough to rattle the sash window frames. The sky was dark and leaden. It was a typical rainy day but Anne hardly noticed it. She was sat at the table in her over crowded room, counting coins into various piles. Her regular chore on the market's half day closing. Elizabeth was with Colin at the market on picket duty. On the market's half day there was a party atmosphere as the young ones took portable radios and the kiosk made burgers for them. Anne smiled at the expression 'picket duty'. Who would have imagined that she and Elizabeth would be embroiled in a dispute with the council? It wasn't the sort of thing ordinary people did. It had been exhilarating though. Anne had been co-opted to talk to the local paper and they had been keen to get information about how the traders were coping. She became friendly with Gill Shaw, the reporter assigned to cover the story. Anne described how they had drawn up a rota for sleeping. At first the men had insisted that only they, not women, be allowed to sleep overnight. Elizabeth had protested that all of them should take equal responsibility and had won the day, or night, for on the third day her name had come to the top of the list and she had shared her duty with Terry O'Malley and Mr. and Mrs. Entwhistle. Elizabeth had taken her flask, biscuits and sleeping bag and gone off as if on a camping trip. The next morning she had met her mother, and, heavy eyed, she had laughed and said;

"Me and my big mouth, mum. I wish I'd left well alone and let the men do the nights."

"What happened?" Anne asked.

"Well, first of all, we sat and talked and Mrs. Entwhistle was really good at making tea while her husband told the most excruciating Christmas cracker jokes. About eight we ladies bedded down. Mr Entwhistle and Terry guarded the doors. You would not *believe* how loud a woman can snore, mum. She began to snore as soon as her head hit the pillow and it got louder as the night went on. I've never heard a noise like it. Then Marmalade had a set to with something. I hope it was only a mouse! As if that wasn't enough, the clock on top of the market hall tower chimed every hour. We ladies had to do the late shift- and the refuse collectors began their rounds about four o'clock, just as the first trains were shunting in the railway. I've never even heard the trains before from where we are but, in the quiet of the night, they sound as if they are about to run through the market. I'm completely exhausted." Anne could not help but laugh. Her daughter's face was stricken. Elizabeth was not good without at least eight hours sleep.

"So you see, Gill," she told the reporter, "I had to send her home and she was only just up and washed when I got in. After that, she volunteered for day duties and no one said a word. They are good people at heart." Gill had written an account of Elizabeth's sleepless night, omitting Mrs. Entwhistle's snores and sympathy for the traders increased. The day after the story appeared business improved, as people came to see "the poor child" at work. The traders had seen only a small reduction in their takings so far. The vast majority of the town's people supported them but some had shown their disapproval of challenges to the council's authority. But Anne, along with all the traders, was desperate to see the situation resolved. The council had hardened their hearts and were refusing to release figures to the local paper. The Editor of the local paper was getting letters every day demanding that he put more pressure on the council to release details. He was caught between his readers and Stewart McIntosh, a man able to use pressure of his own. A local Editor could not afford to completely alienate the Chief Executive of the council. Pondering on how they were going to get out of this dilemma, Anne became aware of a frantic knocking at the front door. As she opened it a gust of wind caught an umbrella, carried by the man standing there, and almost blew him inside her hallway. As she stumbled backwards, she heard him shouting, over the wind,

"Mrs. Patel, Mrs. Anne Patel?"

"You'd better come in," she shouted back, "before you drown." The man backed over the doorstep, shook the rain off the umbrella, placed it gingerly in one corner and turned to face her, his coat dripping on the carpet.

"Thank you, Mrs. Patel, I thought I would drown out there," he said, extending his hand, "allow me to introduce myself." Anne noticed two things instantly. There was barely a trace of accent in his voice, and his clothes were of a quality Anne had never seen on the streets of Lancashire.

"Jonathon Smythe, Her Majesty's Government," he said as she shook his hand, "If you will allow me to remove my coat I will take my credentials from my jacket, where I hope they are still dry." He saw the look of alarm on Anne's face.

"Please do not be alarmed; Mrs. Patel," he said courteously, "you aren't in any trouble." He gave her the faintest of smiles.

"My apologies, Mr. Smythe," Anne said, recovering herself, "please let me take your coat."

"Most kind," said Smythe, struggling out of the sodden coat, "I've forgotten how bad English weather can be." She took his coat and hung it carefully on a coat hanger.

"Please," she said, with a welcoming gesture, "come through to the lounge. Would you like tea?"

"I'd be glad to, Mrs. Patel," Smythe replied, following her along the narrow passageway that led to the lounge. Anne indicated a seat near the fire.

"I'll just warm myself through, if I may, Mrs. Patel," he said. She left him standing in front of the fire while she went and prepared a tray with tea and biscuits, carefully discarding those that were broken. When she returned she saw him looking intently at her wedding photograph, although he had not touched it.

"My husband," she said, placing the tray on a corner of the table, "milk and sugar?"

"One sugar, no milk, thank you," Smythe replied and he took a seat. Taking the tea from her he seemed momentarily to lose his composure as he gazed at the picture. Anne was not unduly concerned. People who came to her house always found the photograph intriguing. She sipped her tea and waited. Moments passed and then Anne gave the gentlest of coughs. The sound startled him. Putting the cup and saucer down by his feet, he reached into his pocket and removed an envelope. It was a thick, creamy-white, expensive piece of stationery and Anne could see a crest in the top left hand corner.

"My credentials, Mrs. Patel," Smythe said. There was nothing more that Anne wanted at that moment but to take that envelope and just feel the luxury of it, but she resisted.

"You are now a guest in my house, Mr. Smythe," she said, "but I am puzzled to know what you want of me." He coughed and cleared his throat.

"I'm afraid, Mrs. Patel," he said, "I bring you news that is not good. It concerns your husband, Mohammed Patel." Anne's eyes went to the photograph and her free hand flew to her mouth, the cup and saucer in her other hand tinkling and rattling as she shook.

"Allow me, Mrs. Patel," Smythe said gently as he took the china from her.

"He's dead, isn't he?" she whispered.

"I'm afraid so," he replied, "Please accept my condolences."

"How long ago?" she asked.

"We're not sure," he said. He reached into his pocket again and took out a large white handkerchief. This was the point when, in his experience of women, the tears began to flow. Anne looked across at him and the handkerchief and smiled, although her face was drawn and pale.

"Mr. Smythe," she said, "you may think it odd that I don't need your handkerchief, but I've cried so many times wondering where Mo is, or what had happened to him. I've seen every single scenario in my dreams. Murdered in cold blood or locked and forgotten in a prison for some trifling offence," she paused and took a deep breath before continuing, "or married again to a woman he met in India. I've even imagined the children he might have had with her. You have no idea what a relief it is to know, to actually have some information, even if bad, after all these years. I'll make us fresh tea and then you can tell me all you know," she said, quickly leaving the room. This was the moment that Jonathon Smythe had been dreading but after meeting Anne Patel he had resolved to tell her the complete and unvarnished truth. It had always stood him in good stead. With fresh tea to hand Jonathon Smythe began telling Anne all about Basil Whicker's trials in India which culminated in himself having to go there and sort things out for the unfortunate Basil. He told her of the shock and horror of all of them at finding the letter after a few days work - only to find that it was dated two years previously.

"Which means Mo died and no one found him for three years?" Anne interrupted.

"I'm afraid so, Mrs. Patel," Smythe replied, "but it does not excuse the fact that you could have been informed much sooner, that blame lies with us."

"But also," Anne said, "it means that, if that cow had not died on that piece of track, his remains might still be there, undiscovered?"

"Well, that's true," Smythe mused, "but the cow *did* die and Mr. Patel *was* found."

"And Mo's few remains can be brought here?" Anne asked.

"It's the least we can do, Mrs. Patel," replied Smythe, "but you must understand that it will not be a full sized coffin. Maybe a child sized one. But if you would like to lay him to rest here, it can be arranged. And you can also have his suitcase. It is stored safely."

"I doubt whether anything in the suitcase would be worth transporting, Mr. Smythe, after five years," Anne said ruefully.

"Oh, you would be surprised, Mrs. Patel," he replied, "In dry, hot conditions, the contents will probably be as perfect as the day they were packed."

"I think, maybe, that you could arrange for some poor man to have the contents, Mr. Smythe," she said, "I cannot even remember what Mo took with him, although I packed the case myself." At this point she looked at the photograph on the mantel piece and broke down. Jonathon Smythe let her weep. He was, in some way, comforted by her weeping. Better tears than hysterics. He had been dreading hysterics. She seemed to have accepted, calmly, the series of events that another might have railed and ranted at. For that he was grateful. Anne's tears ceased and she took the handkerchief he had held out once more.

"Thank you," she said, "that's better."

"Is there anything else I can tell you, Mrs. Patel?" Jonathon asked.

"Oh, yes," she smiled back at him, "tell me what happened to poor Basil Whicker?"

"He arranged a divorce from Mrs. Whicker, citing himself, and is marrying Miss Fitzpatrick. They work together in Delhi. His work is now exemplary but if you wanted to pursue this awful matter further..." he paused, waiting.

"No," she replied, "let it be. No good would come of blaming him. I'm happy for them. We can all move forward now. Will you leave me a telephone number, Mr. Smythe? I'd like to ask Elizabeth if she has any preference to her father remaining where he is, or if she'd like him brought here."

"I understand, Mrs. Patel," Jonathon replied, "but whatever you want, we will facilitate the matter."

"Just one more question, Mr. Smythe," said Anne, "before you go. Do I have to register Mo's death here in England?"

"No, Mrs. Patel," he replied, "all the formalities were completed in India and the details forwarded to England. There is nothing to trouble yourself about. I will ensure that in one or two day's time you will have copies of his death certificate in the post. They will satisfy any authorities." He stood in front of her and held out his hand. She also rose, took his hand in both of hers and thanked him. At that moment a ray of sunshine shone through the window and caught the highlights of her hair. Jonathon Smythe couldn't help but think to himself what a damned attractive woman she was.

"I'll get your coat," she said. Jonathon Smythe left his credentials propped up on the mantelpiece, took a final look at the wedding photograph, breathed a great sigh of relief and followed Anne into the hallway.

"I'm afraid your coat is still damp," said Anne.

"I'll survive, Mrs. Patel," he said. He donned his coat, collected his umbrella and opened the door. Outside the sun was shining, making mirrors of the pavements. He turned one last time and said his farewells to Anne before walking briskly away down the street. She watched until he had turned the corner, and then she looked up into the pale blue sky and whispered, "Rest in peace, Mo." She cleared away the china, sat down in her comfortable armchair and the next thing she knew was the sound of Elizabeth's voice and a gentle shaking of her arm.

"Mum, mum, are you all right?" said Elizabeth. Anne woke fully and shook her head.

"Oh, Elizabeth, darling child," she said, getting up and enfolding her daughter in her arms.

"Mum, what is the matter," Elizabeth asked, "are you ill? You look so pale."

"I'm fine, Elizabeth," Anne replied, "just dreaming. Will you make tea? I have something I need to talk to you about." Elizabeth looked at her mother. Anne's voice puzzled her. She went to the kitchen. There lay the remains of tea for two.

"Have you had a visitor?" she shouted through the open door. There was no reply, so, as the kettle began to hum, she peeped around the door, about to ask again. Her mother was standing in front of the fire with a letter in her hand. She was smiling. Elizabeth shrugged. Anne would tell her about it soon. They had no secrets from each other. She busied herself with the tea tray and returned to the room.

"Shall I pour?" Elizabeth asked. Anne nodded. Elizabeth handed her mother tea and sat down in the chair so recently vacated by Mr. Smythe.

"I have news of your father, Elizabeth," Anne began and held up her hand to stop the immediate question that she saw coming on Elizabeth's face.

"It's not good news, I'm afraid," she added. Elizabeth's face crumpled. Anne slid to her knees in front of Elizabeth, holding out both hands to clutch her daughter's hands and hold them fast.

"Is he..." Elizabeth whispered, and there was no need for her to finish the question. Anne nodded.

"Where?" asked Elizabeth.

"He's in India," said Anne gently. Elizabeth began to cry, gently at first, tears streaming down her face, then the sobs started and she gasped for breath. Anne let her cry.

"I'm never going to see him again," she cried, "Oh, daddy, why did you go and leave us?" Anne folded her arms around Elizabeth and held her until the sobs subsided. Anne passed her a handkerchief and Elizabeth blew her nose.

"Is there any chance of us..." she stammered, but the tears convulsed her again. For minutes Anne could only sit and watch as Elizabeth cried until she was exhausted. Eventually Anne sat back on her chair, releasing Elizabeth's hands.

"There is a long story surrounding your father's death," she said, "is now a good time to tell you, or would you prefer to wait until tomorrow? Maybe you'd like to have some time to yourself." Elizabeth gulped and blew her nose.

"Tell me now," she said. Anne picked up the letter and handed it to Elizabeth.

"My visitor," she said, "was Mr. Jonathon Smythe. He brought his credentials." Elizabeth looked at the royal crest on top of the thick, almost parchment, paper.

"Gosh," she said, "I've never seen paper like this before." She read the flowery, courtier's language and then looked at the signature at the bottom.

"Mum!" she exclaimed, "do you know who has signed this?"

"Yes, Elizabeth," said Anne, with a touch of pride, "The Queen."

"And she 'graciously hopes that we will accept her Special Envoy and show him every courtesy' – did you mum?" asked Elizabeth.

"I gave him tea and biscuits," Anne replied, "just as I would any other visitor." Elizabeth smiled and hugged her mother.

"You'd better tell me about him, and Dad," she said and her lip quivered only slightly. Anne told the story to her daughter and answered all her questions. Elizabeth nodded when Anne told her that she had decided not to pursue Basil Whicker's misdemeanour.

"Where do we go from here, mum?" Elizabeth asked, after a pause.

"In what respect, love?" Anne asked.

"Well, Mr. Smythe wants to know if we leave dad in India or bring him here," Elizabeth asked, "what would you like to happen?"

"We should *both* think about it, Elizabeth," Anne replied, "maybe tomorrow morning, maybe not for a week, but the answer will come to us. Shall we do that? Think about it? There's no rush." Elizabeth nodded and wiped her eyes once more.

"I know," said Elizabeth, "that you can't be happy about the news, mum. But at least now we know. That's something, isn't it?"

"You couldn't have said truer words, Elizabeth. We can now go forward," Anne replied.

"Is it all right if I tell Colin?" Elizabeth asked.

"Yes, of course," Anne replied. Elizabeth hugged her mother. That night Elizabeth said a special prayer for her father and told him that she was happy he was at rest.

Chapter 17

"Elizabeth," the voice she knew so well came down the phone line, "it's Colin. I've had a letter."

"No," said Elizabeth, "I mean, who from?"

"A company called London Swings," he said.

"What does it say?" asked Elizabeth.

"Well, they want me to go down there next Wednesday, see a guy called Jocelyn Fitzgerald, talk with him and discuss my music."

"Wow," said Elizabeth, "that's fabulous. I knew you could do it."

"Will you come with me?" said Colin, "you've never been to London before, have you?" There was silence at the other end.

"Elizabeth?" said Colin urgently, "are you there?"

"Yes, love, yes, I'm here," said Elizabeth.

"Well?" said Colin.

"Are you going there and back.... in a day?" asked Elizabeth warily.

"That's the plan," said Colin, "why?"

"Oh, that's okay," she said cheerfully, "then yes, I'll ask mum if I can have a day off. I'm sure she won't mind."

"You're old enough to make your own mind up about having a day off," said Colin sharply, "and if I was going to stay overnight, I take it you wouldn't want to come?"

"Colin!" said Elizabeth, "that's not what I meant."

"Yes, it is," he said and slammed the phone down. Elizabeth stared at the receiver. All she could hear was a gentle purr – the disconnected tone.

"Who was that?" said Anne, clearing away the last of the breakfast dishes.

"Colin," said Elizabeth.

"So why the long face?" asked Anne, "I thought you two were love's young dream?"

"He just put the phone down on me," she cried, and burst into tears. Anne went across the room and put her arms around Elizabeth.

"Come on," she said, "you were only on the phone two minutes. What on earth can either of you have said to fall out about?"

"He's had a letter," Elizabeth gulped, "from a music agent. He's to go to London next Wednesday and talk to him."

"Well, that's terrific news, Elizabeth," said Anne, "so why the fall out?"

"He wants me to go with him," said Elizabeth. Anne said nothing. Elizabeth disengaged herself from her mother's arms and stood back.

"You see," she said, with a hint of triumph in her voice, "you're thinking the same as I thought." Anne smiled.

"And what would that be?" she said, still smiling.

"That he'd want to stay overnight somewhere," said Elizabeth, "with me."

"And you don't want to do that?" teased Anne.

"Mother!" exclaimed Elizabeth, "you know how I feel about sex before marriage. I want my husband to be the first." Anne glanced at her watch.

"We're going to be late for the market," she said simply, "let's talk later." She turned and gathered their outdoor clothes together, shrugged on her coat and passed Elizabeth's coat to her.

"I can't face him, mum," said Elizabeth, "can I have a day off today?"

"As well as next Wednesday?" said Anne, "no, you can't. Today is Mother and Baby day at the clinic. We'll be busy until lunch time. After that, we'll see." Elizabeth followed Anne out of the house, her face downcast and slightly mutinous. She saw Colin just once that morning, as she was leaving the ladies and he was going into the gents. She studiously avoided his eye, turning to say "hi" to a fellow woman stall holder she hardly knew. He stood, watching her retreating figure, but she didn't turn round.

"Bloody women," he said to Brendan when he got back to the stall. Brendan laughed.

"Don't let Dee hear you saying that," he said to Colin, "who has upset you?"

"Elizabeth," said Colin quietly.

"Oh," said Brendan, stroking his chin, "now that's serious. Want to tell me about it?"

"All I did was ask her to go to London with me next Wednesday," said Colin angrily, "and you'd have thought I was inviting her to a bloody orgy."

"Is that what she said?" said Brendan, a huge grin on his face.

"Not exactly," mumbled Colin, "but she made it clear that if it meant an overnight stay, she wasn't interested. As if..."

"Good on her," interrupted Brendan emphatically, "there's too much of this hanky-panky going on among young folk these days."

"What hanky-panky?" said Terry, coming up behind them. Colin blushed.

"Young Colin here," said Brendan, "is off to London next Wednesday and Elizabeth said she wouldn't go if it meant staying out all night."

"She didn't actually say...." began Colin but Terry butted in.

"Quite right," he said, "you don't want her getting a reputation, do you? It's easy enough you know. Look what happened to..." His voice trailed off.

"Molly and I is what he was going to say," said Brendan, "and he's right. We took some stick for having to get married, as they used to call it. Is it different now?"

"Get round there right now, young lad," said Terry, "and make it up with her. She's a grand girl and she'll get snapped up if you let go. I've seen young Birtwhistle looking all cow-eyed at her."

"Right, dad," said Colin, "and thanks, Brendan." He began to leave the stall when Terry called out to him.

"By the way, you *can* have next Wednesday off!" Colin was still grinning as he approached Patel's Baby Wear.

"Hi, Colin," Anne greeted him.

"Is Elizabeth here?" he asked.

"Just popped to Slinger's for the meat," Anne said, "she'll be back in a minute."

"Did she tell you about this morning?" said Colin quietly.

"She did," said Anne.

"I didn't mean it," said Colin, "I wouldn't do anything she didn't want, you know. I love her."

"I know, Colin," said Anne gently, "but it's not only men who get carried away with their feelings. Women do too..." Colin gasped.

"You don't say!" he spluttered. Anne laughed out loud.

"Here she comes," she said, giggling like a school girl. Colin turned round and saw Elizabeth walking slowly towards the stall. He walked towards her.

"Elizabeth," he said, as they met face to face, "I'm sorry. I shouldn't have said what I did. Forgive me?" He pulled such a funny face as he clasped his hands in a sign of penitence that she couldn't help but laugh.

"You silly.....," she began, but didn't get chance to finish what she was saying. Colin grabbed her, swung her in the air, twirled her round and then kissed her as she landed.

"Mind my pork steaks," shouted Anne.

"Will you come to London *and back* with me next Wednesday?" Colin whispered into her ear, "I promise to fend you off if you get all lovey-dovey on me."

"Can I, mum?" Elizabeth said to her mother.

"With my blessing," said Anne, "bring him back safe."

The train pulled out of the station right on time. Colin and Elizabeth were snuggled together on a seat. The heating wasn't working.

"It's a good job we're both used to getting up early," said Colin, "but it's freezing in here."

"You didn't used to get up early," giggled Elizabeth, "when you were a rock star."

"And now I know why," said Colin, "come here and keep me warm" The ticket inspector came through and punched their tickets.

"Any chance of some heating?" asked Colin.

"Yeah," said the man, looking at their pinched, cold faces, "follow me." They grabbed their bags and followed him.

"In here," he said, opening the door to another carriage.

"This is First Class!" exclaimed Elizabeth, "we've only paid second."

"So," said the man, dismissively, "I know this route. No one travels first class to London on this train. Get in there. You won't be bothered." Elizabeth hesitated but Colin pushed her forward. The warmth enveloped them.

"Cheers mate," said Colin.

"Now this is how rock stars should travel," said Colin. On the way to London they talked endlessly about what might be awaiting them and how it might affect their future.

"Suppose he offers you a contract?" said Elizabeth, "would you move to London?"

"I'll not do anything if it means leaving you," said Colin.

"What about all the groupies," Elizabeth laughed nervously.

"As if I'd even look at them," said Colin emphatically. Four hours later they were standing outside a large detached house, with three plaques on the door.

"Sure this is the right address?" said Elizabeth.

"Absolutely," said Colin, "look, it says London Swings." He pushed at the bell. A disembodied voice came through a tiny grille in the side of the door frame.

"Yah," a bored sounding female voice drawled.

"Colin O'Malley to see Jocelyn Fitzgerald," said Colin, then added, "I've had a letter from him."

"Come," said the voice, "first floor, and turn right. The door's open." They heard a buzzer and the door opened to Colin's touch. Elizabeth giggled.

"Very plummy," she said. They found the door and Colin knocked politely before stepping over the threshold. Elizabeth followed him nervously.

"Hi," said a girl, sitting behind a huge desk, her white boots propped up on it, "Joss isn't here right now. Some important meeting he's been called to. He'll be back in about an hour. Do you want to wait or come back?" She proceeded to file her nails, blowing the debris onto the floor. Colin looked at Elizabeth. She shrugged.

"We'll go and have a coffee," said Colin, "and come back. Do you know a coffee bar nearby?"

"Turn left, turn right, end of the street," the girl said, "it's called The Penguin, but don't ask me why."

They left the room and followed her instructions. They found the coffee bar and sat down.

"I wanted to laugh so badly," said Elizabeth, "what a doddle- filing your nails all day with your feet up. I'm in the wrong job." Colin grinned.

"I once applied for a desk job with an insurance company. They were offering £1000 a year. I nearly took it - then I thought about it. I couldn't sit behind a desk all day. I'd go nuts."

"She's probably his girlfriend," said Elizabeth, "did you see that dress?"

"I think we should eat," said Colin, looking at his watch, "It's half past one now. If he decides to go for lunch, it could be two-thirty before he gets back. We'll need more time to get back to the station in the rush hour." An hour later, they presented themselves back at London Swings.

"Sorry," the girl drawled as they walked into the room, "he's had to lunch with the guys from the meeting. He'll definitely be here at three. I told him you'd been. He sends his apologies. Take a seat." They sat on a leather sofa, so soft they almost fell together. The girl picked up the phone and dialled a number.

"Hi, babes," she drawled, "tell me all about last night." Elizabeth nudged Colin.

"We're not going to have much chance to see London, are we?" she said. Colin shook his head. He passed her a magazine, picked up a music paper and groaned.

"It's last weeks," he whispered to Elizabeth, "but I guess I can read it again." It was half past three before they heard footsteps outside. The girl put the phone down quickly, took her feet off the desk and began shuffling papers around. A thin, blond man walked in and went straight to where Colin was sitting.

"Jocelyn Fitzgerald," he said, "call me Joss, as in sticks." He laughed at his own weak joke.

"So sorry to have kept you waiting," said Joss, "you know how it is. When you're talking to producers, well, you can't just walk away, can you?" Colin struggled to his feet and shook hands with him. The hand shake was limp.

"Cool chick," Joss said to Colin, indicating Elizabeth, "does she sing too?"

"No," said Colin.

"Pity, she's certainly a dish. Very distinctive," said Joss, leering at Elizabeth. Colin said nothing.

"Right," said Joss, turning to his desk, "remind me again of your name."

"Colin O'Malley, I sent you a demo tape." Joss shuffled among a dozen letters wrapped around cassette tapes.

"O'Malley, O'Mara, O, what was it again?" he said

"O'Malley, Colin O'Malley," said Colin as politely as he could. Inwardly he was seething. Not only had this man been late for their pre-arranged appointment, not only had he looked at Elizabeth in a way that Colin did not like, but now he couldn't even remember his name.

"Here we are," said Joss, waving one aloft, "now, let's just listen to it one more time, and then we can talk." He tuned to a cassette recorder and put the tape in. A cacophony of deafeningly loud music came out of the machine. Joss sat back in his chair, closed his eyes and tapped away on the desk in time to the drumbeat. Elizabeth looked at Colin.

"That's not you, is it?" she said.

"No, it is not," Colin said, wincing as the drummer hit his cymbals, completely out of time. Joss was still sitting there, oblivious to anything.

"Let's get out of here," said Colin, "if that's the kind of music he likes, he's not for me." When the music had finished Joss opened his eyes and turned to his secretary with a puzzled look.

"Where did they go?" he said. Colin and Elizabeth were running down the street.

"What a pretentious git," said Colin when they'd rounded the corner and were out of sight of the house, "That music was like half a dozen that were in the charts a year ago. I wonder how many so-called producers are like him." Elizabeth was leaning against the wall, trying to catch her breath and laugh at the same time.

"Come on," he said, grabbing her hand, "we've got exactly one hour before we have to get the train. Let's blow some money and get on one of those red London sightseeing buses." By the time they boarded the train back to Lancashire; Elizabeth had seen all the major sights of London, pointing excitedly as the bus approached each major building. They flopped into their seats. Colin was quiet for some time, biting the side of his finger and thinking.

"Penny for them?" said Elizabeth eventually.

"I'm thinking that rock music might not be all it's made out to be," said Colin, "I'd be giving up a lot for maybe only a year of ...what? Might work, might not. I could get lumbered with the likes of Joss as a manager. Imagine that. Having to be nice to someone who couldn't even remember your name let along find the right piece of music. It's risky. There are so many one hit wonders. Look at the Four Pennies- they've been around for ages but only ever had one number one and that was years ago. I have such a lot now." Elizabeth kissed him.

"Whatever you decide," she said, "I'll be with you all the way. London's a fabulous place, though, we'll have to come again and see it properly."

"We could come here on honeymoon, if you like," said Colin with a grin.

"Was that a proposal, Colin O'Malley?" said Elizabeth.

"Yes," he said, "I love you more than anything in the world. Will you marry me?" She flung her arms around him and kissed him.

"Of course I'll marry you. But I'm not sure how much of London we'll see."

Chapter 18

The four O'Malley adults were having what Colin called a council of war -and it wasn't going well. Brendan and Molly were determined to hold out against the council and the proposed rent increases. Terry had come from the market that day. He had been harangued and harassed by other traders demanding that they move forward, contact the council and try to re-negotiate terms. He was half persuaded and was pleading their cause.

"What have we got to lose?" Terry asked his brother for the second time and his voice was edgy. He hated being at odds with his brother but felt than Brendan was being un-usually stubborn.

"Our self respect," Brendan said quick as a flash.

"And our profits," Terry retorted, "some of the traders are beginning to struggle. Our customers need fruit and veg every week, if not every day. But they don't need other things. People are either not buying or going elsewhere for their non-perishables."

"It's not long since Christmas..." Brendan began feebly.

"And Easter is just around the corner," Terry butted in, "we tried that Brendan and it didn't wash with them."

"The council must give in sooner or later," Molly said quickly, "I've heard that our local M.P. wants answers from McIntosh, and he wants them soon. It's said that even politicians in London have heard about our dispute."

"Heard from who?" said Sharon, "There are so many rumours flying around."

"I can't remember," Molly replied weakly, "and you're right, every day there are more stories and it makes my head spin sometimes."

"Well, at least the paper hasn't turned against us. I expected them to be backing the council by now," Terry added.

"More readers than councillors, I guess," said Colin sarcastically. He was getting fed up with the nights spent in the draughty building and he was missing Elizabeth, who was picketing during the day. They saw each other only in passing, it seemed. The family sat there, silent for once.

"I'll make a drink," said Molly, "tea everyone?" She didn't wait for an answer, merely got up and made her way to the kitchen. She had just put all the crockery onto a tray when she heard the door bell ring.

"Will someone get the door, please?" she shouted through the open door.

"I'll get it," Colin shouted and she heard the door open and a low murmur of two voices.

"Who is it?" she shouted.

"It's a Father Rigby," she heard Colin say from just behind her; "he wants to see Brendan. I've taken him in. He says he'll wait until you are there, just thought you might need another cup." Molly frowned. The priest at their local church was Father Connelly. And what did a priest want Brendan for? She automatically added another cup and saucer to the tray and went into the lounge.

"Good evening, Father," she said, putting the tray down on the table.

"Good evening, Mrs. O'Malley," he replied, "I see you have all the family gathered around you."

"Not all, Father," Molly replied, "our three girls are out in town, seeing a film, I believe." She looked at Brendan, seeking enlightenment for the priest's visit. He shrugged his shoulders.

"I'd better introduce you, Father," Molly said as she handed him a cup of tea. Father Rigby nodded his thanks.

"Brendan, my husband; Terry and Sharon, Brendan's brother and wife; and Colin, their son." Father Rigby shook hands and then looked around for a seat. Colin was elbowed out of his seat by his mother and thrown a look that he recognised.

"Sorry," he mouthed back to his parents. Father Rigby sat down and drank his tea in one.

"Thank you, Mrs. O'Malley," he said, handing his empty cup to Colin. He looked around the room, his gaze landing, for a second or two, on each face. Then he spoke.

"What I have to say here tonight, concerns Brendan O'Malley directly. But the story also is about families. I know this is difficult to ask, before I've spoken, Brendan, but I do have to ask. Do you want me to speak to you alone, Mr. O'Malley, or with your family around you?"

"That's a right dilemma, Father," Brendan said with a nervous laugh, "but my conscience is clear so I'll say go ahead and tell us all, we don't have secrets anyway."

"I'll start at the end of the story then," said Father Rigby, "and show you something I've discovered."

He reached to his inside pocket and drew out an envelope. He handed it to Brendan. Brendan looked closely at the faded ink script.

"It's addressed to Sean O'Malley," Brendan said to the family, "my father."

"Your father?" said Molly incredulously, "where on earth did you find this, Father Rigby?"

"All in good time, Mrs. O'Malley," the priest replied, "but you'll notice the envelope has not been opened. Maybe your husband would like to open it and read whatever is written there. It may, or may not, have some bearing on what else I have to tell you."

"I'm not sure," Brendan said, "It makes me feel odd, seeing my father's name like that." He turned the envelope over and saw there was a tiny seal. The seal was intact.

"Do you have any idea who wrote it?" he asked Father Rigby.

"Your grandmother," the priest paused before adding, "I think."

"Sean's mother, Isabel, who we think died somewhere in Ireland?" Molly asked.

"The same," replied Father Rigby.

"You read it," Brendan said, thrusting the letter into Molly's hand. Molly took it as if it were a piece of glass.

"Are you sure?" she asked Brendan. He nodded and she noticed that his hand shook ever so slightly and his face had lost its colour. Very carefully she opened the envelope. There were three sheets of paper inside and they crackled as she opened them.

"My dearest son," Molly read, **"I have no idea when you will receive this letter, but in all probability I will not be alive when you do and so firstly I want to say**

goodbye. My heart is failing and the doctors say there is no treatment available except complete rest. Rest, my dearest Sean, is something I do not know how to do. It seems that all my life, which began the day I met your father, has been one frantic, joyous, wonderful chase – through countries and against time, always against time. But time has caught up with me at last and I will die in Ireland, where first I saw your father and defied my own. The past may be too painful for your father to speak of, so I will tell you a little myself. Your background should be as important to you as your future and I hope the enclosed will help your prospects. I was sixteen when I first met your father, my beloved Patrick. I literally stumbled into a clearing, while seeking my pet dog, and there he was, stripped to the waist, skinning a rabbit. I had never seen a man half naked before and stood there like a stupid child, staring.

"I'm not a ghost, just flesh and blood, Lady Isabel," he said and he smiled a smile that went right into my heart and stayed there forever. From that day I followed him everywhere around the estate. We laughed, we giggled, and we joked about everything. No one stopped or chastised me. No one seemed to care, least of all my father, Sir Charles Shuttleworth, your maternal grandfather."

"Shuttleworth," interjected Brendan, "there was a Shuttleworth owned all the mines round here at one time. I never knew he was in Ireland too."

"Shush," said Sharon breathlessly, "let her finish." Molly continued to read:

"I turned seventeen, and knew that I loved Patrick and he loved me too. I demanded, like a wilful child,

that Patrick ask my father for my hand in marriage. Patrick knew that Sir Charles would never agree. So we devised a plan whereby Patrick would obtain a considerable amount of money from my father by promising to leave me and Ireland (my dowry I called it). He would then sail to America- and back. In the meantime I would meekly go to Switzerland to finish my education for one year. I promised to meet Patrick in London upon my return from Switzerland. Things rarely go according to plan, my son, and I was twenty years old before I next got word from Patrick. He had gone to America, with my dowry, got involved in some hare brained scheme, lost two thirds of the money and had to work his passage back on a ship-landing in Ireland! I sold some of my mother's jewels and left London, without telling my father, and made my way to Ireland with only my maid for company. Of course my father was not far behind and when he found the two of us together in Ireland he almost went mad with rage. I was not old enough, by a few months, to marry without his permission and he declared he would die before he would give it. Patrick and I went on the run from him. I cut off my hair and dressed as a boy. Patrick grew his and we spent some money dressing him as a gentleman. We travelled as man and page until I was 21 and then we married in a small Catholic chapel in the south of Ireland.

"This is incredible," said Sharon, "like a romantic novel." Her comment was greeted by more "shush" sounds.

"I was 25, your father 29, and still we moved around Ireland, trying to keep away from my father's thugs.

For, yes, Sean, your grandfather had sworn he would not rest until Patrick was dead. We stayed a few months here and a few months there. Patrick would find work and we hoped to settle. But one day we would get word that someone was asking about us in the town. We were always running. We decided to emigrate to America when I discovered that I was pregnant with you, my beloved boy, and the world turned upside down. I was dreadfully ill. Patrick was beside himself so we spent more of our precious money and bought two tickets to England. That journey was horrendous, Sean. I truly thought I would die. But we arrived in England and I threw myself on the mercy of an old friend, whose family land was next to that of my father's land in Lancashire. She and her husband agreed to take care of me until you were born but they would not allow Patrick into the house. He settled as near to me as possible. When you were born, my life was complete. You were perfect in every way. My natural maternal instincts surged powerfully and I was determined to ensure you had your rightful inheritance. Patrick was against my idea from the start. It was probably the only argument we ever had. But I was determined. When you were nine months old I left for Ireland, having ascertained that my father was at his Irish estate. I left nearly all the remaining money and jewels with Patrick. He was lodging with kindly ladies who agreed to wet nurse you and take care of you while Patrick worked. I think I knew, deep down, that my life force was draining. Only the mission I was on kept me going. I met with my father on one of the coldest, wettest, days I ever remember. The very air in the house was frosty. My father was shrunken and looked so much older than he actually was. Bitterness had eaten him away. But as I looked at him, sat in his chair, wrapped in a warm blanket, my heart went out to him.

I remembered how I felt for you and realised that those same feelings were the ones he had felt for me. We were parents wanting only the best for our children. I threw myself at his feet and cried on his knees. “Have you come home, Isabel,” he whispered, taking my face in his hands, “back to where you belong?”

“I came to tell you, father,” I replied, “that you have a beautiful grandson. He is perfect in every way.”

“He’s Patrick O’Malley’s boy?” he asked and his voice was bitter with hate. “Who else, father?” I replied, “I told you that I loved Patrick and I always will. But I want you to acknowledge your grandson. Please, father, cut me off if you will, but acknowledge Sean. He has done you no wrong.” He pushed me hard, Sean, harder than I think he meant to. I tumbled backwards on my heels and fell to the floor, catching my head on the fender. I was unconscious for two days and nights and he sat by my bedside the whole time, refusing to leave me. When I recovered he agreed to send money to England to take care of Sean, “until you get better” and he gave me this document. I’m not sure what it is, Sean, but your father will know what to do with it. My father fell asleep at his desk not a week later, knocked over the candlestick and set fire to his room. He was dead by the time the alarm was raised - and then I discovered that creditors were knocking on every door. I rallied myself to deal with all of them, selling pictures, books, silver, even the carpets under my feet. By the time the house had been

auctioned and the land sold off, every creditor had been paid and my health was spent. I am trying to rally my strength, here in a convent, and the only thing I have from my previous life is the Shuttleworth family bible containing one last diamond that was my mothers. Try Matthew, Chapter 7, Verses 7-8. This is my gift to you. The bible is in the hands of an O'Malley who is inscribing her side of the family tree. My dearest wish is to see you once more, hold you in my arms, kiss your sweet face and hold the hand of my true love, Patrick. God Speed, Sean, I'll be with you soon,

Your loving mother, Isabel Shuttleworth-O'Malley.

The room was perfectly still. It seemed as if no one breathed. Only a gentle ticking came from the clock on the mantel. Molly turned to the last page of the document. She frowned.

"It's a title deed, Brendan, or at least that's what it looks like, for a piece of land in, oh, my goodness, right here in this town."

"Then it's true," Father Rigby shouted, "it's all true." Five pairs of eyes turned his way.

"What's all true, Father?" said Colin.

"You, Brendan O'Malley, as Sean's eldest son, actually *own* the land that the new market hall has been built on."

"That's not funny, Father Rigby," said Brendan.

"It's true, though," replied Father Rigby with a laugh, "look at the title deed properly. I'll bet you the land shown is exactly where the new market hall is being built."

"Priests aren't supposed to gamble, Father," it was Molly's turn to chuckle. She had never seen a priest quite so excited in her life. She handed the paper to Brendan and he peered at it closely.

"You're absolutely right, Father Rigby," Brendan said after a few moments, "the land shown is the site of the new building." He passed the document to Terry who looked at it and whistled softly.

"I think, Father Rigby," said Sharon, "you'd better tell us a bit more about how you came by this letter."

"Yes," added Terry, "what puzzles me is why the letter has only surfaced now. Why wasn't it posted, or sent, after it was written? Where has it been all this time?"

"What can we do about it anyway?" said Molly.

"Here comes the awkward bit," said Father Rigby and he joined his hands together as if in prayer, "Let's just say that a parishioner came across certain information by accident. This person came to me knowing that a wrong was being committed. That person's revelations set me on a voyage of discovery. That voyage ended in Ireland where I obtained the letter from a convent. And believe me; I had to restrain myself all the way back here. I desperately wanted to open the letter. It might not have been anything other than a letter from a mother to her son and then I'd have been hard pressed to come up with an excuse to you all to explain why I had it. But my parishioner and I have been vindicated. A great wrong has been done to you, Brendan. The land is yours."

"Just a moment, Father," Terry interrupted, "are you saying that someone else knows the land is Brendan's?"

"I'm afraid that is the case, Mr. O'Malley," said Father Rigby, "the Chief Executive, Stewart McIntosh, and maybe others, knows that piece of land is your brothers."

"Jesus," said Colin, then clapped his hand to his mouth, "sorry, Father, I forgot." Father Rigby laughed out loud, and to everyone's astonishment carried on laughing.

"I hear that every day, Colin," he said, wiping his eyes, "but rarely the apology after. Forgive my hysterics; I think it is pure relief."

"So, what do we do now?" asked Molly.

"I can help you there, Mrs. O'Malley," said Father Rigby, "you have as your solicitors Grey Brothers on Preston Road, I believe?"

"How do you know that?" Brendan asked, shaking his head.

"A source," replied Father Rigby tapping the side of his nose.

"If you, and maybe I, together, were to visit them with this letter and title deed, I'm sure we can locate some evidence in their archives to support your claim."

"Isn't the deed enough, Father?" said Sharon, "it looks like an original."

"I'm sure it is, Mrs. O'Malley," said Father Rigby, "but remember in those days copies were always made and usually lodged away safely. It won't do any harm to see if there is a letter from Sir Charles, acknowledging his intentions."

"And in the meantime, Father, what do we do?" asked Molly.

"I would suggest we all keep this under our belts, so to speak, until we have proof positive and then we get a solicitor and challenge McIntosh," said Father Rigby, "this will finish him."

"That was said with a modicum of relish, Father Rigby," Colin said.

"Oh," Father Rigby replied with a smile, "I like to see my justice here on earth." And he raised his eyes heavenwards and mouthed "Sorry, Lord." Father Rigby looked at the clock.

"Time I was going," he said. He rose and the O'Malley family got to their feet also. The priest shook hands all round and muttered "Bless you".

"Thank you, Father," Molly said, "for everything, I'll show you out." When she returned all the family were poring over the letter and the document.

"I still don't quite understand why this letter was never sent to England," Terry said, "and did Patrick ever know what happened to his wife? Did he just leave her in Ireland when she died? Why wouldn't he go over there with Sean?"

"Maybe we'll find out later, maybe not," soothed Molly, "but in the meantime I agree with Father Rigby. We should keep quiet until he and Brendan can get to the solicitors. McIntosh and his cohorts may have done something that makes their possession of the land legally binding. We're not sure, are we?" Brendan stood there shaking his head.

"Poor Dad," he said softly, "fancy dying behind a fruit and veg stall, when he could have been a wealthy man."

"Wealth doesn't always bring happiness," Terry said, "and he had a good life. He enjoyed his work and we never went short of anything we really needed, did we?"

"I wanted a new bike when I was twelve," said Brendan with a grin. Terry punched him in the arm.

"If you make anything out of this deal," Terry said, "I'll buy you one."

"Just a minute, Terry," Brendan said, "less of the 'you'. We are both Sean's sons. We go fifty-fifty on anything that comes." He looked at Molly and she nodded her approval. Terry was speechless.

"No buts about it, lad," Brendan said and he reached forward and enveloped his brother in his arms. The door bell rang.

"That will be the girls, back from the cinema," Molly said, quickly gathering up the letter and deed and pushing them in the tiny writing desk.

"Let's keep quiet about what we know," Brendan said, "You know what gossips girls are." Everyone nodded and Molly went to let them in.

"What was on?" Colin asked.

Michelle pulled a face, "Kid's stuff," she said.

"Chitty, Chitty, Bang, Bang," said Barbara as she came in.

"Dad, dad," said Lesley, "I want to be Truly Scrumptious and have a flying car. Will you buy me one? It'll cost loads of money though. We'd have to save up forever." The girls stood in amazement as all the adults in the room burst out laughing.

"What did I say?" said Lesley.

Chapter 19

Michelle O'Malley, eldest daughter of Brendan and Molly, waited at the front desk of the police station where she worked. Her boss was due back from a late afternoon meeting. She was holding the file of statistics he had wanted ready for when he got back. She turned as the door opened and saw a woman struggling with its weight. Michelle went to hold the door open for her, while joking with the desk sergeant:

"It's one way to keep out the public, Joe, but we really should have automatic doors by now."

"All in good time, Michelle," Joe replied, with a smile, "all in good time." The woman smiled her thanks and Michelle could not help staring at her. The woman's clothes were immaculate, but at least twenty years old, and her face was made up as if she was a 1940s film star. Her face was covered in heavy powder, arched eyebrows and a Cupid's bow of bright red lipstick, streaking into the fine lines around her lips.

"Who is in charge around here?" the woman said, looking first at Michelle and then around the reception area. Joe, all six foot of him, coughed to attract her attention.

"I am," he said, "Sergeant Joseph Burns, duty officer today."

"And who is above you, Sergeant Burns," the woman asked.

"Just about everyone," Michelle heard him mutter under his breath.

"Sorry, young man," the woman replied, "you will have to speak up a little."

Michelle smiled as Joe answered more clearly, counting off his senior officers on his fingers, finishing his speech with:

"But you will have to tell me what you want, madam, before I know who to get in touch with." The woman glanced around at Michelle.

"It would have to be in private," she said.

"Don't you worry about Miss O'Malley," Joe said, "she works here in a very senior position, and has signed all the secrets forms." He winked at Michelle, who had trouble stifling a laugh.

"In that case," the woman said, "I wish to report an attempted murder." The woman was gratified to hear Michelle's gasp and see Sergeant Burns stand up a little straighter.

"And," she went on, "a massive fraud that has been taking place over many, many, years."

"Oh, my goodness," Michelle whispered.

"Those are serious charges, madam," said Sergeant Burns, "and will have to be dealt with by a very high authority. May I have your name please?" Michelle couldn't tell if Sergeant Burns was being serious or not but she stepped even closer. There was something familiar about the woman but she couldn't put a finger on what it was.

"Mrs. Susan Mary Sharpe, with an e," the woman replied, "and the charges are to be laid against my son, Nathaniel Sharpe." Michelle drew in her breath sharply.

"Do you mean the Nathaniel Sharpe that is superintendent at the market hall?" she asked. Joe frowned at Michelle but Mrs. Sharpe turned to her.

"The very same," Mrs Sharpe said, "Do you know him?"

"And who is he supposed to have murdered?" Sergeant Burns interrupted before Michelle could answer.

"Attempted murder," Mrs Sharpe corrected him, "I never said he had murdered anyone- yet."

"I'm sorry, Mrs. Sharpe," Sergeant Burns said, "attempted to murder then?"

"Me," announced Mrs. Sharpe triumphantly.

"And just how did he attempt to murder you?" Sergeant Burns said, with a faint smile on his face.

"I'm not sure how he would have done it," mused Mrs. Sharpe, "but believe me, he would have found a way. I know too much, you see." The door behind them swung open and Michelle's boss walked in, looking harassed and hot.

"Ah, Michelle, I see you have the file I need," his voice boomed across the area.

"Ready and waiting, sir," Michelle replied and handed the file over.

"You may go now if you wish," he, nodding at Michelle. He turned to walk up the stairs. Sergeant Burns made a decision.

"Excuse me sir," he said loudly, "but I think maybe you ought to listen to this lady, who says her son is attempting to murder her." The Inspector wheeled around.

"Don't forget the fraud," Mrs Sharpe said to Sergeant Burns, "I may not be dead, but that's been going on for years."

"And she claims to know about a massive fraud perpetrated by her son, Nathaniel Sharpe," Sergeant Burns added.

"Yes, yes," said the Inspector, "I heard the lady." Michelle could almost hear the Inspector's brain ticking away. Finally he spoke.

"Sergeant Burns," he said, "who is relieving you at six o'clock on the desk?"

"No one tonight, sir," replied Burns, "Sergeant Haworth is away on sick leave so I'm doing an extra half shift then a constable is doing the other half." The Inspector frowned then he turned to Michelle.

"Sorry, Michelle, would you take Mrs. Sharpe to Interview Room 2?" he said, "Oh, and could you see that Mrs. Sharpe gets a cup of tea, please." Michelle nodded. After the two women had left the Inspector turned to Sergeant Burns.

"I don't suppose there is anyone in C.I.D. at the moment?" he said. Sergeant Burns shook his head.

"They are all out on cases or gone home," he said.

"Do you think this Mrs. Sharpe is a genuine case?" the Inspector said and he raised his eyebrows.

"Well, Sir," Burns replied, "we're had our fair share of fantasy stories over the years, but they're usually drunks. She obviously isn't."

"I'll need a witness with me," the Inspector said and he frowned.

"Well, sir, if you are going to tape the interview, why not take Miss O'Malley in with you?" said Sergeant Burns, "it is not as if you are going to grill Mrs. Sharpe. Michelle has security clearance for most things. The tape will reveal all that is said. And if you ask Mrs. Sharpe if she minds beforehand, you've covered yourself. She's a victim, not a suspect, if what she says is true."

"It's not strictly correct," the Inspector replied, "but I'll do it just this once. It may end up being something and nothing. Take care of this for me, will you?" He put the file on the front desk and left to join Michelle and Mrs. Sharpe in the interview room.

"Mrs. Sharpe," the Inspector said, "my name is Terence Pope and I'm Inspector here. I'm about to tape what you have to say on this machine here," he indicated the tape recorders built into a console, "and strictly speaking I need a witness. Just to prove that I have not coerced you or led you on in any way. I was going to ask Miss O'Malley here, who is my personal assistant, to stay with us and hear your story. Do you have any objections to that?"

"None at all, Inspector," replied Mrs. Sharpe.

"Michelle," the Inspector turned to her, "I know you are due to finish, but would you mind?"

"No, sir," Michelle replied, secretly pleased at being asked.

"Right," said Inspector Pope, "let's see if we can get these machines working." While he was setting up the tape recorder, Michelle helped Mrs. Sharpe take off her coat.

"Michelle, if you will sit by my side, here," said Inspector Pope, "facing Mrs. Sharpe."

"Are you comfortable, Mrs. Sharpe?" he said. She nodded.

"Right, I'll start, then you just tell us everything you want to," he said and pressed a button. The tape recorder began to whirr and he began to speak into the microphone.

"Interview with Mrs. Susan Mary Sharpe at seventeen thirty hours, in the presence of Inspector Terence Pope and Miss Michelle O'Malley, please tell us what you want us to know, Mrs. Sharpe."

Mrs. Sharpe sat there, for a moment dumbstruck. The Inspector waited.

"In your own good time, Mrs. Sharpe," he said gently, "start at the beginning if you like. No rush."

"Well," said Mrs. Sharpe hesitantly, "I suppose the beginning was when Nathaniel was born."

"Will you tell us, for the tape, who Nathaniel is, Mrs. Sharpe," said Inspector Pope.

"Nathaniel is my son," she replied, "and the son of Mr. Herbert Walker, who was once market superintendent. And I know now that Nathaniel knows that Mr. Sharpe, my husband, was not his father." Inspector Pope looked across at Michelle and he could see that she was as confused as him.

"Can you tell me, Mrs, Sharpe," he asked, "how recently Nathaniel discovered this information? Just to clarify things for me."

"Oh, he's probably known for years. You know what market people are like, a hint here, a word there. I'm sure he found out long ago that Herbert Walker was his father. But I never told him, you see. Not when my husband died, not after the funeral. I just kept quiet." Mrs. Sharpe looked pensive for a moment.

"I suppose I half thought that as Herbert was training him to be market superintendent, it was better that there be only good feelings between them," she continued, "It wouldn't have done for Nathaniel to turn against Herbert, would it? And I suppose I was a bit ashamed as well, although Herbert did the decent thing and moved in with us. So he really was a sort of father to him." Inspector Pope shook his head. The woman was rambling.

"May I ask a couple of questions?" he said. Mrs. Sharpe nodded.

"Just how old is Nathaniel now?" he asked.

"Fifty six. I was very young when I had him," she lied.

"And upon what basis do you think he wants to murder you? That he was not your husband's boy? It would seem that he has known for years," said Inspector Pope.

"Oh," she replied quickly, "it's got nothing to do with that. It's all about the money." Inspector Pope nodded approvingly. It was usually love affairs or money. This he could deal with.

"Tell us about the money, Mrs. Sharpe," he said.

"I won't get in trouble, will I?" she said suddenly.

"Why should you?" asked Inspector Pope.

"Well," she added hesitantly, "I had an inkling, only an inkling mind, of what Nathaniel was up to. But I have been confined to bed for years. My doctor will confirm that. It's taken me months to get myself fit so that I could do something about him. But I couldn't do anything before." She reached into her pocket and drew out a lace trimmed handkerchief and dabbed her eyes.

"Mrs. Sharpe," the Inspector said gently, "you have come here voluntarily to report a fraud you believe your son has committed. I'm absolutely sure that a lady of your years," he coughed softly, "has nothing to fear." The handkerchief disappeared and Mrs. Sharpe took a deep breath..

"I've discovered, "she said, "that my son, Nathaniel, has, over many years, been taking money in a totally underhand way, a totally immoral way, from the traders in the market. He's been charging them for all sorts of offences, some of which he's invented. He's been putting the money away, but I don't know where, and it runs to thousands and thousands of pounds. Now with all this kerfuffle at the site, what with the strike and everything, he's getting desperate. I know he intends to take all this money, and probably my pension money, which are in my bank account, if I'm dead, and run away somewhere." She exhaled a huge sigh and sat back against her chair. The Inspector turned to Michelle, whose mouth was, by now, wide open.

"Some more tea, I think, please, Miss O'Malley," he said and he switched off the tape.

"Why are you doing that?" Mrs. Sharpe asked him.

"We'll just take a break, Mrs. Sharpe," he replied, "and then we'll come back." He rose from his seat, beckoned to Michelle, and left the room. The Inspector motioned her to close the Interview room door. He leaned against the wall.

"Michelle," he said, "I don't know whether to laugh or cry. Is the woman raving mad? Is it possible that what she says could be true?"

"Well, sir," Michelle replied, "my dad is Brendan O'Malley. Our family has run a stall on the market for generations. I've heard him complain about Nathaniel Sharpe over the years but Nathaniel is very clever. He only ever takes small amounts for what he calls infringements of the market rules. Everyone pays up just to get rid of him. They don't like it but the amounts are never worth making a fuss about. Those who have complained, like my father, get left alone. But there are a lot of stallholders who still pay. I guess that over the years he might have gathered together a fair amount of money. But I'm sure he can justify every penny."

"So there could be something in it," the Inspector mused, "but we're going to need proof. I don't think Mrs. Sharpe will stand up against a clever barrister, do you?" Michelle shook her head.

"Will you make tea, please while I think for a moment?" Inspector Pope said. Michelle nodded and went to make tea. Upon her return she found the Inspector sat chatting to Mrs. Sharpe.

"Thank you, Michelle," he said.

"I'm switching the tape back on, Mrs. Sharpe," he said, "so just carry on as before."

"About the money?" Mrs. Sharpe asked.

"Yes, please," said Inspector Pope, "we believe you, but we need proof to get Nathaniel into court."

"What sort of proof?" Mrs. Sharpe asked.

"Well, how did you find out that he was taking this money? After all, he might have been justified in fining the traders and he might have been putting the money into a council fund."

"Oh, no," said Mrs. Sharpe emphatically, "the council wasn't getting the money. It was going into his own pocket. Or a bank account. I've seen his books. It's all written down there, year after year."

"Ah," said Inspector Pope, "now we're getting somewhere. Where are these books?"

"I don't know," said Mrs. Sharpe and her face crumpled.

"So, how did *you* see them?" puzzled the Inspector.

"Well, once a year, at Christmas, when the market is closed, he brings them home and hides them. That's when I saw them. I've been checking them every year since. As soon as he goes back to work, the books go with him. I don't know where he keeps them, but it must be somewhere in the market hall. There must be a safe in the office. I bet you'll find them there."

"Ah, that's better," the Inspector said with quiet satisfaction, "tomorrow I can organise a warrant to search the premises. Someone on the council must have a set of keys and we can find all the evidence we need. Well done, Mrs. Sharpe, and thank you. You have been most helpful." He reached across and switched off the tape for the second time and extracted the tape. He stood up and leaned across the table to shake hands with Mrs. Sharpe. She also stood up but just stood there, looking bewildered.

"Is something the matter, Mrs. Sharpe?" Michelle asked.

"Well, yes, there is," she replied, "where am I to go now? Don't I get protection? I'm in danger. I can't go home, can I?" Michelle heard a noise coming from Inspector Pope that sounded remarkably like a snort, but it may have been a sneeze.

"Bless you," she said. Inspector Pope recovered himself.

"Do you really think your life is in danger?" he asked.

"Yes, young man, I do," said Mrs. Sharpe indignantly, "he's not treated me well for ages now. Hr gives me funny, menacing looks. I know that whatever he's intending to do with the money- it doesn't involve me! The only way he's really free is when I'm gone. You see, I'm not sure if he knows that I know about his books. If he knows I know - then I'm in danger."

"Oh, dear," said Inspector Pope, shaking his head, "I don't believe we have a safe house available right now." It was Michelle's turn to smile.

"What about a nice, quiet hotel on the outskirts of town," suggested Mrs. Sharpe, before adding, "but I have no money, you understand."

"Oh, I'd need authority from much higher up to do that, Mrs. Sharpe," the Inspector frowned.

"A word, sir," Michelle whispered to him and drew him to one side.

"Would it be prejudicial to the case if Mrs. Sharpe stayed at our house just for one night? My two sisters are away so we have spare bedrooms. I'd promise not to ask her any questions," she said.

"But you can't stop her talking," said the Inspector.

"That's true," said Michelle, "it was just a thought. I actually feel sorry for her and I think she may be right. How would it look if we sent her packing and then were attending a coroner's court in a few weeks time?"

"As subtle a piece of blackmail as I've ever come across, Michelle," he smiled at her.

"Then it's settled," Michelle said.

"Mrs. Sharpe," Michelle called across the room, "you will be staying in a very safe house tonight, with my mum and dad. And," she threw a look at the Inspector, "the Inspector here is going to take us there in his own car."

"Delighted to be of service, ladies," the Inspector had no choice but to say, "this way, please." As Michelle let herself in to the house, she heard Molly shout through from the kitchen,

"That was a posh car you came home in, Michelle."

"I've brought a guest for the evening, mum," Michelle called back, "Mrs. Sharpe, Nathaniel Sharpe's mother. Inspector Pope very kindly brought us here." Molly almost ran from the kitchen. She, like her daughter before her, could only stare at the eccentrically dressed old lady.

"Come in, Mrs. Sharpe," she said, "may I take your coat? Would you like tea?"

"Thank you," Mrs. Sharpe replied, "most kind. Tea would be lovely."

Mrs. Sharpe had been right to be worried about going back to the house. During the dispute Nathaniel had tried every way of getting his books and always been thwarted. The last thing he wanted to do was spend time with his mother, the very sight of whom caused him to grind his dentures until his jaw ached. So he had walked miles around the town, discovering places he hadn't known existed before. His life had been the market - and home. But every afternoon he had ended up back at the great Victorian edifice and he had scrutinised the facade for any means of getting into the building undetected. It seemed impossible. The only way was to get in was through the front doors.

He could get out, carefully, by levering open one of the skylight windows and dropping down onto the boxes and pallets stored to the rear but it was a fair drop. It might have to be risked. He had let himself into the house, later than normal, as the pretence of being concerned about his mother had long gone. He made beans on toast without a word, ate his own and then carried the remaining portion upstairs, the toast already cold and the beans lukewarm. She'd have to like it or lump it, he thought. He opened the door to his mother's bedroom and walked in. The tray dropped to the floor and tomato sauce splattered his shoes. The plate cracked and fell in three pieces, hit by the falling cup and saucer. His mother was gone. He crossed to the bed and tore back the bedclothes, as if he would find her hiding there. The bed was cold as ice. He turned and flung open the wardrobe door. Her one set of clothes were missing.

"Damn and blast," he said to the empty space, "I should have got rid of them years ago." He looked around the bedroom and then ran downstairs and searched every flat surface in the house. She had not left a note. Whatever she was up to, Nathaniel knew he couldn't wait to find out. He feared the worst. He had to get out of the house, find a way into the market hall, get his books and get out of town. Quickly he went into his own bedroom and pulled on his heavy coat. It had the advantage of having lots of pockets both inside and out. He was already mentally planning. He worked out that he could stuff bank books into these pockets and with his old leather satchel slung around him, he should be able to carry the money. He slammed the door behind him and set off down the street towards the bus stop. He gave the house, which had been his home for his whole life, not a second glance. The next time he put down roots, where-ever in the world that was; it would be with the sea in front of him and a mountain behind him. The bus came and he was grateful that the conductor was indifferent to his passengers. Nathaniel sat on the back row, collar turned up, trying to look inconspicuous. It wasn't difficult as no one gave the man a second glance. Alighting just yards from the market hall he glanced at the scene. The number of pickets had been reduced to a mere three people, two men and a boy. Nathaniel loitered nearby, but in the shadows. Luck might be with him for he recognised one of the men as Bill Hargreaves, who was known to like a pint. Sure enough, after fifteen interminable minutes, Nathaniel heard Bill say to the boy,

"Will you be all right if me and Sam go for a pint? We'll only be ten minutes and we'll bring you lemonade and some crisps." The boy nodded.

"Aye, dad, there's nothing happening. Make it two bags and you can stay out half an hour." The men laughed. Nathaniel inwardly blessed the boy. Now all he had to do was find a way to distract the boy long enough to get past him. But how? Luck was with him again as a pretty young girl came up and greeted the boy. She wore the shortest of skirts, a thin cotton top and a light raincoat open to show her legs and other attributes.

"You on picket duty, Stuart?" she said, giving him a saucy smile.

"Yes, but I'm alone for the next half hour or more while my dad has gone to the pub. Do you want to come inside and show me your apples?"

"Oh, you cheeky beggar," she sniggered but then she sauntered slowly past him and into the darkness of the market hall.

"Yes," Nathaniel breathed to himself, "I'm in." Like a cat he hugged the walls of the building and slipped in without making a sound. He knew every square inch of the building. While the two youngsters were larking about, he inched his way up the stairs, to his office, listening all the time. He felt in his pocket and found the right key by instinct, put it between two fingers, and grasped the rest of the bunch in his fist. He was surprised to note that his palm was wet. The key slipped silently into the lock and he turned it gently. He pricked up his ears but no one had heard. The door opened. Carefully he closed it behind him and went, completely in the dark, to the safe. He rotated the dial with numbers only he knew and opened the door. His hands felt for the bank books and he extracted them one by one and put them in his pockets. The cash he had already withdrawn he stuffed in his satchel. He left the safe door open and went back to the office door. He opened it and peered down the stairs to the main doors of the building. One lamp cast a gleam on the entrance and his heart skipped a beat as he saw a burly shape there.

"Where the devil are you, lad?" Nathaniel recognised Bill Hargreaves voice.

"Here, dad," came the boy's voice, "I was just taking a leak, without leaving the door unseen."

"Couldn't you have waited until we got back?" his dad replied, "I've brought your pop and crisps."

"You said you'd be half an hour, dad," the boy whined.

"Well, I wasn't," Hargreaves said and Nathaniel saw the man cuff the boy round the head before thrusting the crisps and pop into his hands.

"Stay put, lad," said Hargreaves as he walked away. The boy took up position dead centre of the doors and a few seconds later the girl appeared.

"That was a close one," she giggled, "are you coming back in?" Nathaniel willed the boy to assent but his luck was out.

"No," the boy said, "I'll get a thump if I'm missing next time. But you can share my stuff with me if you want." The girl shook her head, planted a kiss on the boy's cheek, and walked away.

"Bloody girls," said the boy. He tore open the crisps and stuffed them into his mouth.

"Damn," said Nathaniel. He made his way around the balcony. Stopping at the fourth cafe, he opened the door and went in. There was a dim light shining through the skylight. He searched around for a pile of towels and put them on the table nearest to the window and then carried a chair to the table and put it on top. He climbed, without a sound, and reached for the skylight. At first it resisted his efforts, but he hadn't fined the cafe owners for 'windows unable to be opened' for nothing, claiming health and safety regulation. He remembered the words the owner had spat at him:

"No one in their bloody right mind would want to climb out of a window in the roof." Slowly the window opened outwards and Nathaniel fixed the bar onto the latch. He hauled himself up and was half way through the window. He had to pause for breath and he was sure the boy would be able to hear the beating of his heart. Glancing around he shuffled and squirmed until the whole length of his body was flat on the roof. He slid gently down to the guttering and peered over. The pallets and boxes were still in place. His plan was going to work. He felt his heart beating even faster and perspiration was tickling the back of his neck. He righted himself so that he was standing, his feet sideways in the wide stone guttering. He wriggled out of his coat so that it fell across the back of his body and the other arm came out. It was now around his feet and he bent and picked it up. He tucked the empty arms into the pockets and gently threw the coat over the edge of the building. Nathaniel was not to know that inactivity around the market had encouraged pigeons to roost each night on the boxes and pallets. As the coat landed among them, they rose up, flapping wings and making their own panicky noises. They flapped around him and he waved his arms to shoo them away. His heart began to beat as wildly as the flapping wings. He was balanced precariously on the old worn guttering. One brave bird decided Nathaniel was an enemy and flew right at his face. Nathaniel's arms flapped up and down, a huge but ineffective scarecrow on the Market Hall roof. He lost his balance completely and fell, silently, from the building. His life was saved by the leather satchel around his chest but a piece of guttering, dislodged during his fall, followed him to the pallets, smashed his leg and came to rest on his foot, breaking every bone there. Only Marmalade kept vigil all night, mewing and crying to the moon.

The next morning, a mill worker spotted a pair of false teeth on the floor, by the side of a ginger cat. He glanced up and saw a leg sticking out from the pallets. He shouted, but could get no answer. He rang the ambulance and the fire brigade and they retrieved Nathaniel, moaning piteously, together with all his belongings. Nathaniel was in the Infirmary for two days before he was fully conscious, during which time he had surgery. They told him that his left leg had been damaged beyond repair and had had to be amputated above the knee.

"At your age," the consultant had added, "we may get you walking again but I think a chair is a distinct probability for a while. Is there anyone you want to see?"

"Mother," he said weakly. He did not know what else to say. He lapsed back into a deep sleep. The next time he woke his mother was there by his bedside, holding one of his bony hands in her own and muttering endearments at him. But Nathaniel's heart sank as he saw the tall man in uniform standing behind her.

"Mr. Nathaniel Sharpe," the man said, "I'm Inspector Pope and we have a lot to talk about. Your mother has been telling us of your escapades over the past years, and, we have these." Nathaniel watched as the Inspector waved his building society books and patted a pile of his ledgers. For probably the first time in his life, Nathaniel cried.

"There, there, son," cooed Mrs. Sharpe, "you've got me to look after you now." He did not like the look on her face as she said it.

Chapter 20

Anne, Elizabeth, Dave and Colin were in Mr. Singh's restaurant. Anne and Elizabeth had called to see him three days before and told him the news of Mohammed, glossing over the part Basil Wicker had played; they gave him the news of Mo's death. The old man tutted profusely at the news shook his head and wrung his hands together.

"My poor friend, Mohammed," he said sorrowfully, "what a way to die. But it is all in the hands of fate, you know." Anne and Elizabeth smiled.

"We have decided, Mr. Singh, to let Mohammed stay in India. Have we done right?" said Anne.

"Quite right, Mrs. Patel," he replied, "Mo would have wanted that. And at least he'll be warm!"

They smiled again as Mr. Singh shivered. He had never got used to the damp Lancashire air.

"What will you do now?" Mr. Singh asked Anne.

"Keep the business running. Elizabeth has said, quite firmly, that she wants to stay here and work with me. We hope to expand, maybe get a little shop, in time," Anne replied.

"Yes, I understand that, Mrs. Patel, and that is very commendable of Elizabeth," he leaned across and patted Elizabeth's cheek, "but I meant on a more personal level," said Mr. Singh without any trace of embarrassment. Anne hesitated for a moment and slight warmth tinged her cheeks.

"You don't have to tell me, Mrs. Patel," the old man grasped both her hands in his, "you are going to marry that nice Dave, that drives ambulances- and give your daughter a father again. That's very good and to celebrate you must come to my restaurant on Saturday night and I will feed you all a banquet fit for a king and queen."

"Only, Mr. Singh," replied Anne quietly, "if you will do me the honour of standing as my witness at the wedding. You were Mohammed's closest friend in England. He would have liked it."

"I will be delighted to, Anne," he replied and there was the faintest hint of moisture in his eyes.

They had the best window seat, the crispest linen table cloth and napkins. The cutlery was gleaming and the glasses sparkling. The talk was firstly of Anne and Dave's forthcoming wedding. Anne wanted a quiet registry office wedding and Dave had agreed. The sticking point was a reception. Colin and Elizabeth were insisting that the happy couple have a celebratory meal.

"We need to invite all the O'Malley family and a few other market people," said Elizabeth, "and Mr. Singh and his family. You have to feed them after a wedding."

"And there are one or two people from the hospital I'd like to celebrate with me," added Dave, "it's not every day a man gets married. I want to show you off to them all."

"Okay," said Anne, "we'll have a small reception just for close friends. Now go and order some more drinks." Colin went to the bar to order drinks. While he was waiting he glanced at the last edition of the local newspaper and frowned. By this time on Saturday most people had seen the early edition and it was rare for the front page to change.

"May I borrow this for a moment, please," he asked the young man behind the bar.

"Sure," the youth replied, "I'll bring the drinks over to your table." Colin returned to the table, grasping the paper.

"Don't tell me, Colin," Elizabeth laughed, "United scored a late goal in injury time."

"No," Colin said, "but I think you should see this." He thrust the paper in front of Anne.

"I've no glasses with me," she said, "you read it." Colin took a deep breath and read:

Embezzled money claimed by Chief Executive.

"What!" exclaimed Elizabeth.

"That McIntosh has gone completely mad," said Dave.

"You'd better read on," said Anne, with a frown.

Stewart McIntosh, Chief Executive of the borough council, said in a statement released to this paper late today that he would be making a claim on the money embezzled by Nathaniel Sharpe.

Mr. Sharpe is currently in the Infirmary, with his mother by his bedside, unable to walk, following a dramatic fall from the roof of the Market building. He was attempting to flee with money he has misappropriated over years.

"The council feels," wrote Mr. McIntosh, "that, as the money was taken from the traders for infringements of council rules, the proper place for it is in the council's accounts. We will be making a claim to the courts to that effect."

This paper feels that the money should rightfully go back to the traders from whom it was taken, or split between the traders and the council. The role of market

superintendent is in the Chief Executive's hands and we feel that he should accept responsibility for being ignorant of his employee's actions over so many years. This publication has discovered that the Chief Executive did not even know the combination of the safe where Mr. Sharpe kept the records of his ill gotten gains. A dereliction of duty on the part of Mr. McIntosh! Also we have a feeling that many of the so-called infringements may have been "Sharpe" practice by the former market superintendent. As usual, we are happy to receive your comments by letter or by telephone.

A collective groan went up around the table at the pun on Nathaniel's name and Elizabeth laughed.

"Sharpe practice," she grinned, "How corny can you get?"

"It had to come out sometime," Dave replied, "and I doubt that will be the last time we'll hear it."

"Dad and Brendan won't have seen this," Colin said, "They always take home the afternoon edition. Mum and dad are going over to them tonight for a meal."

"I know Mr. Singh won't mind you taking the paper," said Anne, "but what a cheek of McIntosh."

"But we can testify that some of that money was taken without any infringement," Elizabeth said, "He just sort of expected small favours and he got them. I remember when he caught a woman stealing mittens from the stall. He apprehended her and more or less insinuated that he should get a reward. I felt obliged to give him something as he did save us from losing some quite pricey stock. The council isn't entitled to that money. We are."

"And the money he got from the Christmas fly boys," added Anne, "the police were happy to leave them be as long as they weren't selling complete rubbish, but we know Nathaniel used to pressure them into paying him extra, claiming he could make sure they were left alone. I heard him once say to one of the men that he had the power to get him moved on and money changed hands very quickly. Then he walked away with a smirk on his face."

"And we're pretty sure he took back handers from time to time to get people better stalls," said Colin, "but no one could ever prove it."

"I just wonder how long he's been at it," mused Anne, "he's been market superintendent for years now. How much money has he accumulated over the years?"

"I don't know," said Elizabeth, "but the paper said it was thousands and thousands of pounds. I heard that he had at least ten different building society books in towns near and far."

"And there's us," said Colin, nudging Elizabeth, "with just a few miserable pounds put away for our future." Elizabeth blushed.

"Every little counts, Colin," said Anne, "and I'm proud of you both. You've worked hard and honestly. You'll get your reward in time." Elizabeth blushed and Colin leaned over to kiss her cheek.

"It won't take long, love," he whispered into her ear, "then we can get married too."

"Tell me," Dave said, looking at the two young people, "what are you going to do when the time comes for you to take over your respective parent's stalls? I'm not sure white baby clothes will sit comfortably with mucky spuds around." Everyone laughed at the thought.

"Would you like a pound of spuds and a new bib, madam?" Colin said loudly.

"Romper suit and a pound of carrots to match," Elizabeth added. Anne and Dave shook their heads.

"You are a pair," said Anne. The waiter came over to the table.

"Anything else for you?" he asked, "Coffee or tea?" Anne looked at her watch.

"It's almost eleven," she said to Colin, "you'll need to be off soon if you're going to get your bus."

"No," Dave said, "let's have coffee and maybe a liqueur for the ladies, and I'll run him home."

"Four white coffees then, please," Anne said.

"And two Cointreaus," added Elizabeth, "to warm us up before we go."

Across town, in Sharon and Terry's home, Brendan and Molly were also just finishing a meal. They had small-talked about the girls, Dave and Elizabeth, and the forthcoming wedding. Both men had studiously talked about the market, the football results and the weather all night. Dessert had been eaten. The ladies were now getting impatient with their respective husbands.

"I don't care what you say, Brendan," Molly said firmly, "we are not doing the washing up until you and Terry tell us everything. The suspense is killing me."

"I second that, Terry," said Sharon, "you and Brendan have been hugging the news to yourselves since Friday night. You're both up and off before dawn on Saturday and we've been patient long enough. You have to tell us what happened at the solicitor's office that night."

"Fair enough, girls," said Brendan, "but it is only an interim report."

"Yes," added Terry, "the work really begins now and it may take a little time."

"Oh, for goodness sake, get on with it," said Molly, with good humoured impatience.

"Okay," began Brendan, "we met Father Rigby. He had already arranged a meeting with Alan Grey, the elder of the Grey brothers. You should have seen him, Molly, talk about old and dusty like a book on a shelf."

"Get on with it, Brendan," said Molly, punching his arm.

"Okay," he laughed and continued, "It was Wheeler and Blackstone who used to deal with the Shuttleworth family business. All the papers from that time are stored away in a warehouse on the edge of town. But there are ledgers in the office which give details of the files stored away. Mr. Grey had one of his juniors bring them into his office. There were three ledgers covering the time of the Shuttleworths and we all got involved looking through them for the Shuttleworth name."

"I was the one who found the name," interrupted Terry, "and Mr. Grey made a note of the file number. He said he would send two juniors round there first thing on Monday morning to locate the file."

"And the other interesting thing he mentioned, in passing, was that someone tried to get into the container a few months ago," added Brendan, "but they were chased off by the security guards."

"Yes, yes, but what did he think about the letter from Isabel to Sean?" asked Sharon.

"Yes, did he think it was a realistic basis for a claim?" said Molly.

"Sorry, girls," said Brendan, "we should have told you that first. He was intrigued by the letter and fascinated by the story Father Rigby told him about how he had got it. But, yes, he thought there was definitely a claim. He said as soon as we had the file, he could collate all the information and then call us."

"Did he say how long the file would take to locate?" asked Sharon.

"A day, maybe two," Terry said, "was as much as he would say."

"Gosh," said Molly, "can you imagine, the O'Malley brothers actually owning a piece of land?"

"It's hardly an estate, love," said Brendan.

"No," Sharon said, "but value wise, it's better than an estate. It's the prime piece of land in the whole of the town centre. Remember that advertisement we saw last week for plots of land in Rudgefield? They were £1,000 – just for a plot!"

"It's certainly got a value now the new market hall is built on it," laughed Terry, "shall we become landlords or have it demolished?" They all laughed until Brendan held up his hands.

"We're laughing now," he said, "but, we'll have to think very carefully about what happens if, and I say if, Mr. Grey is right. For a start it will be the end of Stewart McIntosh, for sure."

"Aye, and no great loss," said Terry bitterly.

"True, Terry," Brendan went on, "but, do we really see ourselves retiring and collecting rents from our building for the rest of our lives? Or do we sell to the highest bidder? Or -what do we do?"

"Oh, Brendan," Molly said fearfully, "I'd hate it to change us as a family. I mean, it would be nice to have a little nest egg put by for the girl's weddings and maybe a new car- that new Mini you liked was only £560. Oh, and we could go to Ireland to visit the other O'Malleys."

"Oh, yes, Molly," said Sharon breathlessly, "and maybe I could have a new automatic Bendix washer. We couldn't afford 110 guineas last year. And how about buying a TV instead of wasting seven shillings a week on rent?"

"You see," Brendan said to his brother, "we haven't got the money yet- and they've spent half of it!"

"Can't a girl pipe-dream just a little?" Sharon said.

"Of course, Sharon," Brendan said to mollify her, "but I want to be able to hold my head up in this town. I don't want people pointing and staring and saying 'there goes that O'Malley fellow, got a right piece of luck, damn him'. I want people to say 'there go the O'Malley brothers, it's thanks to them that we've got, oh, I don't know, something or other." Brendan scratched his head and looked puzzled.

"I know what you mean, love," Molly said, "well, we could ask folks, once we know what is coming, what they would like in the town to make life a bit better. But please- not a statue."

"Oh, aye," Terry joked, "Brendan and I, holding a cabbage in one hand and a leek in the other, for the entire world to see. Not likely." They all laughed.

"Anyway, only a few more days until we know. Then we can tell the girls. I hate keeping secrets from them;" said Molly, "but Lesley can't keep anything to herself. She came home last week from school with a note from Mr. Sneddon asking me to ring him. When I did, it appears she had been going around telling everyone who would listen that we had a Mafia Godmother sheltering in our house afraid of being murdered. And she was telling everyone that it was a state secret. Mr. Sneddon was most concerned until I put him right. Mrs Sharpe only stayed one night and Lesley wasn't even there." Sharon began laughing until the tears ran down her face, and before long everyone was in stitches.

"Hallo," said a voice from the doorway, "want to share the joke?"

"Come in, Colin," said Terry, "we were laughing about Lesley telling her mates at school about Mrs. Sharpe staying overnight at Molly's house. Apparently they were harbouring a blood member of a criminal gang, the way she told it."

"Well, it's ironic you should be mentioning that particular family, dad," Colin said, putting the late edition paper on the table in front of them all, "have you seen that?" Brendan picked it up and read the front page article out to the others.

"The bare-faced cheek of the man," said Molly.

"The sooner he is thrown out of office the better," added Sharon.

"Does he have a valid point?" asked Terry, "could he really claim the money? Is that fair?"

"Not for at least ninety per cent of the money Sharpe has taken off the traders over the years," said Brendan, "but proving it is going to be a moot point."

"And depending on how long he's been at it," added Terry, "can *you* remember all the traders that have been on the market over the last twenty years?"

"I doubt whether even Nathaniel Sharpe would remember, but the council must have records somewhere," said Molly.

"The traders will just have to find a fair way of distributing the money," said Sharon, "that's if we get hold of it. A judge might agree with McIntosh and say it belongs to the council."

"I'd fight him tooth and nail," said Terry, "and so would all the traders. We know we've been cheated by Sharpe. McIntosh sat in his ivory tower and knew nothing, and cared less, about what was going on in the market hall."

"It explains all the different boys Nathaniel has employed over the years though, doesn't it?" said Brendan, "he must have been terrified one of them would guess what he was up to. None of them lasted long. We all assumed that they couldn't stand the bloke, or were really bad at the job. Now this fraud puts a different light on it."

"It all seems very strange, doesn't it?" Molly said as she looked around the room, "a few weeks ago we were just two market trading families, making do, not going short of anything, content with our lives. Now," she spread her hands wide, "we could be land owners and challengers in a money fraud case. It's all a bit scary, don't you think?" Brendan went across to his wife and put his arm around her shoulder.

"No matter what happens, Molly, love," he said, "we will be family through it and after it. Are we all agreed on that? No one comes between the O'Malleys even if we lose the blooming lot." Every head nodded and Brendan, Terry and Colin shook hands across the room.

"Thanks, everyone," Molly said, with a tear in her eye, "Now, it's time we were off home to bed."

Chapter 21

Police Commissioner Campbell entered the Town Hall, unannounced and accompanied by Inspector Pope and asked to speak to the deputy Chief Executive. He had received them innocently enough.

"Commissioner Campbell," said Richard Day, with a smile, as he rose and went to shake the Commissioner's hand, "delighted to see you again. To what do I owe the honour?" Campbell shook his hand.

"You know Inspector Pope?" he said.

"Of course," replied Day, "he's doing sterling work on the Nathaniel Sharpe case. But surely, that doesn't warrant a visit from you?"

"No, Mr. Day," said the Commissioner, "more serious than that. It concerns Stewart McIntosh."

Richard Day looked puzzled.

"Please," he said, "sit down." The police officers sat and Commissioner Campbell nodded towards the door.

"May we have the door closed?" he said, "This is confidential." Richard Day went to close the door, and called through to his personal assistant.

"No calls, Christine," he said, "and we are not to be disturbed under any circumstances." He returned to his desk.

"You'd better tell me what this is all about," Day said.

"I've been approached by a barrister in Manchester," began the Commissioner, "with a very serious allegation against Mr. McIntosh. It would appear that McIntosh knew, some time ago, that the land, on which the new market hall has been built, was not the council's land to build on."

"What!" exclaimed Day, "not council land. That's preposterous."

"There is evidence," Campbell continued, "and I have seen some of it, that the land belongs to one of your own town's people and at some stage McIntosh discovered this to be the case and he covered up the fact." Richard Day held up his hands.

"Hang on, Commissioner," he said, "let me grasp this. You are saying that someone in this town owns the land?"

"Yes, Mr. Day," replied the Commissioner.

"Then why in God's name didn't they come forward and claim the land once the mines were closed and the houses demolished. Everyone for miles knew the plans for the site. It was no secret."

"Because, Mr. Day," said the Commissioner quietly, "the owner did not know until recently that he *was* the owner of the land. But someone who works in this very building discovered that McIntosh was concealing the true ownership of the land. That person began investigations through a second party. The second party got most of the facts uncovered and the true owner now knows that the land is his."

"Can I interrupt, Commissioner," Richard Day said, "must we keep talking about parties and true owners? Am I to know who the real owner is?"

"Yes," replied Campbell, "but I must insist that you keep the name to yourself. The barrister in question is concerned that as few people know as possible.

The man, who owns the land, by inheritance, is Brendan O'Malley." Richard Day sat back in his chair and shook his head. Then he smiled.

"You have no idea, Commissioner," said Day, "how ironic that name is. Of all the people in this town it has to be Brendan O'Malley."

"I don't understand," Commissioner Campbell said, "you obviously know him."

"Know him?" said Day, "the new market hall was his idea. I remember he came to a meeting once when there was some dispute about the allocation of stalls. He took on Nathaniel Sharpe in front of the council and suggested that the old place wasn't big enough. 'Why not build a new hall?' he said to the whole council. We all sat there and watched the pound signs rolling round in McIntosh's eye balls. Our Chief Executive couldn't believe it. And it turns out O'Malley owns the land. It's unbelievable." It was Inspector Pope's turn to smile.

"It seems that Mr. O'Malley, Mr. McIntosh and Nathaniel Sharpe's lives are inextricably linked."

"Yes," said Richard Day with a wry smile, "and I bet they've never even had a drink together."

"Well," said the Commissioner, "that's as may be, but, back to business. We need to approach Mr. McIntosh today. That's why we are here in your office. It's important that he's not allowed to take any documents from this building. We need you to accompany us to his office and take from him whatever keys and passes he has. Then he can accompany us to the station for an interview."

"Right," said Day, "follow me." The three men left Day's office and ascended the one floor to the penthouse suite.

"Should I knock?" said Day to the Inspector, as he walked briskly past an astonished Mary.

"Not necessary," replied Inspector Pope. For the first time in his life, Richard Day walked unannounced into Stewart McIntosh's office. McIntosh was indulging himself with coffee and a huge cream bun. He almost choked as he saw his Deputy walking in followed by two officers in uniform.

"My God, Day," McIntosh spluttered as he reached for his coffee cup and swilled down the flaky pastry, "you could have knocked." Commissioner Campbell closed the door and nodded at Inspector Pope.

"Stewart McIntosh?" said Inspector Pope in his most official voice. McIntosh had risen from his seat and brushed down his trousers.

"Of course it's me, Pope," he said, "and I see you have the Commissioner with you." He was half way round his huge desk with one hand outstretched to greet the most distinguished of his three visitors. Campbell took one step backwards and allowed Inspector Pope to come between the advancing Chief Executive and himself.

"We'd like you to accompany us to the station, Mr. McIntosh," intoned Pope, "to help us with our inquiries."

"What?" McIntosh blustered, "what am I supposed to have done?"

"You'll find out in due course, Mr. McIntosh," Campbell said from over Pope's shoulder, "but it concerns the validity of the ownership of the land the new market hall has been built on." McIntosh stopped in his tracks. His face turned red and he began to perspire. Then he clutched his chest. He staggered backwards and put one hand on his desk to steady himself.

"Save the histrionics, McIntosh," snapped Inspector Pope as he stepped forward to take McIntosh by the arm. The intended subject of his grasp slipped gently downwards to the floor, and the three men watched as his normally ruddy face turn white.

"Oh, my God," Richard Day shouted, "is he having a heart attack?" Commissioner Campbell opened the door and shouted to Mary.

"Get a first-aider and call an ambulance, quick as you can, young lady." The man on the floor was moaning and Inspector Pope knelt by him and loosened his tie. A little colour returned to McIntosh's face and his eye lids fluttered. They watched as his head began to rock from side to side, then he was perfectly still.

"Someone needs a first-aider?" said one of the porters, entering the room.

"Yes, here," said Commissioner Campbell and he pointed to the prostate McIntosh. The man knelt down and examined McIntosh carefully then he stood up.

"He fainted, as far as I can tell," he said, "his heart is beating normally. Did he bang his head?"

"I don't think so," said Day, "he sort of slipped down the desk to the floor."

"Might have been high blood pressure," the first-aider commented, "Has he had some bad news?"

"Thank you," said Commissioner Campbell; pointedly ignoring the man's question, "we'll have him taken to hospital for a check up, just in case." The man knew he was being dismissed.

"My pleasure, officer," he said on his way out. Mary was standing by the open door to McIntosh's office.

"The ambulance will be here in four minutes, sir," she said, "will Mr. McIntosh be all right?"

"Absolutely fine, I'm sure," replied Inspector Pope, "but as you are here, perhaps you can help us locate Mr. McIntosh's keys for the office and his pass to get into the building. He won't need them for a while. Mr. Day will be taking charge from now on."

"The keys are in his jacket pocket," Mary said as she pointed to the hanger on the back of the door, "and he refused to carry a security pass, he said it was beneath him, as Chief Executive." Richard Day smiled and confirmed that. Commissioner Campbell reached over to McIntosh's jacket and removed the keys there.

"Can you take any key belonging to council premises," he said to Mary, "and we'll make sure Mrs. McIntosh gets the rest. Please phone her and tell her that her husband is being taken to hospital and be sure she knows it is not serious." He had glanced sideways at McIntosh as he spoke and saw the man's eyes fluttering open. McIntosh was conscious and he was listening to every word.

"And it might be a good idea to let Mrs. McIntosh know that her husband will be needing the services of a very good lawyer," Campbell added, "who can meet us at the Police Station as soon as we've had Mr. McIntosh examined in Casualty." A groan came from the floor and four pairs of eyes looked down. Stewart McIntosh knew that his ploy was not going to work and he decided to recover. He got himself into a sitting position, his legs splayed out like a baby in a nappy.

"Would you help me, Richard," he said, holding out one pudgy hand. Richard Day grasped the Chief Executive's hand and hauled McIntosh upwards.

"You can cancel the ambulance, I think," said McIntosh, "I suppose I just fainted."

"It can happen to anyone," said Commissioner Campbell, hiding a smile. He nodded to Mary to confirm that the ambulance could be cancelled.

"Your jacket, sir," said Inspector Pope, as he handed the garment to McIntosh. McIntosh put on the jacket and followed Pope out of the office. Campbell brought up the rear.

"Well," said Mary, "that was an episode I never thought I'd see."

"There's going to be trouble if what Commissioner Campbell says is true," said Day.

"About Brendan O'Malley owning the land?" said Mary. Richard Day frowned.

"Were you listening at the door?" he said. Mary's face turned bright red.

"No, Mr. Day, I wasn't listening," she said, "but I was the one who first heard McIntosh and Wilson talking about the land. He'd left his intercom on and I'd gone to the ladies. When I came back I heard everything. It was me that started the ball rolling, so to speak."

"Jim Wilson is involved as well?" said Day, "Why didn't you come to me, Mary?"

"I wasn't sure *how* many people in the council hierarchy knew about it, Mr. Day. But most of all I was afraid I'd get the sack," said Mary, "I'm sorry."

"Well, that doesn't matter now," said Day, "but it's good you know, because I'm going to need someone very discreet to take minutes of meetings concerning this matter over the next few days. You are perfect for the job."

"Thank you, sir," said Mary.

"And the first one will have to be an immediate meeting with Jim Wilson," said Day, "can you call him up here in fifteen minutes exactly, but don't say I'm in charge. Just ask him to report to Mr. McIntosh's office. And get Mr. Greenwood up here before him. Tell him it's an emergency."

"Yes, sir," said Mary with alacrity. Councillor Greenwood had been briefed by the time Mary glanced at her watch. Jim Wilson was due in one minute. Richard Day popped his head round the door.

"Let him in and then follow him with your shorthand pad and a pencil, Mary," he said. When Jim Wilson arrived in Mary's outer office he was smiling. He didn't think he had a care in the world.

"Go right in, Mr. Wilson," Mary said, "he's expecting you." Jim Wilson gave a cursory tap on the door and went inside. Mary followed him. Without any preliminary greeting, Richard Day went straight for Jim Wilson's proverbial jugular.

"Tell me what part you played in concealing the fact that Brendan O'Malley owns the land the new market hall has been built on. And don't lie or filibuster, Wilson. McIntosh is right now helping the police with their inquiries. So far, they don't know you are involved, but I do. Spit it out-now!" Jim Wilson hesitated for only a few seconds.

"It's true," he said, "I was the one who found the plans with a note attached. The site had been cleared by then and the contractors ready to start. I brought the plans to Stewart and told him what I'd found. He destroyed the note and even went as far as hiring some petty criminal to try and get at the original documents in the storage depot. The man was chased off by security guards. But, how did you find out?"

"Let's just say you weren't as careful as you should have been," said Day quietly, "you might have got away with it but for someone who shall remain anonymous." Mary threw him a grateful look as she scribbled away on her shorthand pad.

"You'll want my resignation," Wilson said, and it was not a question.

"Immediately," replied Day, "and I suggest that you get down to the police station as soon as you can. Confess everything and they might go easy on you. As I said, the police don't know yet that you are involved but I wouldn't put it past McIntosh to drop you right in the mire. I don't see him as the type to take the blame for everything by himself."

"I'm sorry," mumbled Wilson, "if McIntosh had reacted differently and done the honourable thing, I wouldn't have persuaded him differently. But, you know how he is. If I'd gone against him, I'd have been out of a job in no time."

"Don't make excuses, Wilson," Day said sharply, "you had a choice. You made the wrong one. Take the consequences." Wilson merely nodded.

"Mary," Richard Day looked from the stricken face of Jim Wilson to the secretary, "will you call security and ask them to escort Mr. Wilson from the building. Oh, and you'd better call Personnel. We need to be getting replacements. Two senior members of the organisation are not going to be easy to replace. But we must." Mary nodded and left the room. Jim Wilson followed her and sat slumped by her desk until security arrived and took him away. As Mary typed up the notes of the extraordinary event that had taken place just minutes ago she felt a massive sense of relief. At last everything was exposed and she no longer felt in some curious way responsible for the wrong that had been done to Brendan O'Malley. Other people would now take charge and make sure he got his land, or at least some compensation for it. When it was finished she did something she hadn't done for a long time. She made a personal call out of the office to Father Rigby. He answered the phone on the fourth ring.

"Father Rigby," came the familiar voice.

"Good morning, Father, Mary here, from the council," she said.

"You have some news?" he asked.

"Yes, Stewart McIntosh has been taken away by the police," she said, "and Jim Wilson has been sacked and told to go there himself and confess everything before McIntosh incriminates him."

"Wonderful news," Father Rigby replied, "at last, justice is being done. And it's all thanks to you."

"Well," said Mary, "I only wish I'd come to you sooner, Father. I shouldn't have waited so long."

"Nonsense, Mary," Father Rigby replied, "You came to me just in time. If I hadn't been going on retreat days after you told me, it might have taken much longer for events to unfold."

"He works in strange ways, doesn't He?" Mary said.

"You can be sure of that, Mary," said Father Rigby with a chuckle.

The statement from the council to the Press was short and succinct. Mary had taken great delight in typing it and phoning it through to the paper.

"The Council wishes to inform the town that Chief Executive Stewart McIntosh and Planning Officer Jim Wilson are helping the police with inquiries into a matter arising from the building of the new Market Hall. It is not anticipated that they will return to their former duties in this town. The council also wishes everyone to know that the market traders are free to move into the new market hall as soon as is practicable. The rents to be paid will remain as they are at present. Any rent increases will be negotiated in due course with representatives of the traders." Within five minutes the Editor was on the line to her extension.

"Can I have an appointment with Richard Day, Mary" he said, "I take it that he's taking over the running of the council?"

"He is," Mary replied, "but he's got a series of urgent meetings all day, as you can imagine. As soon as he is free, I'll get him to call you."

"Please do," replied the Editor, "this sounds like a big, big, story. I want to be the first to run it."

He put the phone down. Mary chuckled to herself, then collected her pad and pencil and went into Richard Day's office. Life had never been so exciting.

Chapter 22

"You look fabulous, mum," said Elizabeth as Anne twirled around in her new outfit.

"Not a wee bit baggy around the bum?" said Elizabeth with a frown.

"You haven't got one, mum," Elizabeth laughed out loud, "in fact if getting married makes every girl lose weight the way you have, I'm surprised they don't do it more often."

"Once is usually enough," said Anne primly, "for most people."

"I know," Elizabeth replied, "but circumstances aren't always normal, are they?" Anne hugged her daughter tightly.

"You'll put creases down the front," said Elizabeth into her mother's shoulder.

"Come on," said Anne, after a moment, "let me get this back into the wardrobe. Only one more night and I'll be Mrs. Dave Watson." She twisted the wedding ring, which Mo had given her many years ago, and it came off.

"That's the first time since I married Mo that I've taken this off," said Anne, "and I'd like you to wear it, Elizabeth. But not on your wedding finger, please."

"I've got a lovely gold chain in my box," Elizabeth replied, "I'll wear it round my neck."

"Are you out with Colin tonight?" said Anne casually.

"Not tonight, mum," Elizabeth said, "I thought I'd like to spend the night with you. It'll be my last night as well. What's for dinner?"'

"A very special curry, with pineapples," replied Anne, "come on, you can help me make it."

Elizabeth was thinking ahead to the day when she and Colin would walk down the aisle and she would change her name- from Patel to O'Malley. Before bed, the two women hugged each other very closely.

"You know, Elizabeth," Anne whispered, "that you will always be first in my heart. The love I have for Dave is very different to the love I'll always have for you."

"I know, mum," Elizabeth whispered back, "I know. Now, sleep well, we've a busy day ahead."

The next day dawned bright, clear and the sky gave a hint of warmth to come. When she woke, Anne lay in bed watching the tiny clouds gambolling like lambs across the sky.

"Perfect," she murmured. She glanced at the clock. It was seven fifteen. She rolled right across the bed from the window side to the other and then giggled.

"I won't be able to do that after tonight," she said, slipping on her battered sandals.

"And you'll have to go too," she spoke sternly to her footwear, "I think some fluffy pink ones are called for."

"They'll lock you away," Elizabeth's voice came from the other side of the door, "talking to your shoes. Open up, I've got a tray right outside." Anne opened the door and smiled.

"What are you doing up so early," she said.

"Preparing a wedding breakfast for my mum," said Elizabeth, "although it's only orange juice, toast and a soft boiled egg. At least I hope it's soft boiled. Back into bed, please." Anne did as she was told and took the tray. Elizabeth darted back out of the room and came back clutching a handful of envelopes.

"And these are for you, too," she said, "but eat the egg before it goes cold."

"Wonderful, darling," said Anne, "just what the doctor ordered."

"I'll go and make tea while you open your cards," Elizabeth said, picking up the tray. Anne began to open the envelopes. The first three were from fellow market traders. The next one was from Mr. Singh. Inside, in the most perfect script, he had written, *"May your future days be as happy as today."* With best regards from the Singh family. Anne felt a tear start and she sighed as she wiped it away. The next card had a type written envelope and a London postmark. She turned it over and over before opening it. It was a stylish wedding card and inside was written: "With all good wishes on your day, Jonathon Smythe."

"Elizabeth," she called out.

"Coming, mum," her daughter called back and Anne heard her steps.

"I've had a card from Jonathon Smythe," she said incredulously, "how on earth he knew I was getting married again I really cannot imagine."

"I told him," Elizabeth said unceremoniously.

"When?" asked Anne.

"He rang the house a couple of weeks ago. I told him then and he said he would send a card. So I kept quiet just in case he forgot. That was nice of him, wasn't it?"

"But what did he ring about, Elizabeth?" Anne asked perplexed.

"Oh, yes," said Elizabeth, "he wanted to tell you that Basil and his wife are having a baby girl and they are to call her Anne, after you. Mr Smythe said they would send a photo soon." Anne smiled.

"So, if Mr. Smythe had forgotten the card, I've never have known about baby Anne?" she said.

"But he didn't forget, mum," said Elizabeth, "and anyway the photo would have arrived." Anne shook her head.

"Who are the other cards from?" Elizabeth asked. Anne passed over the ones she had opened.

"I haven't finished," she said, "they can't all have come today; the post doesn't come until nine."

"No," said Elizabeth, "I've been collecting them for a week. I thought it would be nice for you to have them all together this morning." The next two were from the O'Malley families and even young Lesley had painstakingly written her name on the card - in six different colours. The last one was from Dave and Anne didn't pass it to Elizabeth. It was too personal. Elizabeth saw her mother smile a smile she hadn't seen before.

"Who's that one from?" she asked, holding out her hand.

"It's from Dave," replied Anne, "and for my eyes only. Sorry, love." She saw Elizabeth's face drop and suddenly felt guilty. This was the first time she had kept anything from her daughter.

"What time is the hair dresser coming?" Anne asked in a light voice.

"Ten o'clock on the dot," said Elizabeth, "we'd better get a move on. I'll run your bath."

By eleven o'clock both women were dressed in their finest and they had half an hour before the taxi, bearing Mr. Singh, arrived to take them to the registrar in the Town Hall. Anne was elegant in a cream silk suit and pale green blouse which she knew enhanced her skin tones. A tiny feathery confection perched atop the swept up burnished copper hair. Elizabeth had been allowed to choose her outfit and had swooped on a rose coloured damask shift dress with a tiny jacket. She refused to wear a hat but had her hair pinned up with one flower at the back. There was a knock at the door.

"If that's the taxi, he's early," said Elizabeth, "I'll go." She came back with the biggest bouquet of roses either woman had ever seen.

"They're for you, mum," said Elizabeth. Anne took the card from the top of the flowers and read it out loud.

"Life may not always be a bed of roses, Anne, but we will always smell the perfume, see the colours and touch the softness - together. With all my love, Dave." Anne's eyes filled up and so did Elizabeth's.

"Don't cry, mum," Elizabeth said, "or you'll set me off too, how romantic."

"I'm so lucky," whispered Anne.

"You deserve to be happy," Elizabeth replied, hugging her, despite the roses between them. Another knock at the door disturbed them and this time it was Mr. Singh. He came into the hallway, resplendent in his national costume. The silks and brocades were multi coloured and in perfect harmony. He looked magnificent. He raised his hands together in greeting and bowed.

"My goodness," he said, "you are like two princesses." Elizabeth and Anne gave him a traditional Indian greeting in return and giggled like school girls.

"You are too kind, Mr. Singh," said Anne, who, like most English women, did not know how to accept a compliment.

"Come, come," said Mr. Singh, "your taxi awaits." He stepped outside onto the pavement and gave Anne his arm to assist her.

"Oh," she said, stopping, one foot still inside the house, "what a magnificent car."

"It belongs to a friend of mine," Mr Singh replied proudly, "and he himself is driving you today. It's a Rolls Royce."

"It's bigger than our kitchen," said Elizabeth over her mother's shoulder, "quick, let me in." All the neighbours, standing on their door steps, applauded as they both stepped into the car.

"Good luck," one shouted.

"Keep him waiting two minutes, no more," laughed another.

"Wave to them, mum," Elizabeth said, as she raised her hand in greeting. Anne raised her hand and gave an embarrassed wave. The car purred forward and within minutes was pulling up outside the Town Hall. The market was trading on Saturday, but it didn't stop many of the workers leaving their stalls and congregating outside to wave, cheer and stamp their feet as Anne stepped out of the car. Butcher's aprons, fish monger's white hats, floral overalls, all were flapped and waved in greeting. Anne waved back, happy to see the familiar faces.

"See you tonight," many called out and she nodded back. The small gathering she had wanted had grown over the weeks, but now she was glad she would be able to share her happiness with them. Colin was waiting at the entrance to the Town Hall; he would escort Elizabeth today. Lesley was to be bridesmaid, and was holding Molly's hand and asking a million questions. Sharon was chatting with Barbara and Michelle. Colin looked decidedly uncomfortable in a suit, white shirt and tie and was tugging and pulling at the knot around his neck. Elizabeth giggled as he came up to her.

"Come here," she said, "let me loosen it a little." He took advantage while her hands were occupied round his neck to lean forward and kiss her.

"This will be us as soon as we can," he whispered into her ear, risking a nibble of her lobe.

"People are watching, Colin," she reprimanded, but she was smiling, "is Dave here?"

"In the room already," said Colin with a grin, "and looking so relaxed I can't believe it."

Anne walked ahead, on the arm of Mr. Singh, Lesley behind them, Colin and Elizabeth fell into step behind Lesley. Mrs. Singh and her two daughters followed with the O'Malleys. As they entered the room where the wedding ceremony was to take place, Dave stepped towards Anne and gathered her in his arms. He whispered something in her ear and she kissed his cheek while whispering back. The registrar, after a moment, coughed gently and asked Anne and Dave to step to one side with him to complete the pre-ceremony formalities. He then turned to the small gathering and called them together. The marriage took place and no one missed a word as Anne and Dave spoke their vows with conviction and commitment.

"You may kiss the bride," the registrar said and Elizabeth burst into tears. Colin searched for a handkerchief and gave it to her.

"You women are soppy," he said, "I've never understood why you all cry when you're happy."

"Neither have I," said Elizabeth with a huge grin, "maybe it's in our genes." The register was signed and the happy couple made their way out of the office.

"Congratulations, Mrs. Watson," Elizabeth said as she hugged her mother.

"Thank you, Elizabeth," Anne said, "but I'm still mum to you."

"You looked splendid," Colin said to Dave, "but these suits are a pain in the neck, aren't they?" He tugged once more at his wayward tie. Dave laughed.

"Come on," he said to the assembled guests, "let's go and eat, I'm starving."

"No breakfast this morning?" Anne asked.

"Too nervous," he replied, with a grin, "but Rover ate for both of us." As they reached the steps of the Town Hall he whistled loudly.

"What's this?" he said, looking at the Rolls Royce, parked right in front.

"My carriage for the day," Anne said, "compliments of Mr. Singh."

"Very nice," said Dave appreciatively, "and no more than you deserve." He opened the door of the car; made sure she was settled and went round to get in the other side.

"Perfect," Anne said dreamily.

"We're here," Dave said, breaking into her reverie.

"Welcome, Mr and Mrs Watson," the manager of the hotel said, "and congratulations from the staff of Park Lodge. We hope to make your day even more special," he glanced at the Rolls Royce parked outside, "if that's possible." They were a small gathering and the men folk were outnumbered. The Singh daughters and the O'Malley girls chattered away about different wedding traditions. They discussed the dresses they would wear and impulsively invited each other to their weddings.

"We've got to find a man first," giggled Barbara to Michelle.

"We don't have that problem," said Meena Singh, "our mother and father will do all that for us."

"Lucky you," said Michelle, "any chance of finding one for me? Preferably rich and very good looking." They all giggled. Mr. Singh made a shushing sound to his daughters.

"Quietly, girls," he said. He turned to Anne, seated on his left, "I'll be glad to see them settled," he said.

"They are so beautiful," Anne replied, "will you be arranging their marriages soon?"

"Yes, and no," Mr. Singh said. Anne raised her eyebrows.

"They will be found husbands, Anne," Mr. Singh continued, "but they must also like and respect them before I'll sign a contract. That's only fair, isn't it?" Anne nodded.

"It would never have happened in my day," Mrs. Singh spoke across Dave to her husband, "I think you are being too soft on them. They have to learn."

"Not every man is as good as I am," Mr. Singh laughed, "and I love them too much to see them unhappy. Besides, we have seen that other ways can be as good as our own."

"You've lived here too long," said Mrs Singh, shaking her head.

"My wife is very old fashioned," said Mr. Singh to Dave, "but a dutiful woman."

"Don't you believe it," said Mrs. Singh to Dave quietly, "but he's right in one thing. I do have a husband that I have grown to love and respect very much. But I still say it was my parent's good fortune first - in finding him. Not mine."

In the evening they moved into a room where a D.J. was selecting records and a buffet had been laid out on the side tables.

"Don't touch that food;" said Molly as Lesley made a bee line for the tables, "It's for much later when the people who have been working arrive."

"I've been working, mum," protested Lesley, "it is not easy being a bridesmaid, you know."She fingered the tiny gold locket around her neck that had been Anne and Dave's gift to her.

"Yes, Lesley," said Molly, also looking at the locket, "and you've been paid handsomely. Leave the food alone." Guests began arriving and Anne and Dave were overwhelmed by greetings and gifts. Terry, Brendan and Molly were almost the first there.

"How did you get away so early?" said Molly.

"Dee is the one who managed that," Brendan chuckled, "she had a huge banner draped across the stall saying' *'We've a wedding party to go to- so shop here first!"*

"Well done, Dee," said Molly, "now, come this way, Sharon has saved a table for us."

"Don't you want some privacy?" Dee said, "I know you'll be talking about the trip to Ireland."

"Dee," Molly answered, "you're as much family as anyone in this room, and you know it." Dee coloured ever so slightly but followed Molly willingly. The O'Malley adults were soon around the table, glasses of Buck's Fizz in their hands.

"Can we drink this up and get something else?" said Brendan with a grimace.

"I'll second that," said Terry.

"Oh, give it here, you philistines," said Sharon, "honest, you'd think it was poison. You might have to get used to the champagne life soon."

"God forbid that day ever happens," said Molly.

"Did I hear my boss's name called?" said a voice from behind her shoulder.

"Father Rigby," laughed Molly, "I didn't know you had arrived. I wasn't blaspheming, honestly."

"I know, I know," he said, "May I join you here?"

"Please do, Father," said Sharon, "Terry, will you get Father Rigby a drink while you are going."

"A pint, please," said Father Rigby to Terry, looking askance at the champagne and orange juice.

"Right," said Terry, getting up from his seat, "three pints of best bitter."

"Are you all ready for Monday?" said Father Rigby, looking at Molly and Brendan.

"We are, Father," replied Brendan, "and we'll be glad to have your company. We neither of us have been to Ireland and we're glad you know where we're going. It will make life easier for us."

"It's hardly a foreign country," said Colin, who had sat, with Elizabeth, at the end of the table.

"Wait until you hear the natives speak," said Father Rigby, "you've to take time tuning in to the accent and, believe me, after a day or so, you find yourself adopting the brogue as if you were born there. But, they know you weren't."

"Where are you going first?" asked Dee.

"To the convent," replied Father Rigby, "I'm sure I can persuade Mother Superior to let in a couple of lay people. She'll be dying to know the news. I've written to let her know we're coming."

"Will I have cousins and things over there?" piped up Lesley.

"Possibly," said Brendan, "but we're not sure."

"Can I go there for holidays if you find some?" asked Lesley. The adults laughed.

"You may not even like them," said Elizabeth, "families aren't all like yours, you know. They might not like you when they meet you."

"Not like *me*?" Lesley replied, as if the idea was preposterous, "why on earth not?" The whole table laughed and Lesley looked crestfallen.

"Come here, darling child," said Terry, "and give your uncle a big hug. I don't care if the whole world doesn't like you, I always will." Lesley ran to Terry and jumped on his knee.

"Mind the beer," he said, "there is love and there is spilling a man's beer."

"Can I taste it?" said Lesley with a grin.

"No!" exclaimed Molly, "you can't, no alcohol until you're eighteen."

"It's a pity you are going to miss the beginning of Nathaniel's trial," said Dee.

"Well," said Brendan, "Terry and Sharon will be there, we'll keep in touch by phone and please, keep all the papers for us. I want to read them. But we can't put off this trip; we've tickets and accommodation reserved."

"And I'm staying with Terry and Sharon and Colin," said Lesley, "who has promised to play his guitar just for me."

"You two had better keep the place tidy," Molly said to her two elder daughters.

"Mum," said Michelle and Barbara together, with a simultaneous groan.

"Sorry," said Molly sheepishly, "I know the house will be perfect when I get back."

"Well," said Barbara, "I wouldn't go that far."

The DJ tapped his microphone in time honoured tradition: "One, two, one two."

"Your attention, please," he said, "The bride and groom will now lead the dancing." Anne and Dave took to the floor and the whole room applauded as the song began to play Louis Armstrong's "What a Wonderful World."

"Oh, you women," said Colin as handkerchiefs were dabbed to eyes once more.

Chapter 23

When Molly set foot on Irish soil, her heart beat faster.

"Oh, Brendan," she said, clutching her husband's arm, "do you feel it? Do you smell it? Can you taste it?" Brendan smiled.

"It's me that has the Irish blood, Molly," he said, "but yes, I do. It feels different to England."

"I believe you're captivated already," said Father Rigby, "and not two minutes in the place."

"It's definitely different," said Molly dreamily, "I feel that here you could be at peace."

"Yes, well, we can be at peace when we have found The Patrick Hotel," replied Father Rigby, "and got ourselves settled in. We've a long drive tomorrow if we're to make the convent at a reasonable hour." They ate well in the Hotel restaurant and went to bed early.

The following morning they checked out of the hotel and went to collect their hire car. Molly sat in the back and watched intently as Brendan navigated his way through Dun Laoghaire and took the road South towards Kilkenny. They stopped for a pub lunch and Father Rigby asked Molly if she'd heard from Terry about Nathaniel's trial.

"Yes, Father," said Molly, "Terry said there was not much happening yesterday, but Nathaniel has changed. All his hair, and there isn't much of it, has turned completely white. He's lost all his self confidence. Maybe it's because he only has half a leg now. Terry said his eyes were almost empty, except when he looked at his mother. Then it was as if he was afraid. Terry found it odd and a bit creepy."

"Well," said Brendan, "that's hardly surprising, is it? He was going to murder her. I'm only amazed he can look her in the eye at all."

"Yes, but he said she was acting like royalty," said Molly, "waving gloved hands at people and whispering to the barrister as if they were bosom buddies. She's been spending money around town, too."

"So, how far did they get?" said Father Rigby.

"They read out the indictment," said Molly, "and that took forever. Terry said the people in the public gallery kept 'oh-ing' and 'ah-ing' so often, the Judge had to ask them to be quiet."

"Nathaniel's been stealing from you all for a long time, hasn't he?" said Father Rigby.

"Since he took over from Herbert Walker," said Molly, "it was confirmed he was Nathaniel's real dad."

"So," said Brendan, "they actually said that in court. I wonder how Mrs. Sharpe took that."

"Brazened it out," said Molly, "as if she had a valid excuse for being unfaithful to her husband."

"What happens next?" asked Father Rigby.

"Nathaniel's solicitor has asked that Nathaniel go into the witness box first. He's going to plead guilty as charged but Terry thinks the solicitor is going to try and make the jury feel sorry for him," said Molly.

"Sorry he's lost half his leg," said Brendan bitterly, "or sorry he got caught?"

"The Judge said he would decide tomorrow," said Molly, "so we'll have to wait and see."

"Anything else?"said Father Rigby eagerly.

"Only that Stewart McIntosh will be called to give evidence," said Molly, "but that won't be for a few days. He's in serious trouble with the land business though. He's a shadow of himself, Terry says, and he's been barred from the golf club."

"I bet that hurt him more than anything," said Brendan.

"We'd better get on," said Father Rigby, checking his watch, "I'll drive now." He took the road to Tipperary. Molly couldn't help singing, 'It's a long, long way to Tipperary', much to the amusement of the men. They stopped one more time for a drink and to check their route and then the signs for Tralee began. Soon they were on the road to the Convent and Molly began to ask questions.

"Will they know we are coming, Father?"

"Yes, Molly," he replied, "I wrote and said we'd be here today, sometime."

"Will they let us, that is, Brendan and me, in?"

"I'm hoping so," the priest replied, "I'm sure they will. It's not as if you are heathens, is it?"

"Will we be able to talk to Sister Marie Julie that was an O'Malley?"

"I don't know about that," Father Rigby replied patiently, as Molly had asked all these questions before, "but I'm hoping you can at least see her." The Convent was suddenly in front of them. Father Rigby parked the car.

"Come on," he said, "I know the drill." They approached the huge door and the priest rang the bell. They all heard the rosary beads and the gentle flip flop of sandals on the pathway. The tiny grille opened and a nun nodded to Father Rigby.

"We're here to see Mother Superior," he said, "I wrote to say we were coming today. She is expecting us." The door opened.

"Easy," said Father Rigby. They followed the nun into the convent and to the door Father Rigby recognised as Mother Superiors. The nun knocked twice and then came the first surprise. A deep bass voice said: "Come." Father Rigby looked at his companions.

"That's definitely not her voice," he said as he opened the door, letting Molly go through first. She was met by the sight of a tall, thin, distinguished looking man, dressed in the purple of a bishop.

"Mrs. Brendan O'Malley, I take it?" the bishop said, as he moved forward to greet her. Molly wasn't sure whether to shake his hand or bend her knee and kiss his ring.

"Don't worry about tradition, Mrs. O'Malley," he smiled at her and held out his hand.

"Thank you," Molly said as she shook his hand.

"You must be Mr. Brendan O'Malley" the bishop said, "as you're not wearing a dog collar." Brendan shook his hand.

"Father Rigby," the bishop said. Father Rigby couldn't help himself. A lifetime of obedience took over. He dropped to one knee, took the bishop's hand, kissed his ring and whispered: "Your Excellency."

"Please, Mr and Mrs O'Malley," take a seat," the bishop said, "tea and biscuits are on their way. Will you sit beside me, Father?" The visitors were bemused. They weren't expecting a bishop. They followed his directions and were seated when there was a knock at the door.

"Come," the bishop said. A nun entered with a tea trolley. The china rattled as the castors navigated the old oak parquet flooring.

"Thank you, sister," the bishop said, "We'll manage now." The nun bowed her head to acknowledge the bishop and left the room.

"Will you pour, Mrs O'Malley?" the bishop said, "and then we can begin." Once they had tea, the bishop sat back in Mother Superior's chair.

"I'm not going to pretend this is easy," he began, "but, these things happen. After your visit, Father Rigby, I had a call from Mother Superior. She told me she wished to discuss a matter of importance, but not urgency. I foolishly thought one of the nuns was thinking of leaving the order and wanted some guidance. It was two weeks before I could visit her. When I arrived here, she made a full confession to me." Molly gasped and put down her cup and saucer.

"Before you think I am breaking a sacred trust," the bishop went on, "she did say that you were to know the truth. It is not good news I'm afraid. Sister Joseph, as she has reverted to being, is now in India, working with the poor and sick. She will remain there until she dies." Father Rigby crossed himself.

"Father," said the bishop, "remember her in your prayers. It won't be easy. I have made sure of that." Brendan shook his head slightly.

"That seems hard to you, Mr O'Malley?" the bishop questioned.

"Well," Brendan hesitated, "that depends on what she's supposed to have done. I mean, how can anyone do anything that wrong stuck out here in a convent?"

"It's you she has wronged, Mr O'Malley," said the bishop quietly.

"Me?" said Brendan, "How?"

"I'm afraid to say it, but let me ask first. Is your visit here to do with the Shuttleworth family bible?" Brendan nodded.

"And the bible, you believe, holds a gem, some would say more precious than the words therein?" the bishop asked gently. Brendan nodded again and his heart sank.

"I thought so," the bishop said, "well, Sister Joseph discovered the gem some years ago. She was once a missionary in Africa and became used to seeing diamonds, both cut and uncut. When she took over the convent here, she examined the bible, probably with the purest of motives, and discovered that a diamond was set into one of the illuminated pages."

"Matthew, Chapter 7, verses 7-8," said Father Rigby, "Seek and you shall find."

"Exactly, Father Rigby," said the bishop.

"She took the diamond," said Brendan, and it was a statement, not a question.

"I'm afraid so," said the bishop, "and there are no excuses. If you want, I will tell you her reasoning." Father Rigby stood, went to where Molly was sitting and took her hand in his.

"Do you want to hear this?" he said quietly, "it won't bring the diamond back."

"Yes," said Molly.

"Brendan?" the priest looked at the man who had come all this way with high expectations.

"Yes," said Brendan.

"Very well," said the bishop as Father Rigby nodded to him, "not long after Sister Joseph had discovered the gem, the convent fell upon hard times. It's not unusual. We're not attracting younger women into convent life. Many of them brought in good incomes, teaching, nursing or selling handmade vestments and embroidered altar cloths etc. Sister Joseph found herself in a convent of older nuns, past their working life. Funds were running short and she was desperate to keep them together in the only community most of them had ever known. If the convent closed they would be scattered all over the world. It's something they would have accepted, but she loved them all - like a good mother. So, when her funds were almost exhausted, she took the diamond, changed into civilian clothes and went to Belfast. There she sold the diamond, bought a good fake, and the convent has been running on the proceeds ever since. There is still some of the money left."

"My God!" exclaimed Brendan.

"Brendan!" Molly said sharply. The bishop allowed himself a small smile.

"I don't blame you, Mr. O'Malley," he said, "and if Sister Joseph had put that much money into the convent accounts, we would have noticed it straight away and challenged it. But she used the money cleverly and wrote the amounts up as donations, legacies and such like. She also asked for permission to sell some convent assets and she hid the items away and put money into the account."

"She must have been worried sick when I turned up," said Father Rigby.

"I think your visit to the convent precipitated a bout of conscience, Father," said the bishop.

"Oh, the poor woman," said Molly.

"Don't feel sorry for her, Mrs. O'Malley," said the bishop, "what she did was wrong. It was stolen property she was using, whatever the motives. She did show true contrition though, so I was able to absolve her. She told me to tell you she was truly contrite and suggested, quite rightly, that the assets she had hidden away, be given to you. I agreed with that." Molly and Brendan sat there, in front of the bishop, dumbstruck.

"Father Rigby," the bishop said, "would you join me in the chapel. Please," he inclined his head towards Brendan and Molly, "follow when you are ready."

"Your Excellency," the priest replied, shaken to the core by the tale of the former Mother Superior. When the door had closed behind the clerics, Molly turned to Brendan.

"What are you thinking?" she asked.

"I'm thinking that our lives are being turned inside out by the wrong doing of others. Firstly, Stewart McIntosh tries to cheat us. Secondly, Nathaniel Sharpe almost got away with cheating us. And now, thirdly, we have a nun - she's robbed us too! Can it get worse?" he said angrily.

"I understand your anger, Brendan," said Molly, "but look at it the other way. Apart from Nathaniel, who has been found out, we are actually no worse off than if we had never heard the name Shuttleworth. If Mary hadn't followed her conscience and told Father Rigby, we would never have known anything. So, you see, one person doing good has brought all this out into the open."

"There is a crooked sort of logic in that, Molly, my dear," said Brendan with a wry smile, "and one of these days I'll work out what it is."

"Let's go and find the clergy," said Molly, "and we'll ask if we can speak with Sister Marie Julie. We've found one O'Malley, which is better than money. We may find some more." They left the room and wandered down the first corridor to the left until they came upon a nun.

"Please can you direct us to the chapel?" said Molly. The nun smiled and beckoned them to follow her. The chapel was austere but had the most delicious scent of beeswax and incense. Every pew gleamed. Molly could hear the bishop and the priest talking and followed the sound.

"Father," she said softly, entering a vestment room to the side of the chapel. Father Rigby and the bishop turned round.

"Ah, you are here," said the bishop, "come and see your treasures." Molly and Brendan entered the room and were confronted by a wall to wall cupboard with four doors. It reached from floor to ceiling.

"There is a lovely pair of candlesticks here, gold plated, supposedly sold four years ago," said the bishop, "and an illuminated Gospels worth around three thousand pounds, I remember Sister Joseph asked if she could sell this only two years ago."

"And here we have a silver monstrance," said Father Rigby, "the like of which I haven't seen in ages."

"And a solid silver altar plate set," went on the bishop, "quite a haul."

"Where did it all come from originally?" asked Brendan.

"Gifts from wealthy patrons, mostly," said the bishop, "people think they can buy their way into Heaven." Father Rigby chuckled and so did Molly.

"We're not touching any of this," said Brendan vehemently, "not one piece." The bishop raised his eyebrows at the vigour with which Brendan spoke.

"It is yours, Mr O'Malley," the bishop said softly, "we, that is the church, would rather you take this than," he hesitated, "than sue us for the money that is rightfully yours."

"I'll not be suing the church, bishop," Brendan said, "if you will promise me to sell all this again and keep the convent alive for longer. And keep the rest of the money too. One of my relatives lives here. I'll not see her homeless."

"That's very generous of you," the bishop said and the relief on his face was apparent.

"May we talk to Sister Marie Julie?" Molly said to the bishop, "will you give her permission, just for a short time?"

"Certainly," said the bishop, "come with me now and we'll find her." They found the tiny nun in her cell. She was reading her tattered, worn old Bible. The bishop coughed gently to attract the nun's attention.

"Sister Marie Julie," the bishop said, "will you come and talk to our visitors. They are O'Malleys from England. Maybe you'd like to show them the rose garden. I hear it is a favourite place of yours."

"Thank you, your Excellency," Sister Marie Julie's voice was surprisingly firm. She led Molly and Brendan out through a side door and walked quickly to the garden.

"Here," she said, indicating a bench, "you sit either side of me and we'll talk. Do you know about the diamond?" Brendan was shocked. There was a look on the nun's face that was inappropriate to her surroundings. It was definitely not a demure look. Her eyes glittered. Molly just nodded.

"We O'Malley's knew about it long ago," she said, with a gleeful grin, "and we were waiting for someone to claim it. Now it is yours."

"Oh," said Molly, "you don't know that it is gone- sold by Mother Superior." The tiny nun's face was stricken.

"Gone?" she said eventually, "the Shuttleworth diamond, gone." Tears filled her eyes.

"Oh, my," she said, "I'm so sorry. It was beautiful. I'm afraid I coveted it. I confessed my fault but the priest couldn't understand what I coveted so badly." She giggled unexpectedly.

"There isn't a lot to covet here," she said, "and I thought I was the only one who knew about it." She stood.

"You'll want to go back inside then," she said, "now the diamond is gone?"

"Actually, no, Sister," Brendan said, "we would like to know about our family, the O'Malleys. You are an O'Malley by birth, aren't you?"

"Oh, I can reel off the O'Malley family to you right away, but it's all in the back of the Shuttleworth bible. Patrick, the O'Malley that ran away with Isabel, had one son, Sean. You'll know more about that side than me. Patrick's brother Casey had two children-Alan and Erin; His other brother, Kevin had two children, Liam and Niamh and his sister Siobhan had two also, Connor and Mairead. Now, the children of those three were..." Molly interrupted the nun in mid flow.

"I'm not sure we can remember all this, Sister," she said, "but what we really want to know is, why did Isabel's letter stay here? Did anyone contact Patrick when she died? We'd have thought he would have come over to claim her body. Or at least taken Sean to Ireland just once! Why was Sean left in ignorance of his inheritance?"

"Ah, so many questions, Mrs. O'Malley," Sister Marie Julie smiled, "and ones that have perplexed generations of O'Malleys in Ireland. We think that Patrick was getting his revenge on Sir Charles. In a twisted way, because Shuttleworth cut off Patrick and Isabel, we think Patrick tried to deny his son the knowledge of his maternal grandfather. Patrick knew of the letter, and the title deed, because one of the priests here wrote and told him. Patrick wrote back and said that Sean would collect it when he was twenty one. But Sean never came. Patrick stayed in England to look after the boy and that was it. The O'Malley's over here never heard from him, or Sean, again."

"How sad," said Molly.

"But now we've found you," added the nun, "I'll copy out all the O'Malley addresses I know and send them to you." The nun's face was animated. She had found family.

"How do you do it, sister," Molly asked gently.

"Do what?" Sister Marie Julie replied, tucking her hands away in her copious sleeves.

"Well," said Molly, not sure of which question to ask, "live here; cut off from the world, not speaking, not being able to communicate with your family, all of it?" Sister Marie Julie sat for three seconds only before answering:

"I've never known anything else," she said simply, "since I entered as a novice. This is life, isn't it?"

Later that evening Molly found Brendan deep in thought.

"Penny for them?" she said, sitting beside him on the bed.

"Just the one question I'm wracking my brains to answer. Why didn't Patrick tell my father, when he turned 21, to go and find the family bible? He could have been rich beyond his wildest dreams. Maybe he wouldn't have died at 45 behind a market stall." Molly sat and thought about Sean.

"I can't answer that, Brendan," she said, "except that maybe Patrick died before Sean was 21, maybe he didn't want Sean connected to the Shuttleworth family, maybe it was as simple as wanting his boy to make his own way in the world. We'll never know. Leave it at that." Brendan kissed his wife gently.

"You're right, Molly," he said, "We'll leave them to rest in peace."

Chapter 24

"So, your honour," the barrister said, "we plead that the defendant, Stewart McIntosh, be found not guilty of fraud. His motive was to secure the new market hall with no further expense to the already over burdened people of this town. He made a serious error of judgement that is all. We ask for his complete acquittal." The barrister sat down and wiped his face, knocking his wig slightly. The court room was packed to capacity and he was amused to hear cries of 'never' and 'lock the bugger up' coming from the public gallery. The Judge nodded and turned to the jury.

"You have heard my learned friend for the defence give his summing up. You have heard the case for the prosecution. I do not feel that you need to be guided by me. Retire for lunch, come back refreshed to the jury room, and return to the court when you have reached a verdict." The Judge rose and left the bench. Both sets of barristers were hurriedly trying to get to their feet before the Judge had left. The prosecution barrister turned to his clerk.

"Goodness," he said, "no guidance. He's definitely expecting a conviction."

"What other verdict could there be? It's cut and dried," replied the clerk.

"McIntosh was already tarnished before he came here," added the barrister, "he was castigated at the Nathaniel Sharpe case. Even if M'Lud directed the jury not to link the two cases together, it's certain that most of them will have heard the result of that little fiasco. McIntosh was practically accused of allowing the whole decades of fraud to continue by not being in control of his staff."

"Let's go for lunch," said the clerk, "I don't think the jury will be out for long."

"Down to the Court Inn?" said the clerk.

"Why not," said the barrister, "we can eavesdrop to our heart's content." There was hardly a need to eavesdrop from the table they had reserved in advance. Every voice was giving an opinion, some of them quite loudly.

"I seem to recognise the people at the table behind you," said the barrister. The clerk dropped his knife on the floor and glanced around. He nodded.

"They are the O'Malley family, who were not only being cheated by McIntosh, but being robbed by Sharpe."

"Unfortunate," tutted the barrister, "let's listen."

"I can't understand how people can defend criminals like McIntosh," Brendan was saying, "have they no shame?"

"Someone has to do it, dad," said Michelle, "not everyone is articulate or confident enough to get up in court and defend themselves. Don't forget we're innocent until proved guilty."

"After Jim Wilson had confessed and Mary had told the Judge what she heard, how has the man the nerve to plead not guilty?" said Molly, "what good will it do him? I'd have thought he'd get a lighter sentence if he held up his hands and confessed." The barrister nodded to the clerk as he put a huge piece of steak pie into his mouth.

"If the jury do reach a verdict today," said Colin, "will we have to wait before sentencing, that's what I want to know?" The clerk shook his head at the barrister as he took a sip of water. The barrister smiled and made a sign across his throat with his finger as if he were cutting it.

"Hey," said Colin, glancing at his watch, "time to go back to court." The jury deliberated for less than two hours before returning a unanimous verdict of guilty, as charged, on Stewart McIntosh. The defendant stuck his chin one degree higher in the air and then closed his eyes as the judge sent him down for eight years. The Judge's final words were a direction that the O'Malley family be awarded compensation from the council. Mrs. McIntosh, who was sat with the rest of the public, broke down and sobbed.

"You stupid man," she wailed at her husband, "I'll never be able to show my face in the tennis club again." The judge thanked the jury, the usher banged his gavel, called out, 'all rise' and it was over. Brendan, Molly, Terry, Colin and Michelle O'Malley stood and watched as Stewart McIntosh was taken down.

"That's it," said Molly, with a sigh, "he got what he deserved, twice as long as Nathaniel got. But I think the judge went easy on Nathaniel because he'll probably never walk again."

"It all seems a bit of an anti climax," said Michelle.

"Two court cases down," said Terry grimly, "and one more to go, if the council wants to play it that way."

"We'll know in a few days," said Brendan, "so let's just all get home to Sharon and the girls and enjoy the rest of the day, together."

Three days later a letter arrived at Brendan's home, from the council's solicitor. The solicitor was requesting a meeting, that same day, at the council offices. Brendan rang to accept the time of the meeting and then rang Terry.

"We're on for this afternoon," Brendan said to his brother, "I'll pick you up."

"Should we have our solicitor there?" asked Terry.

"Definitely," said Brendan, "I'll ring them next. See you at two o'clock." He dialled Grey Brothers and got through to Mr. Grey.

"We've had a letter," he said, "from the council. They want to meet this afternoon at 2.30pm. Can you make it? I know its short notice."

"A typical tactic, courtesy of their solicitor," replied Mr Grey, "don't worry, I'll be there. See you outside the main door at 2.15 pm." The three men met up on time. Brendan and Terry were uncomfortable in their best suits. Mr Grey shook their hands, hoisted his file up under his arm and said:

"I've got all the notes here. If you want to speak to me, ask for an adjournment. We can talk freely outside the room. Leave it to me. Ready?" They nodded. Brendan desperately wanted a drink and gulped.

"Don't be nervous, Mr O'Malley," Mr Grey smiled at him, "you know most of the men who will be in the meeting better than I do."

"Yes," replied Brendan, "but we've always been working and trying to get things done- together. I've never been in a situation like this before."

"Well, I know the solicitor," said Mr. Grey, "he's sharp and comes across as belligerent. But he knows the score. The council haven't got a leg to stand on. Believe me; the only dispute will be about how much they are prepared to pay out. I'll settle, after consulting you, of course, for about three times what they first offer. And don't forget one important thing- its Public Liability insurance money. The people of this town will not be losing their rates to you."

"Can we make sure the public knows that when they find out," said Terry with a grin. They walked together into the reception area.

"Please go directly to the Chief Executive's suite, gentlemen," the receptionist said. They arrived outside Mary's office and Mr Grey knocked once on her door and walked in.

"Good afternoon, Mary," he said.

"They're waiting for you, Mr Grey," she replied, "I'll bring drinks through."

"Thank you, Mary," said Brendan, "I've a dry throat."

"Don't you worry, Brendan," Mary replied, "I've said a prayer for you this morning."

"Every little helps," said Terry, smiling nervously. They walked into the room, where the council's solicitor, Mr. Johnson, was sitting in McIntosh's old chair. Brendan knew the other men - the Acting Chief Executive, Richard Day, and councillors Greenwood, Smith and Bates. Richard Day rose and welcomed the three men, shaking hands all round. Mary came in with a tray of coffee and water and organised a drink for each man.

"No calls, Mary," said Richard Day.

"Of course not, Mr. Day," she replied. She closed the door behind her.

"Shall I begin?" said Mr. Johnson.

"Please do," replied Mr Grey.

"Mindful of the fact that only Stewart McIntosh and Jim Wilson knew of the fraud, the council, as a body, deny responsibility." He sat back and leaned on the chair, his hands clasped in front of him. Brendan looked sideways at Mr Grey and noticed that his brother, sat the other side of their solicitor, was doing the same.

"You are prepared to go to Court, I take it?" Mr Grey said smoothly, "for which course of action we will be requesting costs, and the services of the best barristers in London. I think the High Court is the proper place, don't you?" Brendan saw Richard Day's face blanch and Councillor Bates began to bluster. Mr Johnson looked at Richard Day and they all saw the slight shake of his head.

"In that case," Johnson went on, as if nothing had happened, "the council will discuss compensation terms - with your clients."

"You'll discuss them with me, Mr Johnson," said Mr Grey firmly, "as from experience, we *both* know that fairness is accomplished when *both* sides have legal representation."

"Obviously, once we have agreed a sum of money," said Mr Johnson, "the title deed to the land will be handed over to the borough council at no extra cost." Mr Grey looked at Brendan, who nodded; he then looked at Terry, who did the same.

"As long as the council pay the costs of the transfer," replied Mr Grey, "we agree."

"A trifling sum," said Mr Johnson sarcastically.

"Then it won't be a problem for the council," replied Mr Grey calmly.

"Then, Mr Grey," said Mr Johnson, "pray tell us what amount your clients are seeking." Mr Grey shook his head.

"Oh, no, Mr Johnson," he replied quickly, "you and the councillors are the experts in land values. The council knows what the land would cost if it had to buy on the open market. The most lucrative site in town was stolen from my clients by your ex-Chief Executive. Also, don't forget punitive damages for the distress my clients have experienced."

"Then my clients are offering £10,000, without prejudice," said Mr. Johnson. Brendan gulped. Terry gasped. Mr Grey looked sharply at them both and then rose from his seat.

"Come, gentlemen, we'll leave the councillors and their professional adviser. May I remind you, Mr Johnson, that £10,000 wouldn't buy my clients a new house each in the best part of town? See you in court." Brendan and Terry were half way out of their seats when Richard Day intervened.

"Please, Mr O'Malley, Mr Grey," he said, "do sit down. I think Mr Johnson was joking. At least, I hope he was." Richard Day threw a look of pure astonishment at Mr Johnson. Johnson returned the look with a shake of his head.

"Shall we take five minutes outside," asked Mr Grey, looking not at his clients, but at the councillors, "while you remind Mr Johnson of my client's losses?" Brendan and Terry stood once more, Mr Grey between them.

"No need, Mr Grey," soothed Councillor Greenwood, "we have a figure in mind that we feel is fair. Would £30,000 be more appropriate?" Richard Day let out an exasperated sigh.

"No," said Mr Grey," but £60,000 and we have a deal." Brendan sat down heavily on his chair. The figure was more money than he could have dreamed the land would be worth. Before they were compulsorily purchased the houses there were changing hands for less than £2,500 each. The room was deathly quiet. No one spoke a word. Terry realised he was holding his breath and let the air out of his lungs quietly. At last Richard Day spoke.

"You have a deal," he said, "Mr. Johnson will prepare the contract immediately. Once it is signed, to everyone's satisfaction, the money will be transferred within four days." He stood up and offered his hand to Mr Grey. Mr Grey looked once at Brendan with raised, questioning, eyebrows. Brendan nodded. He repeated the gesture to Terry who also nodded. Mr Grey then took Richard Day's outstretched hand and shook it firmly. The O'Malleys also shook Richard Day's hand. Brendan found himself saying, "Thank you."

"Don't thank me, Brendan," the man said, "You were the wronged party. Sorry about the tactics. They were Johnson's idea, not mine." Brendan and Terry walked out of the room in a daze.

"Tell me one more time, Brendan," said Terry, "how much did they say? I can't believe it."

"£60, 000," whispered Brendan.

"We'll never need to work again," said Terry.

"We've customers to deal with tomorrow," said Brendan quickly, "and don't you forget it!"

"You're right, brother," said Terry, but he still punched the air and hissed "Yessssss."

"Congratulations," said a voice from behind them.

"Mr Grey," Terry said, a trifle embarrassed, "we owe you. I still can't believe it."

"I'll get my fee," the solicitor said quietly, "and you have got justice. That makes my job worthwhile. Now, how are you fixed for buying one thirsty solicitor a drink?" Brendan looked at his watch.

"It's gone three o'clock," he said, "the pubs will be closed." Mr Grey winked at him.

"Not if you know the manager of a certain hotel across town," he said, "who, if anyone asks, will swear I'm resident there." They walked out of the town hall, crossed the road, and walked into the hotel, like three school boys on the last day of term.

"Leave this to me," Mr Grey said. He approached the manager, who was reading a racing paper.

"May I bring two friends in for a very quick drink, Arthur?" he asked.

"Sure, Mr. Grey," said Arthur, "go through to the small saloon bar. What will you be having?"

"Three pints of your best bitter and three tots of your very best whisky," replied Mr Grey.

"I'll bring them through," said Arthur, "and ignore the lady in there; she'll be asleep by now." Mr Grey beckoned the O'Malley brothers, who were hovering by the front door. He entered the small saloon bar and laughed, quietly.

"Look what we have here, gentlemen," he whispered, "Sleeping Beauty." Brendan and Terry peered around his body and they too had to smile. Propped up on a corner of the padded seat that ran around the room, her mouth wide open and her hat covering one eye, was Mrs. Sharpe. By the time the three men had consumed four pints each, always with a whisky chaser, Mr Grey was transformed. Brendan and Terry were holding their sides with laughter and saying 'no more' to every joke that Mr Grey was digging up from his youth. Mr Grey's face was anything but gray- his cheeks had turned ruddy, his nose was actually glowing and he had discarded both jacket and tie.

"And then there was the one about the criminal..." he started,

"Eh, what's that?" came a plaintive voice from the corner. The three men turned and saw Mrs. Sharpe roused from her slumber.

"Oh," she said, suddenly awake, "it's you, is it? The O'Malley Brothers no less, put my boy away in prison, didn't you? But I'm going to get him back, worse luck."

"Not me," said Brendan, failing to stop a hiccough.

"Not me, neither, or is it either?" said Terry laughing.

"Oh, yes you did," she stood up and came over to them, swinging her handbag. The first blow landed on Brendan's shoulder. The second blow on Terry's knee.

"You miserable buggers," she panted, swinging away wildly, "you were the ones who suggested the bloody new market hall in the first place. But for that he wouldn't have panicked and tried to get the money away." She stopped her assault suddenly and collapsed onto a chair next to Mr. Grey.

"Madam," said Mr Grey, in a stern voice, "pull yourself together. This is not how a lady acts. These good men probably saved your life- or have you forgotten that."

"I'd rather have died," she cried, "than know that I'm still trapped. I come here," and she waved her arms around wildly, "and all my new friends, bugger them, they never stay. They don't want to come to visit me at home. They just drink my money and go." The tears flowed down her cheeks, leaving tiny pink rivulets where they coursed through the rouge. Her mascara smudged as she dabbed her eyes.

"And, to cap it all," she sobbed, "I'll have to look after him for the rest of his natural. I won't make a good martyr, you know. I wanted cruise ships and Carr..bir..ean, Cab..bi, oh, you know, them islands. I wanted some life."

"Time to go home," said Mr Grey, smiling, "will you help me, Brendan?"

"I'll call a taxi for her," said Terry.

"Better call three, if you can," said Brendan, "one for us and one for Mr Grey." They half carried Mrs. Sharpe, still weeping and wailing, through to the entrance of the hotel.

"Oh, dear, Mrs Sharpe," said Arthur, tut tutting, "got ourselves upset again, have we?" Half an hour later Brendan, with Terry just a pace behind, was trying to get a key into the lock of his front door. He was failing miserably. The door opened suddenly and he almost fell into the hallway.

"I take it you had good news," said Sharon, "or have you been drowning your sorrows? Molly's making strong, black coffee." She hauled Brendan over the doorstep and then assisted Terry into the house.

"Where have you boys been?" came Molly's voice from the kitchen, "we've all been dying to know what happened today." Brendan went into the lounge and was confronted by his three daughters and Terry's son.

"Oh," squealed Lesley, "you look awful, dad."

"A little the worse for wear," added Barbara.

"And Uncle Terry isn't much better," said Michelle.

"They've had a skin full," said Colin, accusingly, "and never even invited me."

"Get those down you," said Molly crossly to Brendan and Terry, handing them coffee, "and then tell us your news."

"Our news, darling wife," smiled Brendan, "sorry, we just sort of went for one drink with Mr Grey and one drink led to another." Sharon looked at Molly and they both shook their heads.

"Dad" said Lesley, "are you going to tell us how rich we are, or not?"

"Money is not everything, child," Brendan began sternly, "why only an hour ago we bumped into Mrs Sharpe. She has money now, and she is not happy, not happy at all."

"Dad," said Michelle, "please will you tell us or do we have to beat it out of you?"

"OK," said Brendan, "Terry and I will have £30,000 .... each."

"No!" said Molly, covering her mouth with one hand.

"Oh, my goodness," Sharon said, and burst into tears.

"What's the matter with mum and Aunt Sharon?" Lesley asked her sisters. She turned to Barbara and Michelle, who were both sat with their mouths wide open.

"Is that a lot of money?" she said plaintively to Colin, the only mortal who seemed normal right now.

"It's a great, huge, mountain of money, Lesley," he said to her.

"Oh," said Lesley, "that's all right then. I'm going upstairs to finish my book."

The new market hall was formally opened six months later by the town's M. P. He also officially opened a new playground, built with a donation from the O'Malley families. It had been named "The Shuttleworth Memorial Play Park.". Molly held on to Brendan's arm.

"It's lovely," she said, "and I'm so glad the people chose to have something for the children."

"Our children" whispered Elizabeth to Colin, "one day."

THE END.

Made in the USA
Monee, IL
04 November 2026

67381749R00177